Karam Nayebpour

Mind Presentation in Ian McEwan's Fiction

Consciousness and the Presentation of Character in *Amsterdam*, *Atonement*, and *On Chesil Beach*

Karam Nayebpour

MIND PRESENTATION IN IAN MCEWAN'S FICTION

Consciousness and the Presentation of Character in *Amsterdam*, *Atonement*, and *On Chesil Beach*

ibidem-Verlag
Stuttgart

Bibliographic information published by the Deutsche Nationalbibliothek
Die Deutsche Nationalbibliothek lists this publication in the Deutsche Nationalbibliografie; detailed bibliographic data are available in the Internet at http://dnb.d-nb.de.

Bibliografische Information der Deutschen Nationalbibliothek
Die Deutsche Nationalbibliothek verzeichnet diese Publikation in der Deutschen Nationalbibliografie; detaillierte bibliografische Daten sind im Internet über http://dnb.d-nb.de abrufbar.

ISBN-13: 978-3-8382-1029-2

Printed in the United States of America

Our Stories Are Interwoven—

to

Naghmeh

and

to Our Burgeoning *Narrative*—

Nahal

TABLE OF CONTENTS

List of Abbrevations **9**

Acknowledgements **11**

1. Introduction **13**

1.1 Reading McEwan as a Cognitive Novelist 23

1.2 Mind Representation in *Amsterdam, Atonement* and *On Chesil Beach* and the Aim of this Study 26

2. Cognitive Narratology and Consciousness (Re)Presentation **31**

2.1 Cognitive Narratology and Narrative Experience 32

2.1.1 Fictional Minds and Cognitive Reader 39

2.2 Alan Palmer's Approach to Fictional Minds 48

2.2.1 (Doubly) Embedded Narratives 52

2.2.2 Fictional Minds and Theory of Intermental / Intramental Thought 57

2.2.3 Modes for Presenting Fictional Minds (Consciousness) in Fiction 63

2.3 David Herman's Approach to Narrative and Narrativity 71

2.3.1 What It's Like or Qualia 84

3. *Amsterdam* **91**

3.1 Intramental Characterization and Consciousness Presentation: *AM* 91

3.2 The Passage from Intermental to Intramenal Minds: Clive Linely's and Vernon Halliday's (Doubly) Embedded Narratives 98

3.3 The (Im)Balance between Intermental and Intramental Thoughts: Representation of the Impact of Narrative Events and Situations on Clive Linely's Mind 114

3.4 The Egocentricism and Intermentality: Representation of the Impact of (Intentional) Intramentality on Vernon Haliday's Thoughts and Actions 152

4. *Atonement* **177**

4.1 An Intramental Thought against Intermental Minds: *AT* 177

4.2 Briony Tallis's Intramental Mind and the Order of the Real World 186

4.3 In Search of Love: Constructin of an Interminal Mind between Cecilia and Robbie 196

4.4 The Destructive Impact of Briony's Intramental Thoughts on the Emerging Intermental Bond between Cecilia and Robbie 211

5. *On Chesil Beach* 225

5.1 A Narrative of Unfortunate Misreadings: *CB* 225

5.2 The Imbalance in the Intermental Unit between Edward and Florence 231

5.3 What It's Like to »Love, and Set Each Other Free«: Florence Ponting's Passage from Intermentality to Intramentality 249

5.4 The Question of Aspectuality in the Embedded Narratives: Edward Mayhew 275

6. Conclusion 299

7. Bibliography 309

LIST OF ABBREVATIONS

AM	*Amsterdam*
AT	*Atonement*
CB	*On Chesil Beach*
CN	Cognitive Narratology
TR	Thought Report
FIT	Free Indirect Thought

ACKNOWLEDGEMENTS

My research was informed by a great variety of sources. I would like to express my gratitude to all the authors and colleagues who helped me along the way, most notably I would like to thank David Herman, Alan Palmer, Monika Fludernik, Gerald Prince, Marco Caracciolo and John Pier for their illuminating insights about (Cognitive) Narratology and the significance of mind, consciousness and character (re)presentation in narrative literature. I would also like to thank Prof. Mustafa Zeki Çıraklı for his significant contribution to this project.

1. INTRODUCTION

> [T]he novel is a special case. As a form it's so rich in explicit meaning, so intimately concerned with other minds, with relationships, and with human nature, and so extended too—tens of thousands of words—that the writer is bound to leave his or her personality behind on the page. There's nothing we can do about it. The form is total in its embrace. (McEwan, »Art of Fiction«)

Ian Russell McEwan (b. 1948) is one of the »highly respected professional« (Malcolm 6) contemporary British novelists. He has already »established himself as one of the world's most celebrated writers in English« (Wells, »Ian McEwan« 250). McEwan's writing career began in the 1970s and has undergone profound thematic and technical transformations. His earlier works—*First Love, Last Rites* (1975), a collection of short stories; *The Cement Garden* (1978), McEwan's first novel; his second short story collection *In Between the Sheets* (1978); and his second novel *The Comfort of Strangers* (1981)—are mainly concerned with the effects of instinctive desires and socio-cultural pressure on human behaviour. Their subjects include: »sexual abuse« in early adolescence; the »desire to destroy« inherent in human nature; familial relationships with »dislocated children« whose uncontrolled behaviour threatens the established social as well as domestic patriarchal units; and the »perversion and psychosis operating« in the absence of a »social context« (Cochran 391, 398, 392, 400). Because of these themes, critics, according to Wells, labelled early McEwan »one of the *enfant terribles* of the British literary scene« and nicknamed him »Ian Macabre« (»Ian McEwan« 250, 252).[1] In his later works, however, McEwan deals with mature characters, giving up the »exploration of grotesque and disturbing themes« (Groes 1) as well as the »exteriorized narration of events« (Wells, *Ian McEwan* 17).

---

1 Peter Childs also points out this, »at the start of his career, Ian McEwan appeared to reviewers to be one of the *enfants terribles* of a new kind of writing that was emerging in the 1970s« (*The Fiction* 1). McEwan, however, could »hardly complain about the ›Ian Macabre‹ tag« (»Journeys« 130).

McEwan's second phase of writing[2] began with the publication of his third novel, *The Child in Time* (1987), »hailed as a turning point in McEwan's career« (Wells, »Ian McEwan« 250). It marked »a point of change« in his fiction »with its positive, adult ending« (Malcolm 5). The novel is also considered as a »radical shift in stylist posture« (James 81). In an interview with Lynn Wells, McEwan himself points to the importance of what Wells calls his »evolving literary techniques« (Wells, *Ian McEwan* 18). His interest in the novel as a moral or ethical form, he states,

> has certainly changed from the work I did in the 70s and early 80s. Then I was more interested in the surfaces. I thought it was almost cheating to let the reader know what a character was thinking. It seemed antiquated, a dead aesthetic, to provide paragraph summaries of someone's states of mind: I thought a subjective state had to be conveyed through observed details or simply by what people said and did. Later this existential kind of writing came to seem very self-limiting, and my fiction began to change around the time of *The Child in Time*. What fiction does better than any other art form is present consciousness, the flow of thought, to give an interior

---

2 As central concerns of his works written after 1987 McEwan recently pointed out the »representation of consciousness« as well as his recognition of the possibility that the novel as a genre provides in order to »access to the minds of others«:
I fall in and out of love with things. There was a kind of writing, for example in the 1970s, that I adored and tried to imitate. It had a kind of existential quality. I thought that you broke your own rules if you ever thought you could describe someone's thoughts. I thought that is against rules. What people said and what did, and then I described physical details to generate a kind of mood, a kind of … a penumbra of consciousness around things, but never would I say *He turned away and thought to himself she is not for me.* Then I realized, when I came too late, by the time I was thirty, I thought there is a warmth and richness to the literary tradition that has given us, especially since Joyce, access to conventions to convey the flow of consciousness and how can you deny yourself this. You who walk around with thoughts and why not let your characters walk around with your thoughts. So, I drew away and in the last novel I wrote like that was *Comfort for strangers*, 1981 or 1982. And when I came back to the novel, there was a five-year gap when I did other things, with *The Child in Time*, it was much more informed by something which seems to be warmer and richer and more entangled with the presentation of consciousness. So that was a falling out of love and at the same time a falling in love with the greater possibilities. […] We have not yet invented another art form that allows us such access to the minds of others and to the nature of consciousness, movies cannot do it, even the theatre cannot do it, that it has to remain on the outside of things. That interior sense the novel gives, only poetry also can excel in. (»On Making«)

> narrative, a subjective history of an individual through time, through every conceived event, through love, or moral dilemmas. This inner quality is what I now value. (*Ian* 126)

Shifting from the »surfaces« to »interior narrative[s]« is the most outstanding characteristic of McEwan's later work. Further, representing a »world beyond the trauma of violence and the cynicism of public life« and plumbing the »depths of individual subjectivity« (Cochran 402), McEwan in *The Child in Time* was inclined to »be rather dark, rather interior and rather more concerned with the pathology of the mind« (qtd. in Cochran 400), he told the (London) *Sunday Times*. Such characteristics are recurring tendencies in McEwan's later narratives too. There, he mainly represents symbiotic relationships between exterior factors (embedded in the social contexts) and interior ones or the subjective (re)constructions of them. In other words, the novels written in his second phase are, in his own words, »the representation of states of mind and the society that forms them« (qtd. in Brooker 54). Moreover, what is highlighted more in McEwan's later writing period is the vulnerability of the seemingly safe urban life because the works written in this period are »noted for the revelation of psychological and emotional disturbances beneath an ordered social veneer« (Head, *The Cambridge* 217). In *The Child in Time*, McEwan, as Cochran says, uses new narrative techniques and subjects: »The central calamity« in this narrative, »occurs at the beginning of the work rather than at the climactic moment near the end« and its main concern is »human suffering« (402). Moreover, events in this narrative, according to Brooker, are »subjectively experienced« (202).

Set against the historical backdrop of European and global history of World War II, McEwan's next two novels are primarily considered explorations of the central characters' selves. The self in these narratives, however, is mostly determined by the historical forces and the exploration of the interdependent relationship between them is their main concern. *The Innocent* (1990) »develops tunnelling into a motif for Leonard's gradual exploration of his own potential. [. . .] [He] begins to unearth aspects of his personality that before his journey he could only have guessed at« (Cochran 403). In *Black Dogs* (1992), the main narrative concern is »a deep-seated connection between the personal and the political« (Cochran 403). In his next novel, *Enduring Love* (1997)—hailed as an »ethical turn« (qtd. in Wells, *Ian McEwan* 11)— McEwan left political and historical themes and instead concentrated on human relationships. The central concern in this novel is the »difficulties of conveying the truth in narrative form« (Wells, »Ian McEwan« 251). Alan Palmer, in his article »Attributions of Madness in Ian McEwan's *Enduring Love*,« explores how Jed's madness affects »the perfectly sane intermental unit of Joe and Clarissa« (291). Moreover, the central characters in this novel are »almost entirely removed« from the historical, political and social »determinant« present in McEwan's early novels. Such factors are »of secondary importance to the novel's presentation of Joe's and Jed's minds« (Malcolm 8). Possibly, it is in consideration of this fact that the critic Andrew Gaedtke writes: »Among the most formally ambitious examples of contemporary literature's engagement with cognitive science is McEwan's *Enduring Love*« (187). Analysing third-person narratives only, this study, however, does not include a discussion of *Enduring Love*.

Likewise, McEwan's focus in his last novel in the twentieth century—*AM*—is »on the present and on certain psychological states« (Malcolm 8).[3] In his interview with Jon Cook et al., McEwan, referring to the period when his four previous novels were published, states that:

> During that period, before I actually started work, many of the notes, the messages I sent to myself were about finding dramatic or sensual ways in bringing ideas to life rather than about characters or settings or plots. In other words, I set out to make a novel of ideas [. . .] But then I abruptly fell out of love with that notion. When I wrote *Amsterdam*, I had no specific ›ideas‹ in mind. [. . .] *Amsterdam* was a form of farce—I abandoned myself purely to the possibilities of its characters. Although I gave them ideas [. . .] they seemed subsidiary. *Amsterdam* was light-hearted, and it liberated me from abstraction. (»Journeys« 7)

Despite David Malcolm's wonder in 2002—»How this aspect [presentation of the characters' psychological states in *AM*] of McEwan's fiction will develop in the new century is far from clear« (8)—it is now obvious that the

---

3 Peter Childs also argues that *AM* »shows McEwan's continuing skill at providing macabre twists to debates over contemporary social issues« (*The Fiction* 5).

primacy of fictional minds (consciousness) and their psychological presentation increasingly continues in McEwan's narratives published after 1998, particularly in *AT* and *CB*.

McEwan's novels written after 1998—*Amsterdam (AM), Atonement (AT), Saturday, On Chesil Beach* (*CB*), *Solar* and *Sweet Tooth* —reveal a particular concern with the presentation of the characters' internal or psychological states. Dealing with the characters' mental workings strongly cues the reader's scripts and world models. In this way, it firmly anchors the reader's experiential repertoire to the fictional models. The result of such a technique is a narrative with high degrees of narrativity or fictionality and worldmaking. These features are both textual and thematic. The main characters' mental functioning are largely presented in these narratives such that the reader encounters fictional event sequences mostly through the experiencing characters' or focalisers'[4] consciousnesses. Despite this, an omniscient narrator orients the transfer of information whenever the focalisation shifts. In such a representational mode of consciousness and through following the characters' thoughts and actions, the reader also gets to know the ways characters come to terms with their own pasts, with the others, the way their minds bring self and other together and finally their (mis)interpretations and (mis)readings. At the centre of *AM, AT* and *CB* a mind in action is presented dramatically—a socialised consciousness or centre of consciousness heavily busy with the social and familial relationships—and a mind interrelated

---

4 This is a debatable term in English language narratology since, according to Margolin, there are many terms for it each designating a particular aspect of the concept:
– mirror, screen, reflector, filter, prism stress the mediating role;
– angle of vision, point of view, origo, focus, vantage point, window and perspective stress the specific situatedness of the agent: spatial, temporal but also conceptual, cultural and epistemic;
– viewer, perceiver, cogniser, and experiencer point to aspects of the mental activity involved;
– (finally) center of subjectivity, awareness or consciousness and mediating consciousness remind us that a human or human-like mind is behind most focalisations in literature. (»Focalization« 45)
In this study, the concept of focaliser, and hence focalisation, refers to the »aspects of the mental activity« in Margolin's list.

with the other fictional minds through regular visions and revisions.[5] Further, the narrators of these narratives are extradiegetic or non-character narrators who recount the story from outside the fictional world applying variable focalisations.

AM, one of the three main subjects of this study, »has strong elements of the psychological novel« which is the »traditional genre in British fiction« too (Malcolm192). It is focalised intermittently from an eminent composer's, Clive Linely's, as well as from the professional editor's, Vernon Halliday's, perspectives. The central concern in this narrative is a personal or private issue. It presents the way the two friends Clive and Vernon are deteriorated by their own »greed, corruption, self-interest [...and] masculine egotism that is in direct contrast to the principles of compassion and generosity« (Wells, »Ian McEwan« 251). Pursuing an intramental way of thought without »compassion« for others brings about their final calamity. Their destiny mainly derives from their orientation to break down any potential intermental unit with each other throughout the storyworld or the world evoked by the narrative. Moreover, the communication among them fails because the intramental side of their mental functioning overcomes the intermental one. Helga Schwalm illustrates this with the following scene: »in the key scene of the novel set in the Lake District, when the composer Clive witnesses the assault on a woman, he fails to overcome his egoistic concerns and decides not to help a female stranger« (175).

The difficulty of constructing intermental units in the first part of *AT* seems to be this novel's main concern too. Briony Tallis's (imaginary) relationship with Robbie Turner and his relationship with Cecilia Tallis are strongly under the influence of their primarily intramental behaviours, which bring about the ensuing disintegration. Briony Tallis spends her life trying to reconstruct the breakdown and compensate for the terrible lie[6] with which she ruined her sister and Robbie's lives. She seeks her atonement and act of repentance in fiction, which is hardly recognisable from truth. All

---

5 Palmer calls this kind of mind ›social mind‹ (*Social* 39–63).

6 »Briony wilfully misidentifies Robbie Turner as her cousin Lola's rapist« (James 93).

in all, the narrative, as Bentley points out, »deals with ideas of memory, historical truth and the fictionalizing of the past« (128). Further, in *AT* everything begins with an initial misreading which leads to deadly consequences. The whole narrative can be summarised in Bentley's words:

> After misreading the first stages of a love relationship between Robbie and Cecilia, Briony mistakenly accuses Robbie of attacking Lola by the lake in the grounds of the country house. She has observed Lola's attacker in the half-light and because of her feelings toward Robbie at this time mistakenly assumes that he is the culprit. (150)

Thus, the central narrative concern in *AT* is, as David K. O'Hara points out, »The same uncertain relationship between selves and others. [. . .] Over the course of McEwan's perspective-shifting narrative, we find characters, again and again, realizing that they are bounded by otherness, by other minds with their own plans, their own interiorities, their own ways of perceiving the world« (75). From this perspective, the first part of *AT* is a rich narrative. Therefore, in this study the focal character's, Briony's, mental functioning and its impact on the emerging intermental unit between Cecilia and Robbie are analysed.

This study does not include McEwan's next novel *Saturday* (2005), although it »is uniquely placed to enable us to know ›what it is like‹ to experience the mind of another« (Green 58–59). The narrative has been so far the subject of some studies in terms of consciousness and the intermental breakdown as its focal concern. Caracciolo regards it as »a brilliant example of internally focalized narration« (»Phenomenological« 62). Having been »consciously about consciousness [...and] a critical participant in the quest to understand the mind« (Green 58), the narrative during twenty-four hours pursues the social events that construct or affect the central character's consciousness. In other words, consciousness in *Saturday* »has central stage« (»Phenomenological« 61). Perowne fails to communicate whenever he becomes a »subjective first« character. The omniscient narrator represents the way Perowne reacts to the exterior threats represented by mentally ill street-thug Baxter. Perowne's reflection on his wife, children, Baxter and the social events are suggestive of the way his mind functions in different situations.

In *CB*, McEwan's next novel and the second narrative analysed in this study, Florence Ponting's and Edward Mayhew's mental workings derive from their socio-cultural contexts. Their intramental or subjective first mode of mental functioning, however, brings about their separation eventually. Applying an omniscient narration, internal mode of focalization is pursued in this narrative through representing two central characters alternately. Florence and Edward are unable to consummate their marriage because of different reasons since above all their attributions of mental states—such as intentions, beliefs and desires—to each other are not congruent with their true feelings and thoughts. As mentioned by Wells, »as it is common in McEwan's work, there are self-reflexive elements in *On Chasid Beach*, with couple's dilemma paralleling the difficulties of ›reading‹ the other, and of communicating adequately with language« (»Ian McEwan« 252). Furthermore, although the manner of Edward's and Florence's mental functioning, among the other factors, basically derives from the defining discourse of the time they live in, the early years of 1960s, it is in fact their intramental or subjective first side of mental functioning that at last brings about their separation. This is also the main reason of their inability to construct a shared, communion or intermental unit. Moreover, this narrative, like *AM*, anchors itself strongly to the reader's world models by presenting a worldly known script—the difficulties of a wedding night. Narrative reader's initial expectations and inferences of the subject, however, are reconstructed through the progression of narrative sequences. Thus, this study investigates the two central characters' mental states or functioning as well as the impact of the particular moments on their consciousness.

McEwan's next narrative, *Solar* (2010), is not also included in this study because it seems that gaining access to the mental functioning of the central characters is not primarily necessary for narrative understanding since there are only few passages of mental readings. Michael Beard, scientist and the noble prizewinner, is a self-oriented character whose mentality is to great extent busy with his own desire. He is revealed to be a symbol of »exploitation« (Wells, »Ian McEwan« 252) since he is mainly concerned with his self-interests leading him to his final destruction. His self-centeredness in pursuing both fame and pleasure, regardless of the other social minds, brings him finally to a deadly consequence. His mind dominantly functions intramentally without considering a possibility of communication with the other social minds in the fictional world. Likewise, the study does not include McEwan's last published novel, *Sweet Tooth* (2012), for the simple reason that it is a first person narrative and the study's priority is third-person narratives. The study, in this case, agrees with Palmer's distinction between homodiegetic narratives (where narrator is a character in the story being narrated) and heterodiegetic ones (where narrator is not a character in the story being narrated). As Palmer says, »there are various complexities inherent in this apparently simple distinction« (Fictional« 25).

This study, thus, explores the manner of central characters' »mental functioning« (Palmer, *Fictional* 25) as well as »the impact of [narrated] situations and events on the minds experiencing them« (Herman, *Basic* 147) in Ian McEwan's three narratives—*AM, AT* and *CB*. The processes through which these narratives engender »experience« (Herman, »Cognitive« 30) in the interpreter's mind as well as the nature of this experience will be explored. In other words, this research applies the terminology of cognitive narratology (CN), a subdomain of postclassical narratology, to the analysis of some *cognitive* aspects of the characters in *AM, AT* and *CB*. The term ›cognitive‹ in this approach has no connection with a »neurological description of the reader's brain«; rather, it refers to the »reader's subjective experience« during the reading act (Bernaerts et al, 3, 8). »Readers,« as cognitive narratologist Monica Fludernik understands, »do not see texts as having narrative features but read texts as narrative by imposing cognitive narrative frames on them« (»Narratology« 926). Related to this, Alan Palmer's terminology explains how the reader's mind (re)constructs fictional minds and how fictional minds operate. He defines fictional minds as »semiotic constructs that form part of an overall narrative pattern. They are elements in a plot as well as centers of consciousness« (*Fictional* 191). Narrative readers mentally simulate such experiencing consciousnesses within the storyworlds in order to understand or experience narrative events and situations. Moreover, to experience narrative, a typical reader undergoes the some mental processes in order to reconstruct fictional minds based on textual (semiotic) cues. In a similar manner to Palmer, David Herman explores how fictional characters' lived experiences influence their thoughts and behaviour and how narrative experience takes place in the interpreter's mind. Concerning the construction of fictional minds, both cognitive narratologists allow for some similarities between real or actual minds and fictional minds. That is mainly because, as Palmer points out, »Just as in real life the individual constructs the minds of others from their behavior, so the reader infers the workings of fictional minds and sees these minds in action from observation of characters' behavior and actions« (*Fictional* 246).

This study specifically applies Palmer's and Herman's theories of fictional minds and narrativity in order to explain the manner of central fictional minds mental functioning in McEwan's *AM, AT* and *CB*. The study, furthermore, analyses the way they experience particular events and situations and their impact on their thoughts and behaviour. To this end and before discussing the narratives, the following theoretical issues are examined at first: the cognitive approach to literature or CN; the role of the reader in narrative understanding; intermental (joint, group, shared, or collective) thought / intramental (individual or private) thought; the modes of presenting fictional minds in narrative; and narrativity (or narrativeness). This is preceded in the following section with a review of the role of mind or consciousness representation in McEwan's fiction.

The presentation of the characters' mental workings and the impact of narrative events and situations on their minds as observable from their actions and behaviour, are central to *AM, AT* and *CB*. Accordingly, applying the terminology of CN to the analysis of these narratives seems appropriate since, as David James points out, the »McEwan we have seen emerging over the past fifteen years is a complex figure requiring rigorous narratological focus« (81). The present narratives have been chosen for this study, because the characters' mental workings as well as the impact of some decisive narrative moments on their consciousness seem to be their central concern. Furthermore, these are the basic characteristics for a cognitive approach. Avoiding generalisations and following a slow analysis methodology, the present study mainly focuses on the passages of internal focalisation within the selected narratives in order to examine the manner of fictional minds' mental functioning.

Critical approaches to McEwan's novels demonstrate the growing importance of character, fictional minds and consciousness throughout his writing career. It is believed that socio-historical (external) circumstances and their pernicious impact on children's and young adults' behaviour are central concerns in his earlier novels. Moreover, the representation of the impact of narrative events and situations on the fictional minds' consciousness appears to be the crucial concern in McEwan's later narratives published after *The Child in Time* (1987). After a discussion of these issues, the cardinal questions of the present study, the approach it applies in order to examine and explore the mental workings of the chosen fictional minds are given at the end of the following section.

1.1 Reading McEwan as a Cognitive Novelist

McEwan's fiction has evolved thematically and technically during the nearly four decades of his writing career. He »has been considered [a] shocking« writer in his early career and a »serious and contemplative novelist« (Childs, *The* 2) with respect to his later work. In his later novels, McEwan has paid close attention to the presentation of fictional minds. He uses the omniscient third person narrative mode in *AM* (1998), *AT* (2002), *Saturday* (2005), *CB* (2007) and *Solar* (2010) as well as diverse consciousness (re)presentation[7] methods—direct thought, indirect thought and particu-

---

7 In relation to »consciousness representation« and »fictional minds,« Marco Caracciolo criticises Herman and Palmer, respectively, for two different reasons. He criticises Palmer, as well as Lisa Zunshine, for not discussing the »consciousness proper« in narrative in their analyses of fictional minds. Likewise, he criticises Herman for his argument over the »representation of consciousness« primarily based on the textual cues. Caracciolo argues that Palmer in *Fictional Minds* and Zunshine in *Why We Read Fiction* never use »representation« in tandem with »consciousness,« instead what they focus on is »the reader's attribution of mental states to the characters; they do not seem to devote special attention to consciousness proper« (»Fictional« 42). In other words, applying a functional approach and relying on the characters' actions and focusing on »the reader's attribution of mental states to the characters,« they did not »devote special attention to consciousness proper.« (»Fictional 142). Therefore, according to Caracciolo, they only explore »what [David] Chalmers

calls ›the psychological mind‹« which is involved with »the mind's role in influencing behavior« (qtd. in Caracciolo, »Fictional« 42); so, they leave »the issue of fictional consciousnesses unsolved.« Nevertheless, modifying their approaches, Caracciolo (»Fictional« 43) states that »defining fictional characters in functionalist terms has yielded deep insights, well exemplified by Palmer's and Zunshine's books. And yet, it is important to remind ourselves that readers do not just attribute mental states to fictional characters—they attribute to them mental states with a qualitative aspect. I'd like to see the original text of this quotation in full. In short, they attribute to them a consciousness« based on the textual cues. Therefore, Caracciolo argues that »we should not view characters' consciousnesses as ›things in the text.‹ Readers can enact a fictional consciousness, they can perform it on the basis of textual cues [...] I will call (this phenomenon) consciousness-enactment.« Following that, Caracciolo's chief complaint against Herman is that »consciousness (be it fictional or not) cannot be represented« (»Fictional« 43) but it can only be »enacted« or performed. Accordingly, he concludes that »Palmer, and Herman have proposed an excellent representational model of how readers conceptualize characters' psychological states and traits, but that they miss the mark when it comes to consciousnesses. [...] fictional consciousnesses cannot be represented (neither in the text nor in the reader's mind), since consciousness and subject experience seem to be largely impervious to representationalism« (»Fictional« 46). Moreover, Caracciolo argues that in a similar manner to consciousness which is not representable in the text, experience also »cannot be subsumed under the framework of representationalism« (»Fictional« 59). Instead, it is narratively constructed since »narrative texts are experiencing-providing machines,« therefore, the »experiential direction of flow is not only from the reader to the text, but also from the text to the reader [...] the characters' experiences cannot be represented—they are not *things in the text*. These new experiences are undergone by readers, and by no one else« (»Fictional« 54–55). Thus, according to Caracciolo, in an imagining process, readers, based on their actual world experiences and the textual cues, not only attribute consciousness to fictional minds, but they also enact or perform the consciousness itself. Therefore, consciousness-enactment, according to Caracciolo, »is always complemented by consciousness-attribution: our consciousness merges with the consciousness attributed to the fictional character, and we experience a fictional world through the narrow gap between being ourselves and not being ourselves« (»Fictional« 59). In other terms, we, through imagining, firstly attribute an independent consciousness to the characters and then gradually »shape our own consciousness until it merges with the consciousness we attribute to the character. It is through this reshaped consciousness that we experience the fictional world« (»Fictional« 57). Accordingly, the nutshell of Caracciolo's hypothesis is that characters are not only »as psychologically ›minded‹ beings (functionally analogous to humans), but also as beings capable of having conscious mental states, or of undergoing subjective experience« (»Fictional« 58). It follows that according

larly free indirect thought (FIT). These techniques allow him to report focalised characters' inner perceptions in order to involve the reader in the mental functioning of the fictional characters. With their high degrees of fictionality and narrativity,[8] moreover, these narratives are potential to anchor themselves firmly to the readers' real world knowledge, experience and mental models, or to their so-called frames and scripts. Therefore, McEwan can be considered as a cognitive novelist.

McEwan's central narrative themes and techniques, according to Angus R. B. Cochran, should not be analysed apart from

> a tradition of twentieth-century European novelists who took it upon themselves to expose the cynicism and corruption of government, patriarchy, class division and nationalism. Furthermore, his influences—Kafka, Woolf, Joyce—proposed that individual psychology was inextricably bound up with such large-scale social forces. (407)

One should also include in this list of influences Henry James as »something of a mentor.« McEwan, however, as Brooker adds, has »imaginatively engaged with the politics of the present« (53, 54) in his works. Exploration of the individual psychology becomes central in McEwan's later fiction in which he primarily »illuminates the cavernous makeup of the mind by using his own instrument, his penetrating prose. The place he discovers there is both dark and elegant« (Cochran 407). Even though this statement by Cochran predates the novels discussed in this study, it fits them as well. They are predominantly concerned with the representation of the fictional

---

to Caracciolo, reader, not the textual cues, should be considered as the focal point in the realization of narrative experience and fictional minds since, based on his/her actual experiential repertoire, s/he can both attribute and enact or perform consciousness to characters. For example, it is only based on the dialectic exchanges with the presented experiences within *AM*, *AT* and *CB* that the fictional minds such as Clive, Vernon, Edward, Florence and Briony are shaped in our minds. Nevertheless, following Palmer's and Herman's discussion, fictional minds and consciousness-related issues in this study are used respectively in tandem with »presentation« and »representation«.

8 Herman defines the term narrativity as »what makes a story (interpretable as) a story« or »what makes a narrative a narrative« (*Basic* x, 1)

characters' mental functioning. Moreover, they explore the destructive impact of fictional minds' intramental thoughts on their inter-personal relationships. Likewise, McEwan, according to Wells,

> combines a contemporary sensibility about the power and limitations of narrative with a keen sense of his characters' inner lives and their struggles to deal morally with one another. His work demonstrates an impressive variety of generic styles and a wide historical range while consistently providing his readers with points of identification and reflection about their own lives. (»Ian McEwan« 252)

Through presentation of their mental functioning, McEwan's consciousness narratives present the characters' inner lives showing the nature or mode of their thoughts and the way(s) they deal with the other fictional minds. As Matt Ridley states, »The novelist's privilege, according to Ian McEwan, is to step inside the consciousness of others, and to lead the reader there like psychological Virgil« (vii). Similarly, McEwan in *AM, AT* and *CB* steps inside the central characters' consciousnesses and in this way enables the reader to compare and contrast the presented perspectives.

1.2 Mind Representation in *Amsterdam*, *Atonement* and *On Chesil Beach* and the Aim of this Study

Presentation of the characters' mental functioning is the central narrative concern in McEwan's *AM, AT* and *CB*. In the first part of *AT* Briony, is represented as yearning to impose her mental order on her surroundings. Likewise, McEwan's two other narratives, as Wells states, »have a number of things in common despite their very different subjects and generic styles. Both focus on a small number of characters engaged in tightly formed relationships and lead to intense dramatic action and climactic endings« (*Ian McEwan* 84). This study maintains that whenever the main characters in the chosen narratives become too much intramental pursuing only their own interests or perspectives, they finally face excruciating pain and failure. Although the fictional minds in *AM* are situated and constructed socially, the communication among them fails mostly because the intramental side of their mental functioning overcomes the intermental one or the balance between them is disrupted. The reader mainly becomes aware of such situations through both the narrative presentation of the concerned characters' unuttered thoughts and their behaviour. For example, in *AM*, »As the novel proceeds, the reader enters the minds of the two protagonists and some other characters, too, and follows their moods, uncertainties, and intimations of mortality and immortality« (Malcolm 192). In other words, »In both books, the characters are either unwilling or unable to recognise the needs of others, and remain trapped within modes of self-serving behaviour that ultimately harm them as well« (Wells, *Ian McEwan* 85). Moreover, the primary focus of these narratives seems to be character presentation. According to Palmer »characters« in these narratives »face sharp and painful dilemmas relating to attempts to exercise control over other minds and the motives in trying to doing so« (*Social* 64). This characteristic, presentation of characters' or selves' relationships with the others, is in fact in line with McEwan's style too. Pascal Nicklas refers to this case stating that: »At the heart of McEwan's poetology is the desire to look through the eyes of someone else. The confusion of the self and the other [. . .] in general opens up for Ian McEwan the ethical dimension of literature« (9). Further, the main problem in these narratives arises when the rift between the central characters' intermental units and their intramental orientations is left unfilled causing disequilibrium in the narratives. This brings about a situation when the central characters are unable to come to terms with their own problems or, recognizing them, they are unable to cure them through having a real affiliation between their private selves and the social cognitive networks. In other words, they are unable to construct a permanent balance in their intermental units. It is mainly because of such paucity that their relationships are likely affected adversely.

This study explores the mental functioning of the central characters in McEwan's three narratives. As it is shown in the discussion chapters, the main reason for the disruption of fictional intermental units in *AM*, *AT* and *CB* appears to be the central characters' intramental dissents. The possible worlds in these narratives, moreover, anchor themselves strongly to the reader's world knowledge, experiences or models. This happens because the narratives primarily represent the impact of the presented events and situations on the central characters' consciousness throughout their life courses. This characteristic makes the mentioned narratives more narratives or narratives with high degrees of narrativity because they closely portray the characters' consciousness or the quality of what it's like to undergo some experiences. The difficulty of constructing stable intermental relationships or cognitive units between and among these minds, however, appears to be the main reason for the destructive consequences in these narratives. The »reflector-characters«[9] in these narratives, furthermore, appear to prefer their single subjectivity over (re)constructing intermental units. They are depicted as relying mainly on their own (mis)interpretations of the other(s) as well as on their own minds or highly aspectual perceptions. That seems to be the fundamental reason in bringing about the lack of a unified social or intermental unit in these narratives or annihilating any established one(s) within them.

As this study argues, the workings of the fictional minds in *AM*, *AT* and *CB* reveal both intermental/social and intramental/individual aspects. It is,

---

9 Coined by Franz K. Stanzel in *A Theory of Narrative* (1979 [1986]), the reflector-character, as a mode of narrative transmission, is defined in contrast to the other mode, teller-character. Its main function, according to Stanzel (1981), »is to reflect, i.e., to mirror in his consciousness what is going on in the world outside or inside himself. A reflector-character never narrates in the sense of verbalizing his perceptions, thoughts and feelings, since he does not attempt to communicate his perceptions or thoughts to the reader« (7). Likewise, Manfred Jahn—who develops Stanzel's theory in his discussion of third-person narrative situations as frames: authorial, authorial-figural and figural—argues that »reflectorial seeing includes perception, imaginary perception, thought, feelings, and other mental processes; and the product of these mental activities will be summarily referred to as a character's *consciousness-data*. In reflectorial mode, a reflector's inside views are shown from within,« the text foregrounds the reflector's consciousness-data, the narrative tempo is scenic, and the reader is cast into the role of a witness« (»Frames« 445). Moreover, having reviewed the earlier models, particularly Stanzel's, Jahn continues his argument that »a flexible frame system [...] is actually needed in order to account for the internal dynamics of the narrative situations as well as the various diachronic and synchronic transitions« (»Frames« 448). Accordingly, the narrative situations in *AM*, *AT* and *CB* move from authorial to authorial-figural to figural narratives overtime and following of the characters' mental functioning becomes the reader's primary purpose.

nevertheless, the negative emotional consequences of their subjective first position, or intramental side of their mental functioning, that fundamentally orient their mental states. This also finally brings about the fatal imbalance to their relationships. In *AM,* this situation ends at Clive's and Vernon's double murder and in *CB* in Edward's and Florence's separation before consummating their marriage. This study explores the way(s) fictional minds within these narratives operate when they encounter with challenging conflicts as well as the impact of those momentous conflicts on the operation of their consciousness. Following such a process, the study explores how narrative experience takes place too. To do that, the study, in a combining manner in the discussion chapters, uses the terminologies provided by Palmer and Herman about the workings and presentation of fictional minds as well as the impact of the dissenting events and situations on their experiencing consciousness within *AM, AT* and *CB*. Accordingly, two subjects are explored in the theoretical part of this study: the relationship between narrative meaning or experience and fictional minds as well as the connection between any narrative reader's cognitive abilities and her/his understanding of the fictional minds. In analysing the three selected narratives, this study focuses on three points. Firstly, it examines the narrativity level of each narrative. Secondly, it explores the way fictional minds in them are presented and the manner of their operation. Finally, the study analyses the impacts of central characters' thoughts and (mental) experiences on their and the other characters' (individual and social) behaviour/actions as well as relationships.

2. Cognitive Narratology and Consciousness (Re)Presentation

> Situated at a point where the narrative and cognitive turns meet, cognitive narratology provides a meeting ground for many disciplines, including literature, history, linguistics, pragmatics, philosophy, and psychology. (Jahn, »Cognitive« 67)

> Interiority, experientiality, and fictional minds are, after all, a good part of what we read novels for. (Palmer, *Fictional* 38)

> The research at issue suggests not only that narrative is centrally concerned with *qualia*, a term used by philosophers of mind to refer to the sense of what it's like for someone or something to have a particular experience, but also that narrative bears importantly on debates concerning the nature of consciousness itself. (Herman, *Basic* 144)

This chapter explores the fundamental questions of CN, the approach to fictional minds according to Palmer's theories as well as the concept of narrative and narrativity from Herman's perspective. These subjects are the basic theoretical issues for the analysis of the central characters' mental functioning in *AM*, *AT* and *CB*. Under the first subframe, Cognitive Narratology and Narrative Experience, the fundamental questions of CN are examined and then, under a sub-subframe, Fictional Minds and Cognitive Reader, the role of narrative reader is examined within that framework. Further, under the second subframe, Palmer's Approach to Fictional Minds' Mental Functioning, the concepts of fictional minds, their workings within the storyworlds, their presentational modes and their construction and understanding by the reader are discussed. Finally, under the third subframe, Narrative and Narrativity, the concept of narrative and its most important element, what it's like or qualia, as well as reader's narrative experience are explored according to Herman's theories.

2.1 Cognitive Narratology and Narrative Experience

As an important branch of postclassical narratology, CN has been developing from the classical narratology since 1980s. Analyses of the fictional characters' cognitive aspects in postclassical narratology, according to Palmer, take place within two conceptual frameworks: possible-worlds theory and cognitive science. While the former one »regards the fictional text as a set of instructions according to which the storyworld is recovered and reassembled,« the latter, »derived from cognitive science, studies how various cognitive frames and scripts which are made up of real-world, stereotypical knowledge are applied to the reading process« (»Thought« 606). Moreover, considered »as a subdomain [...and] still an emergent trend within the broader domain of narratology,« CN[10] »at present constitutes more a set of loosely confederated heuristic schemes than a systematic framework for inquiry.« The lack of a »systematic framework,« however, does not mean that the related works in this field are disconnected. According to Herman, the »mind relevant aspects of storytelling practices« is a »trait shared by all this work [cognitive approaches to narrative fiction].« Following that, CN is defined as »the study of mind-relevant aspects of storytelling practices« (Herman, »Cognitive« 30–31). It is so because in CN »representation of minds are [considered] fundamental to stories« (Herman, »Cognition« 257)[11]. In

10 Herman defines CN as »A strand within postclassical narratology that focuses on mind-relevant dimensions of storytelling practices, wherever—and by whatever means—those practices occur« (»Cognitive« 182). Likewise, Palmer states that »cognitive narratology takes narrative in general as its object of study—it is as interested in film as in print, as interested in nonfiction as in fiction—but most of its work up to this point has focused on novels and short stories« (»Social Minds in Fiction« 199).

11 Furthermore, elaborating on the importance of »mind-relevant« aspects in CN, Herman holds that ›mind-relevance‹ can be studied vis-à-vis the multiple factors associated with the design and interpretation of narratives, including the story-producing activities of tellers, the processes by means of which interpreters make sense of storyworlds evoked by narrative representations or artifacts, and the cognitive states and dispositions of characters in those storyworlds. In addition, the mind-narrative nexus can be studied along two other dimensions, insofar as stories function as both (1) a target of interpretation and (2) a means for making sense of experience—a resource for structuring and comprehending the world—in their own

addition, reader experiences storyworld mainly through following the cognitive aspects of narrative.

Narrative, according to Herman, is a »cognitive activity« (*Basic* 98) since its »meaning potential requires the cognitive activity of readers« (Herman, »Cognitive« 33).[12] Furthermore, mind, as claimed by Herman, is crucial to storyworld since »stories both shape and are shaped by what minds perceive, infer, remember, and feel« (»Cognition« 257). Likewise, representation of the experiencing minds is considered to be one of the key concerns in McEwan's work since, as maintained by Nicklas, »The genome and theories of the mind and brain as well as Darwinian evolutionary models or ecological problems of climate change are the background to much of McEwan's fiction and his many articles« (10). CN is, furthermore, concerned with questions that in general deal with narrative production, the nature of fictional minds' functioning as well as their presentation in narrative and narrative understanding. Moreover, in the opinion of Palmer, »One of the concerns of cognitive narratology is the relationship between consciousness and narrative« (»Attributions« 292) which is central to this study too. The following questions, which, according to Herman, »still suggest themselves

---

right (*Basic* 85). By the same token, the primary aim in this study is the analysis of the fictional characters' cognitive states since the study begins with the assumption that, through the examination of the ways fictional characters' make sense of their own and the other characters' experiences, narratives can help the readers to understand their real experiences because it presents the possible situations of human beings' interactions.

12 Lisa Zunshine in *Why We Read Fiction: Theory of Mind and the Novel* (2006) lists a series of critics »working with cognitive approaches to literature«: Porter Abbott, Frederick Louis Aldama, Mary Crane, Nancy Easterlin, Elizabeth Hart, David Herman, Patrick Colm Hogan, Alan Palmer, Alan Richardson, Ellen Spolsky, and Blakey Vermeule (ix). Supporting this approach, in terms of her own Theory of Mind (ToM) she, moreover, states that as »an evolved cognitive capacity« it enables »both our interaction with each other and our ability to make sense of fiction« (13). Likewise, Palmer points out the centrality of cognition within narratives arguing, »Narrative is, in essence, the description of fictional mental functioning. In my view, readers enter the storyworlds of novels primarily by attempting to follow the workings of the fictional minds contained in them [...] In fact, we have to be cognitivists« (*Social* 177).

to the cognitive narratologists« (»Cognitive« 31), are also the fundamental questions of the present study:

> How exactly do stories function as tools for thinking? Is it the case that [. . .] narrative is a mode of representation tailor-made for gauging the felt quality of lived experiences? More radically, do stories afford scaffolding for consciousness itself—in part by emulating through their temporal and perspectival configuration the nature of conscious awareness itself? In other words, are there grounds for making the strong claim that narrative not only represents what it is like for experiencing minds to live through events in storyworlds, but also constitutes a basis for having—for knowing—a mind at all, whether it is one's own or another's?[13] (Herman, »Cognitive« 32)

CN, as Herman understands, intends to evaluate narrative as tools for thinking[14] meaning that any narrative provides some cues that initiate the reader's cognitive activities while experiencing narrative. In addition, it is a medium of experience representation and representation of the impact of represented events and situations on characters' consciousness. CN, moreover, intends to connect the storyworlds to the readers' actual world knowledge and experiences treating fictional minds' operation partially like the mental functioning of the actual minds in many respects. It is concerned with the relationship between narrative or storyworld presentation and the actual lived experiences. It examines the relationship between the nature of fictional minds' functioning, the way they are presented as well as their consciousness and the manner they are actualised or configured in the reader's

---

13 In addition, the following questions, according to Herman, are among the key questions for CN:
What cognitive processes support narrative understanding, allowing readers, viewers, or listeners to construct mental models of the worlds evoked by stories? How do they use medium-specific cues to build on the basis of the discourse or *sujet* a chronology for events, or *fabula* (what happened when, or in what order?); a broader temporal and spatial environment for those events (when in history did these events occur, and where geographically?); an inventory of the characters involved; and a working model of what it was like for these characters to experience the more or less disruptive or non-canonical events that constitute a core feature of narrative representations. (*Basic* 31)

14 Similarly, according to Matt Ridley, McEwan also »uses fiction to understand the mind and to explore human nature, as well as uses words to alter readers' consciousness« (viii).

mind while experiencing narrative[15]. All in all, CN-based analysis presupposes the affinity between the storyworld and the actual one and hence attempts to analyse, in Herman's words, the »mind-relevant aspects of storytelling practices« (»Cognitive« 31) in the former one based on the principles of the latter. That is so, because, as Herman suggests elsewhere, fictional minds' examination »entails giving an account of readers' minds, too—of how readers interpret particular textual details as information about characters' attempts to make sense of the world around them« (»Cognition« 245). Likewise, the central concern in *AM, AT* and *CB* seems to be the fictional minds' reactions to the challenging situations and events or their mental functioning in different situations. In other words, they both »replicate consciousness in text« (Ridley vii). In *AM,* for example, Clive-Vernon relationship is mostly represented through their internal broodings both about each other and about themselves. In the same way, the bedroom scene and the beach scene in *CB* are represented primarily through Edward's and Florence's internal perspectives focusing on their intramental evaluations of the conflicts. Likewise, in *AT* the narrative mainly shows how Briony's perspective at some particular moments (for example in the fountain scene) is in conflict with that of the others. As a result of this characteristic, these narratives are rich in terms of tools for thinking, experience, consciousness, mindreading and the other cognitive related issues.[16]

The attention to the importance of mind, experience, consciousness as well as the reader's function in narrative interpretation and finally his/her narrative experience are mainly notable within the postclassical phase of narratology. With an autonomous and self-sufficient understanding of the text, classical narratology was limited to the textual framework. According

---

15 Such emphasis on experience representation is in agreement with Ian Watt's statement that »the novelist's primary task is to convey the impression of fidelity to human experience« (13).

16 As illustrated by Orhan Pamuk, representation of fictional world information through internal focalisation adds to the reader's engagement with the selected narratives because »the real pleasure of reading a novel starts with the ability to see the world not from the outside but through the eyes of the protagonists living in that world.« Besides that, »reading a novel means looking at the world through the eyes, mind and the soul of the novel's characters« (11, 60).

to Jahn, it attempted to refute as far as possible any extraneous factors ignoring »the forces, and desires of psychological, social, cultural and historic contexts.« Therefore, it rejected the idea that »texts« should be »reconstructed in an ongoing and revisable readerly process« (»Cognitive« 67) as pursued by the postclassical approaches to narrative. Further, the abstract nature of classical models, in terms of story and text, is believed to »ignore(s) experience, ideology, and other so-called subjective and contextual elements as much as possible« (Herman and Vervaeck 104). The early narratologists, or Francophone Structuralists, were influenced by the Russian Formalism through Vladimir Propp's *Morphology of the Folktale* (1928). After Tzvetan Todorov proposed the term narratology in 1968, they came to be known as structuralist narratologists. They emphasised on narrative form, its intrinsic constituents and common ingredients in order to define a universal pattern or grammar for the understanding of narrative function. The structuralist-inspired narratology, as Gerald Princestates, was »text type rather than context, grammar rather than rhetoric, form rather than force« (*A Dictionary* 66).

Postclassical narratology, however, has made efforts to extend the focus of analysis in the process of narrative experience beyond the textual frames of narrative though including the contextual elements such as the importance of author, reader, history, class, gender etc. Nevertheless, postclassical narratology, as Herman points out, is not considered as a negation of the classical one but instead it »draws on concepts and methods to which the classical narratology did not have access to« (»Scripts« 1049). Moreover, it:

> contains structuralist theory as one of its »moments« but enriches the older approach with research tools taken from other areas of inquiry. Or, to put the same point another way, postclassical narratology expands the scope of narrative analysis and its applicability. The result is not simply new ways of getting at old problems in narrative analysis but a rearticulation of those problems, including the root problem of how to define stories. (»Scripts« 1057)

Therefore, in spite of the fact that »The postclassical approaches partly resist structuralism,« or the so-called classical narratology, »but at the same time rarely if ever make a complete break from it« (Herman and Vervaeck 103).

One of the ›research tools‹ that in postclassical narratology has been included in narrative analysis approaches comes from cognitive psychologists. Cognitive approach to narrative, accordingly, argues that narrative readers—who experience narrative using their actual experiences and cognitive abilities—undergo nearly the same experiences as represented in the storyworld or experienced by the fictional characters.

Accordingly, »Cognitive dimensions of stories and storytelling,« according to Herman, »has become an important subdomain within the field of narrative analysis.« It is »concerned both with how people understand narratives and with narrative itself as a mode of understating« (»Narrative: Cognitive« 452). Cognitive approaches to literature, therefore, intend to analyse the (cognitive) techniques readers apply in order to experience narratives. It also explores the ways narrative itself can be taken as a mode of understanding (the minds and experiences) or as a tool for thinking. Hence, the presupposition behind Herman's statement is twofold.[17] Firstly, fictional minds and storyworld as a whole can be treated as well as analysed like actual minds or actual world entities. Secondly, it is implied that from the perspective of cognitive approach to literature, narrative reader or audience is central to the process of decoding narrative information. In the same way, Palmer, as a follower of cognitive theories and approaches, underlines the fundamental role of the reading processes of real readers. He remarks that »the constructions of the minds of fictional characters by narrators and readers are central to our understanding of how novels work, because readers

17 Herman's concept of story is also illuminating in this case since he holds that »stories are the result of complex transactions involving producers of texts, discourses, or other semiotic artifacts, the texts or artifacts themselves, and interpreters of these narrative productions working with cultural, institutional, genre-based, and textspecific protocols« (*Basic* 17). Therefore, Herman in his last work, *Storytelling and the Sciences of Mind* (2013), explores the processes of what he refers to as *worlding the story* and *storying the world*. For example, in its chapter eight, »Storied Minds (or Persons and Reasons Revisited): Narrative Scaffolding for Falk Psychology«, using McEwan's *CB* he explores the »ways in which narrative can function as a folk-psychological resource [...or discusses] how narrative's capacity to maintain time [...] makes stories an ideal environment for modeling the motivations, structure, and consequences of the conduct of persons« (19).

enter storyworlds primarily by attempting to follow the workings of the fictional minds contained in them« (*Social* 7). However, considering the symbiotic relationship between the diegetic feature (that is narrator) and extradiegetic feature (that is real readers) of the narrative, Herman's and Palmer's stances are unlike those of the classical narratologists. Classical or structuralist narratology inclined to constrain the active role of reader in narrative comprehension by its over emphasis on intradiegetic or textual features.[18]

---

[18] The implied analogy between real people and fictional characters adopted by narratologists within cognitive perspective, including Palmer, however, has been evaluated disapprovingly by many critics. Marisa Bortolussi, for example, remarks that: He [Palmer] simply assumes that readers form a theory of mind for characters as they do for real people and, therefore, that the mechanisms for »reading« fictional characters are the same as those involved in dealing with real people. But what Palmer presents as a foregone conclusion, is in fact an empirical question for which there exists empirical evidence to the contrary. [...] A fundamental difference between real people and literary characters is that we deal with the former directly and with the latter only through the intermediary of authorial or narratorial direction. Characters do not have theories of mind of other characters; they only think or know what the narrators tell us, or insinuate, that they think or know. And because it is the narrator who provides the information that leads readers to draw particular kinds of inferences about characters, the crucial question is how readers process the narrator. Rather than form a theory of mind for fictional characters, readers may simply construct a representation of what the narrator might intend for us to understand. (285)

Nevertheless, Margolin, drawing on the recent insights by James Phelan and Jens Eder on the »readerly engagement« with the character, proposes a »systematic map« by the help of some terms obtained from the medieval philosophy. According to him there are four modes of readerly engagement with the fictional characters: *de sensu, de dicto, de re* and *de se* modes:

De sensu mode (Characters as Semantic Items) means we are dealing with the senses or meanings of *expressions*. *De dicto* (Characters as Object of Thought) means dealing with the *content or intensions (meanings, senses) of propositions* which in their turn are conveyed by expressions related to one another in some formal logical ways. In the *de re* mode (Characters as Existents in Worlds) we are concerned with the *truth value* of the claims made by propositions, and with the corresponding *states of affairs and individuals* described by them, hence with references or extensions as well. Finally, in the *de se* mode (Fictional Characters in Our Lives) the *claims, individuals, and states of affairs* projected by the propositions are related to the cogniser's own correspond-

2.1.1 Fictional Minds and Cognitive Reader

Fictional minds are modelled by the help of readers' cognitive abilities based on the semiotic features provided by the author in the narrative text. Accordingly, CN considers fictional character, not plot or sequence of events, as the central part of narrative through which reader's experience of fictional world is realised. That is so because narrative plot is primarily shaped by what happens to characters within the storyworld or by the events that become their experiences. It follows that, narrative is in fact representation, as well as analysis, of the impact of narrative events and situations on fictional characters. That is so because, as Palmer says, »events in the storyworld are of little importance unless they become the experiences of characters. We follow the plot by following the workings of fictional minds« (»The Lydgate« 156). At the centre of Palmer's research lies the question »how fictional minds work within the context of the storyworlds to which they belong« (»Construction« 29). According to him, fictional minds are the product of both story level and the discourse level of narrative:

> I have been asked whether fictional minds form part of the story level (the content plane, the narrated, the »what,« the *fabula)* or the discourse level (the expression

---

ing mental attitudes, activities and experiences, such as beliefs, desires, and intentions, and to his emotions and actions in the actual world. (»From Predicates to people Like Us« 401)

Palmer's concept of fictional characters seems to be closer to Margolin's second mode, *de dicto*, which holds that »there is possibly in some domain an individual who is designated by the given individual referring expression and who is thus and so« (»From Predicates to people Like Us« 406). Likewise, Palmer reiterates that fictional minds *possibly* exist in some world. For instance, Clive, Vernon, Edward and Florence may or may not exist in a world although the existence of such storyworlds is taken for granted. Thus, understanding of such beings, as Schneider emphasises, »requires our forming some kind of mental representation of them, attributing dispositions and motivations to them, understanding and explaining their actions, forming expectations about what they will do next and why, and, of course, reacting emotionally to them.« Palmer emphasises on frames instead of mental models implying partly the same concept that Schneider was following: »I will therefore explicate my proposal to conceive of literary character as a mental model that the reader construes in the reading process through a combination of information from textual and mental sources« (608).

> plane, the narrating, the »how,« the *sjuzhet).* The answer involves two separate but related issues: One is the story-level issue of the nature of the fictional minds constructed by the texts, the *what* that is the content of those minds; the other is the discourse-level issue of the techniques used to represent consciousness in narrative, *how* minds are presented in the discourse. It quickly becomes apparent, however, that it is difficult in practice to maintain a distinction between the two. I focus primarily on the first issue, the *what,* but it is impossible to talk about the *what* without detailed consideration of the *how.* To describe the contents of fictional minds is to focus on how those minds are presented in the text. Also, the techniques that are used for fictional mind presentations will determine, to a certain extent, what thoughts are described. (»Social Minds« 205)

Therefore, narrative reader experiences fictional minds through following both narrative content and its techniques. Moreover, in CN any undertaken narrative analysis is based on the representational or mimetic concept of character since from mimetic perspective, as Uri Margolin put, a character is treated »as a human or human-like entity« (»Character« 53).[19] Following that, narrative reader is able to experience narrative using her/his own universal knowledge structures (schemas, scripts, and frames). As a result, within the theoretical paradigms of cognitive approach, a »character is seen as a mental model of a storyworld participant, constructed by the reader incrementally in the course of reading (text comprehension) on the basis of constant interplay between specific textual data and general knowledge structures stored in the reader's long-term memory.« The constructed mental model, however, is based on nothing other than the textual or semiotic data or clues which orient the reader's mental map of a character as a »conceptual unit« (Margolin, »Character« 54). As Margolin continues, having gathered the scattered but related properties of a character within the text following a »bottom-up or data-driven processing, [. . .] they often activate

19 This perspective, according to Rimmon-Kenan (34), is similar to the »realistic« approach to character. Likewise, he compares the mimetic approach to character with the semiotic one as following, »Whereas in mimetic theories (i.e. theories which consider literature as, in some sense, an imitation of reality) characters are equated with people, in semiotic theories they dissolve into textuality« (35). In the same way, Mieke Bal in her discussion of character takes an »anthropomorphic« approach stating that »a character is the effect that occurs when a figure is presented with distinctive, mostly human characteristics« (*Narratology* 112–113).

a knowledge structure stored in long-term memory under which these properties can be subsumed and integrated into a character model« (»Character« 54–5). Further, the constructed knowledge structure which triggers a unique character category in reader's mind can be, other than the literary models, based on actual-world models. In that case, the readers, following a top down model besides the bottom up one,[20] experience the text with an already established mental model or categorization. As a result, according to Margolin, they »fill in or complete their mental model of the individual, formulate expectations about further textual information about it, and explain previous information« (»Character« 55). Nevertheless, the reader's mental model of a character does not stay fixed throughout his/her narrative experiencing. It is exposed to refreshment or reconstruction and disruption or change. That is mainly because they ascribe different properties to a particular character based on both the explicit textual data and their own inferences as well.

Therefore, the reader[21] is considered as the main part of narrative understanding or experiencing in cognitive approaches to narrative. This is a result of the fact, that encountering the fictional minds, they use their default experiences. They also use their ability of constructing theories of mind, as they do in their actual relationships, in order to gain access to the manner of fictional characters' mental functioning. At the same time, they experience the ways fictional characters make theories of minds about the other characters. In the same way, reader is central to Herman's and Palmer's cognitive

---

20 Readers in CN are considered to be using the two processing methods simultaneously. Therefore, as Ralf Schneider states, from such a perspective:

Text understanding always combines top-down processing, in which the reader's pre-stored knowledge structure are directly activated to incorporate new items of information, and bottom up-processing, in which bits of textual information are kept in working memory separately and integrated into an overall representation at a later point in time. Top-down and bottom-up processing continually interact in the reading process on all levels. (611)

21 The concept of reader, in both Palmer's and Herman's theories, refers to a correlation of both implied reader and the real or historical one. The former is the effect of the overall narrative structure constructed based on the textual implications while the latter takes into consideration the psychological states of the real readers.

approaches to narrative. They attempt to show how readers utilise their everyday cognitive frames, which have default values too, and scripts or their world knowledge and models in order to interpret the fictional minds or, in the opinion of Palmer, »to fill gaps in storyworlds« (»The Lydgate« 154).[22] Although Herman's area of concern is much broader than that of Palmer's, their approaches highlight some of those universal frames. Herman's theory is in agreement with Palmer's statement that »fictional beings are necessarily incomplete, frames, scripts, and preference rules are required to supply the defaults that fill the gaps in the storyworld and provide the presuppositions that enable the reader to construct continually conscious minds from the text« (*Fictional* 176). Therefore, these are the central questions to both Herman and Palmer: how readers accept storyworlds as plausible possible worlds with possible beings, how they make sense of stories and how they utilise their cognitive potentialities in order to access the plausible characters' minds are central.

Palmer pursues a parallel approach[23] to the fictional minds. Calling this approach »criss-crossing of the field [. . .] an interdisciplinary project« (*Fic-*

---

22 These gaps, according to Palmer:

> constitute the difference between, on the one hand, the combination of the story and the discourse that constitutes the text; and, on the other hand, the storyworld. No discourse could ever be long enough to say in its story all that could be said about the whole storyworld. As a result, fiction is necessarily incomplete. The reader can cope with the gaps in the continuing consciousnesses of fictional minds because, in the real world, we experience gaps in other, real minds too. (»The Lydgate« 154)

23 Palmer's approach to fictional minds foregrounds the similarity between fictional and actual minds by postulating that »fictional minds [...] have to operate very much like actual minds.« Palmer expands his analogy by arguing that »Just as in real life the individual constructs the minds of others from their behaviour, so the reader infers the workings of fictional minds and sees these minds in action from observation of characters' behavior and actions« (*Fictional* 202, 246). Therefore, Palmer's main concern is the analysis of the way(s) fictional minds are constructed by both the narrators and the readers because, according to him, they are »central to our understanding of how novels work.« (*Fictional* 12). His tendency to anthropomorphise fictional minds, however, does mean going beyond the concrete text considered by the classical narratologists as a systematic whole providing narrative

tional 3–4), he argues that the same techniques people apply in order to understand other people's minds are automatically applied when they, as readers, try to understand the fictional minds through attributing mental states to them. In Herman's words:

> Palmer (2004) also draws on elements of the early work on knowledge representations, studying how readers' world-knowledge allows them to make sense of a variety of techniques for representing fictional characters' minds. Palmer explores how readers construct inferences about fictional minds by using various textual indicators, including thought reports, speech representations, and ascriptions of behaviors that span the continuum linking mental with physical actions. (»Cognitive« 34)

Moreover, having called his approach to the fictional minds »external,« Palmer elsewhere uses the term social mind to »describe those aspects of the whole mind that are revealed through the externalist perspective« (*Social* 39)[24]. His concept of social mind in fiction, nevertheless, is within the context of »the cognitive turn in humanities, or, more specifically, what has come to be known as cognitive approach to literature« (Palmer, *Social* 198). Moreover, he chimes on the »traditional narratological approach to the representation of fictional character,« which, according to him, is »internalist one that stresses those aspects that are inner, passive, introspective, and individual«

meaning primarily by itself. About seventy responses to Palmer's theory, *Social Minds in Fiction*, were published in the prestigious journal *Style* 45(2): Summer 2011. Palmer's answer to the question, »Are you saying that fictional minds are the same as real minds?, comes as following: »*I am not saying that fictional minds are the same as real minds. I am saying that fictional minds are similar to real minds in some ways and different from them in other ways. We will not understand fictional minds unless we understand both of these aspects: both their similarities to, and their differences from, real minds*« (emphasis original, »Social Minds in Fiction« 205).

24 This concept is related to Palmer's externalist approach which, he believes, has been ignored in earlier approaches to novel studies. It supposes that cognition, (fictional) consciousness, action and identity are socially distributed or situated. This study uses both external and internal perspectives. Although the main part of narrative events and situations in *AM*, *AT* and *CB* are recounted internally throughout the characters' embedded narratives, still their states of minds are revealed in the other characters' perspectives too. In other words, the fictional minds' mental functioning in these narratives is revealed through both their own broodings and the other character's perceptions about them.

(*Social* 39). Thus, according to Palmer, in the previous narratological approaches to the fictional characters, either »the social nature of fictional thought has been neglected« or »little narratological work has been done on social minds in the novel« (*Social* 39–40, 45). Thus, exploration of such aspect of fictional character should be included in the narratological approaches because an externalist perspective »stresses the public, social, concrete, and located aspects of mental life in the novel« (Palmer, 2010a: 40). Accordingly, when referring to the intermental and intramental thoughts,[25] which are the important parts of Palmer's social mind theory, a complementary approach is thought to be an appropriate narratological approach to the fictional minds. It should combine internalist perspective with the externalist one. Considering the two perspectives on mind—INTERNALIST PERSPECTIVE and EXTERNAL PERSPECTIVE [capitals are Palmer's]—Palmer suggests that:

> A good deal of the significance of the thought that occurs in novels is lost if only the internalist perspective is employed. Both perspectives are required, because a major preoccupation of novels is precisely this balance between public and private thought, intermental and intramental functioning, and social and individual minds. Within

---

25 As Herman states, »interpreting fictional and other narratives requires making sense of how they portray supraindividual or group-level forms of sense making, or what Palmer calls intermental thought« (*Storytelling* 249). Likewise, equating it with »*socially distributed, situated* or *extended cognition* and also as *intersubjectivity,*« Palmer considers intermental thought as an important part of the social mind (»Social Minds in *Little*« 28). Moreover, according to Palmer, »The relationship between intra- and intermental activity, between social minds and individual minds, between the internalist and the externalist perspectives, is a complex and fascinating one. It is central to narrative fiction« (»Social Minds in Fiction« 198). Similarly, the primary purpose of this study is to examine the relationships between these polarities in *AM, AT* and *CB*. Nevertheless, some of Palmer's critics reject his definition of intermental thought. Hogan, for example, argues that, »it is difficult to say just what this [intermental thought] might mean. Despite Palmer's assertions, cognitive science offers no help here. If we follow the standard neuro-cognitive view that the mind is a function of the brain, then there has to be a brain for there to be a thought. But the point of an intermental thought is, presumably, that it is not found only in brains« (244).

this balance, I will be emphasizing social minds because of their past neglect. (*Social* 42)

Therefore, from Palmer's perspective both internalist and externalist perspectives are required for the proper analysis of the fictional minds' mental functioning as it is followed in this study too.[26]

A character's mind is modelled based on some sources. His/her inner speeches can delineate his/her mental life including feelings, beliefs, intentions and internal perceptions regarding the other characters' thoughts and actions. Similarly, the way a character appears in the minds of the other characters or is thought by them, his/her place in the community, his/her actions etc. can define and clarify the manner of his/her mental functioning. Moreover, drawing on the textual cues and the real world experiences, the

---

26 Also related to this discussion, Palmer elsewhere states that:

In considering mental functioning in fiction, we need to use both an internalist and externalist perspective. An internalist perspective stresses those aspects of cognitive functioning that are inner, introspective, solitary, private, individual and mysterious. By contrast an externalist perspective stresses those aspects of mental functioning that are outer, active, public, social, behavioral and evident. It seems to me that an internalist perspective will not tell us much about the mental functioning [... but] the complex, dialogical relationship between the two [will do so]. (»Storyworlds«185)

Drawing on Antonio Damasio's suggestion, »The study of human consciousness requires both internal and external views« (qtd. in Palmer, »Small« 163), Palmer, moreover, considers the two terms »more of a continuum than an either/or dichotomy« (Palmer, »Small« 163). Nevertheless, he believes that »We all study the workings of fictional minds and think of novels in terms of the mental functioning of characters« (»Social Minds in fiction« 200). Herman, however, in his response to Palmer's social minds and applying a post-Cartesian approach to fictional minds, seeks to »replace the internal-external scale with a continuum stretching between, at one pole, a tight coupling between an intelligent agent and that agent's surrounding environment, and, at the other pole, a looser coupling between agent and environment [...] The new scale stretches between, not inner and outer worlds, but rather relatively fine-grained and relatively coarse-grained representations of the way intelligent agents negotiate opportunities for action and interaction« (»Post-Cartesian« 269–270). The approach to the fictional minds in this study is also similar to Herman's understanding regarding internal-external scale.

reader attributes mental states to characters. Palmer examines this issue under attribution theory[27] or »the study of how attributions of states of mind are made« (»Attribution« 293). These attributions are possible because of the existence of »theory of mind« in human beings. According to Palmer, it is »used by philosophers and psychologists to describe our awareness of the existence of other minds, our knowledge of how to interpret other people's thought processes, our mind-reading abilities in the real world.« For this reason, Palmer argues that:

> Readers of novels have to use their theory of mind in order to try to follow the workings of characters' minds. Otherwise, they will lose the plot. The only wayin which the reader can understand the plot of a novel is by trying to follow the workings of characters' minds and thereby by attributing states of minds to them. This mind reading involves trying to follow characters' attempts to read other characters' minds. (»Attribution« 293)

The central characters' attributions of states of mind to each other in *AM, AT* and *CB* appear to be inaccurate and unsuccessful. Such false attributions, as a result, lead the bond between Clive and Vernon as well as Edward and Florence to total breakdown or annihilation.

Palmer's theory regarding the function of reader in narrative experiencing derives partly from the traditional reader response theory. Recognizing the »intense power of reader response to fictional minds,« he alludes to the »sheer scale of the input required from readers in constructing minds from novels« (*Fictional* 4, 3). This means that he believes in the »creative nature of the reading process.« According to him, the textual signs are loaded with real human imagination or they are coloured with real life knowledge and experiences. A »text is simply [considered] the scaffolding on which you build the vivid psychological processes that stay with you for so long afterward« (Palmer, *Fictional* 4). Palmer's preference of the study of character to the study of narrative plot, action or event, which is the main concern in classical narratology, according to Stockwell, suggests that »narrative

[27] It includes the following questions: »How do narrators attribute states of mind to characters? How do characters attribute mental states both to themselves and to other characters? How do readers make attributions and thereby build up a sense of a character's whole personality?« (Palmer, »Attributions« 293)

should be regarded as being driven not by event but by person.« Thus, pursuing his central concern in his studies on social and fictional minds, as Stockwell put, »Palmer's approach rests on the evident truism that narratives are about relationships between people« (288). Therefore, the primary concern of the critic/reader in CN appears to be a thorough analysis of the relationship between fictional characters' thoughts and their actions or the effect of their own or the other characters' actions on their thoughts.

Accordingly, either from Herman's perspective or from Palmer's—which are congruent with the general inclination of the postclassical or contextual approaches to narrative—a reader experiences narrative by the help of his/her every day, non-literary or anthropomorphic experiences. In this way, he/she unfolds the possible meanings of a narrative or communicates with it. Therefore, the narrative readers' main responsibility is not the discovery of the narrative grammar through a systematic approach to narrative text, as the structuralist narratologists supposed it should be.[28] Rather, their primary function is to participate in the construction and realization of the narrative meaning using their own real world knowledge and experiences mostly in the forms of scripts and frames they use in everyday communications. The focus of narrative analysis, therefore, changes from text to its receiver who, referring to his/her own anthropomorphic characteristics, constructs the narrative meaning depending on the semiotic features of the narrative text itself. This postclassical understanding of narrative analysis is at

[28] As Herman and Vervaeck summarise, Structuralist narratologists such as Gerard Genette, Mieke Bal and Shlomith Rimmon-Kenan categorised the narrative text into three levels although with different labels:

	GENETTE	RIMMON-KENAN	BAL
Story	histoire	story	fabula
Narrative	recit	text	story
Narration	narration	narration	text

They all, nevertheless, intended to »combine all aspects of narrative analysis in a convenient system« (Herman and Vervaeck 45). Following that, the narrative reader was supposed to derive its embedded meaning by following the textual (through examining the *narrative* and *narration* levels) and extratextual (in the *story* level which is an abstract construct based on the concrete text) markers and accordingly finding out their systematic relationships.

the heart of the new definitions of fictional character, fictional minds, narrative and narrativity or the constituent elements that make a narrative narrative. In the following part, therefore, first Palmer's terminologies regarding the construction, presentation, workings and comprehension or experiencing of fictional minds are analysed. Then, the concept of narrativity and the role of reader in accepting a narrative as narrative as well as its basic elements are discussed.

2.2 Alan Palmer's Approach to Fictional Minds

Palmer in *Fictional Minds* (2004), chapters six »The Fictional Mind« and seven »The Fictional Mind in Action,« gives the outline of his »newly expanded, postclassical narratology of the fictional mind« approach which relates »some cognitive science notions to the specific area of reader comprehension of fictional minds« (17, 175). The previous approaches, according to Palmer, have ignored the central role of the workings of characters' minds while they should be the primary concern of any theoretical analysis of fiction. Palmer builds his approach to fictional minds on five main previous concepts within narrative theory—Story Analysis, Possible Worlds Theory, Characterization, Focalization and Cognitive Science and Frames. However, he finds their attention to fictional minds, which »adjuncts to those other fields,« insufficient. Ignoring the workings of characters' minds, they were primarily concerned with »the analysis of spoken speech in the case of the speech categories; various aspects of discourse analysis in the case of focalization; intertextuality in the case of characterization; classical structuralism in the case of story analysis; and modal logic in the case of possible-worlds theory« (Palmer, Fictional 2). Palmer, however, turns to account some of the fundamentals of these approaches in order to propose a new subject area within narrative theory. In that case and in order to handle his interdisciplinary project, he makes use of what he calls »the parallel discourses[29] on real

---

29 As Palmer states: »They are parallel discourses because they contain a very different kind of picture of consciousness from that provided so far by narratology« (»The Lydgate« 153).

minds« (»The Lydgate« 152). His approach to fictional minds, therefore, includes some of the notions of reader response theory, some of the disciplines related to real minds, (folk) psychology, philosophy of mind, psycholinguistics, cognitive science etc. The questions in his theory address subjects: How fictional characters' minds operate in the chosen narratives? How narrative provides reader with the necessary interpretational tools? How a reader understands them? By what means? Palmer's theory deals with the textural features and textures that provide cues for the readers in order to analyse the presentation of the characters' minds as they are presented by the narrators as well as are judged, thought, perceived etc. by the characters themselves and by the other characters within the storyworld. His theory, furthermore, underscores the role of the readers' stored knowledge or experiences in his understanding of the fictional mental functioning. Palmer, furthermore, points out some of the similarities between the real minds and the fictional ones regarding the same cognitive techniques that they both put to use in order to figure out the mental functioning of the other (real/fictional) people.[30]

Palmer's primary concern is to show how cognitive science notions—frames, plans and scripts—can add to the reader's understanding of fictional minds. The main cognitive notion in his theory is *continuing-consciousness frame*[31] by applying which readers, according to Palmer, are able to construct

---

30 Likewise, considering the close relationship between the real world and the fictional one, Pamuk, the noble-prize winner Turkish novelist, holds that »the fictional world we encounter and enjoy is more real than the real world itself. That these second lives can appear more to us than reality often means that we confuse them with real lives« (3).

31 It is a key cognitive frame, according to Palmer, which makes it possible for the readers to ascribe consciousness to the fictional minds. They utilise their actual world experiences to construct the fictional minds or process the fictional knowledge in a similar manner they construct other real minds through processing knowledge about them and:

Because fictional beings are necessarily incomplete, frames are required to supply the hat fill the gaps in the storyworld and provide the presuppositions that enable the reader to construct continually conscious minds from the text. One key default

characters' minds based on their scattered embedded narratives. Palmer explicates the relationship between the continuing-consciousness frame and the notion of embedded narratives as following:

> the former is the means by which we are able to construct fictional minds; the latter is the result of that construction. Embedded narratives are the product of the application of the continuing-consciousness frame to the discourse. The term *embedded narratives* is intended to convey the point that the reader has a wide range of information available with which to make and then revise judgments about characters minds. (Fictional 183)

Reader, according to Palmer, constructs any fictional mind though obtaining dispersed information regarding that character from different parts of the narrative. The result of this construction is the characters' embedded narratives, which mainly derive from three sources: the relationship between thought and action, intermental or group or shared thinking and doubly embedded narratives. Readers are familiar with these techniques since they »utilize fundamental aspects of our real-world knowledge of the mental functioning both of ourselves and of others« (Palmer, *Fictional* 205).

Considering the importance of characters' actions, Palmer emphasises that »constructions of fictional minds are inextricably bound up with presentations of action« (*Fictional* 211). Therefore, the decoding of actions, the thought-action continuum, indicative descriptions and causation are some of the textual features that can help the readers to construct fictional minds and experience the manner of their functioning (*Fictional* 210–218). Clive's and Vernon's as well as Edward's and Florence's actions and interactions reveal generally the traits of their thoughts. As the second subframe of the continuing consciousness frame, Palmer discusses intermental or joint thought as opposed to intramental or individual thought focusing on the

---

> setting is the assumption that a consciousness will continue throughout the text until interrupted, as in life, by death or absence. Another is that characters will think and act in certain fundamental respects like real people. (»The Lydgate« 155)

Therefore, Palmer's continuing consciousness frame »enables readers to generate so much information from so little source material.« Palmer, moreover, considers Fludernik's *experientiality* and Bal's emphasis on the centrality of *subjectivity* in narrative as the aspects of continuing consciousness frame.

communicative action and relationships between intramental thinking and group norms. With Palmer's differentiation between intermnetal and intramental thought in mind, this study aims to show how the construction of new intermental units or maintenance of already existing fragile intermental units is nearly impossible among the central characters within *AM*, *AT* and *CB*. Palmer's third subframe, doubly embedded narratives, refers to »a character's mind as contained within another character's mind.« In this case and using the term »situated identity,« in order to refer to the contextual nature of a character's identity, he argues that »a fictional character's identity consists, not just of his or her own embedded narrative, but of all the doubly embedded narratives of which he or she is the subject« (*Fictional* 231). Palmer discusses this subframe in terms of three kinds of relationships: individual-individual, individual-group and group-group. Regarding the fictional minds in McEwan's *AM*, *AT* and *CB*, it is arguable that there are a good deal of doubly embedded narratives of individual-individual type while a very little evidence of intermental thinking and acting. In other words, in many cases within these narratives the stimulated versions of the fictional characters exist in the minds of the other characters. That, however, does not stop the fragmentation of intermental bonds in their relationships because, after the disappearance of their already existing but delicate intermental bonds, they intramentally dissent rather than assenting.

Finally, concerning the representation of fictional characters' mental functioning, Palmer finds the conventional modes, or the so-called Speech Categories, as insufficient since they do not represent the comprehensive aspects of characters' mental functioning. Undervaluation of the Thought Report (TR) mode in the categories, according to Palmer, has marginalised fictional minds' contextual nature. That is so because the »*linking function*« (*Fictional* 76) of TR helps narrators to bind the characters' thoughts or mental functioning to their environment or surroundings delineating their both inner lives and social aspects. It, therefore, encompass all aspects of the mind, private and social, in comparison to the other two modes labelled as direct thought and FIT. This, nevertheless, does not mean they should be subordinated to TR mode. As they are thought to imitate the fictional characters' internal and external discourses, TR can similarly present fictional characters' perceptions and dispositions in both private and public domains. The third person narrators in McEwan's narratives primarily use a mixture of the three modes. Still, in the chosen narratives, the TR mode is combined with FIT or perception mode. For example, as Malcolm points out, in *AM* the »Extensive sections of free indirect thought in the form of indirect internal speech, but without any ›he said that/he thought that,‹ which at times gets very close to free direct thought, set out the principal characters' emotions, worries, jealousies, doubts, and grandiose plans« (192). The combined nature of the modes, moreover, adds to the rich delineation of the characters' mental functioning because they describe both the characters' inner lives and their physical environments too. Since the chosen narratives in this study are analysed using Palmer's terminologies such as doubly embedded narratives, intermental/intramental thought and consciousness presentational modes—TR, direct thought and FIT, therefore, they are respectively discussed in length in the next part.

2.2.1 (Doubly) Embedded Narratives

Palmer uses Marie-Laure Ryan's original term *embedded narrative* as a tool in order to analyse fictional minds.[32] His embedded narratives approach »emphasize the centrality of fictional minds to the reading process.« They are the result of some textual cues based on which readers create the »effects of characters' mental functioning (*Fictional* 189 and 175). To create such »effects,« the readers, according to Palmer, utilise their cognitive frames, which are »crucially related to the mental functioning of characters: their goals, desires, plans for achieving them, and so on.« The embedded narratives are the result of applying continuing consciousness frame to the narrative. As an effective cognitive frame, it emphasises the »ascription of consciousness

---

32 »In using this term I am following the narratologist Marie-Laure Ryan, who introduces it in an article entitled »Embedded Narratives and Tellability« (1986) and later in her book, *Possible Worlds, Artificial Intelligence, and Narrative Theory* (1991)« (Palmer, *Fictional* 15). Palmer's definition of the term, however, is the extended version of, in terms of its both content and approach, Ryan's definition which is »any storylike representation produced in the mind of a character and reproduced in the mind of the reader« (qtd. in Palmer, *Fictional* 188).

to narrative agents« and therefore »is required for constructing fictional minds from narrative« (Palmer, *Fictional* 183, 178). This frame, moreover, makes it possible for the readers to use their actual world knowledge repertoires in order to (re)construct the fictional minds through building up their embedded narratives. Therefore, Palmer's embedded narrative approach pursues a »detailed, precise, functional and inclusive approach towards the whole of a fictional mind in its social and physical context« (»The Lydgate« 159). Furthermore, according to Palmer, the:

> combination of all the embedded narratives in a text forms the plot of the novel. A complete picture of an aspectual, subjectively experienced storyworld results. The storyworld is aspectual in the sense that its characters can only ever experience it from a particular perceptual and cognitive aspect at any one time. (»The Lydgate« 159)

For example, to figure out such fictional minds as Edward and Florence in *CB* and their mental functioning, reader deconstructs the temporal and spatial dimensions of the narrative through combining the characters' embedded narratives together. To do that, s/he uses his/her continuing consciousness frame. This is an influential step of experiencing narrative because, according to Palmer (2004), it is »the whole of a character's various perceptual and conceptual viewpoints, ideological worldviews, and plans for the future considered as an individual narrative that is embedded in the whole fictional text« (*Fictional* 15).

Through the analysis of a character's embedded narratives, the reader moreover gets to know his/her mental states such as intentions, motives, desires, hidden plans, judgments etc. because »The mental events, processes, and states that distinguish actions from mere doings are crucial to the concept of embedded narratives« (Palmer, *Fictional* 122). For example, between the bedroom scene and the beach scene, McEwan in *CB* embeds the characters' whole lives after and before their encountering. It is only through examination of the embedded stories that reader can make out the reasons for the characters' actions in their present stern situations. The reader, according to palmer, »uses a variety of information about a character from which to infer the underlying mental reality that over the course of the novel becomes that character's embedded narrative.« The reader, therefore, gets familiar with the future result(s), or »The teleological implications of embedded narratives« (*Fictional* 140, 166), of the character's past and present actions.[33] Or, to put the same point another way, Palmer's embedded narratives make it possible for the reader in order to investigate »narrative in terms of its final purpose or ending« (15). For example, in the *AM* the news related with the medical scandal in Holland, Clive's indifference to a raw scene in the rocks etc. carry highly teleological importance. Likewise, in *CB* recounting of Florence's trip with her father, Edward's inability to control his anger when a passer-by hits his Jewish friend Harold Mather etc. are telologically important for the unfolding of the narrative actions. Furthermore, Briony—the-author's first person narration at the last part of *AT* shows the impact of some of her adolescent experience, such as her approach to the romantic relationship between her sister and Robbie, on her adult psychology. Accordingly, the readers, according to Palmer, read the »plot of a novel as the combination of the concrete expressions of the embedded narratives of all of its various characters: the thoughts they think and the actions they take.« Palmer's teleological approach to the characters' embedded narratives, moreover, helps the reader to construct the narrative plot. In other words, it »forms a conceptual framework within which texts can be analysed to show how particular examples of access to characters' minds contribute to the presentation of the plot-forming process« (*Fictional* 190). The approach, therefore, is an essential method for the perception of narrative plots whose construction is the final purpose of the embedded narratives approach as it is obvious from Palmer's teleological model,

> desires and beliefs —> intentions and motives —> inner speech and self-regulation —> decisions —> action and behavior —> long term plans and goals —> embedded narratives —> character —> plot (*Fictional* 192):

This approach, accordingly, considers character, or more particularly character's mind, as the main narrative element. Reader constructs a narrative

[33] This aspect, *teleology*, is Palmer's modification of Ryan's theory. Palmer extends Ryan's theory in order to »mean the whole of a character's mind in action« (*Fictional* 183).

plot through its characters' embedded narratives following the characters' thought and actions as presented by the narrator, his/her intermental thoughts and doubly embedded narratives. When an embedded narrative of a character exists inside another character's mind, the second version of the former character's embedded narrative is called doubly embedded narrative. In other words, it means, »versions of characters exist within the minds of other characters.« Within the framework of a single narrative or a frame narrative, however, there may be several embedded narratives.[34] The embedded narrative approach, moreover, takes into account the narrator's description of the characters' mental states as well as their physical actions since »A description by a narrator of a character's action is a description of the development of that character's embedded narrative.« Considering the role of a character's embedded narrative in delineating his/her mental states, Palmer propounds that »The reasons, motives, intentions, purposes, and so on behind the action may be explicitly specified by the narrator, they may be implicit but understood by the reader, or they may remain mysterious. However, they are always there in the storyworld« (*Fictional* 122). Additionally, the embedded narrative approach brings together the characters' inner states, visible actions and their relationships to other characters since, as Palmer says:

> The core of the embedded narrative approach is the systematic analysis of the structure of mental events that lies behind the decisions that lead to actions and, specifically, of how this is presented in the discourse by the narrator. This causal, mental process is the embedded narrative in action. In addition, physical action is the point at which different characters' embedded narratives entangle. Descriptions of joint actions in particular reveal the enmeshing of the various mental networks of two or more characters. (*Fictional* 122–123)

Therefore, the characters' private and public spheres meet in their embedded narratives. Their embedded narratives, for example, interweave when they »undertake joint actions« and »overlap during the extent of their joint purpose before diverging again.« In the opinion of Palmer, the embedded

---

34 This is very true in terms of *AM, AT* and *CB* in which the frame narratives are mainly composed of the characters' intermittent narratives which gradually reveal their aspectalities, different understandings of ethics and different characters.

narrative approach, moreover, along with Mikhail Bakhtin's dialogic approach, locates

> individual consciousness in its social context; use[s] a functional approach toward characters' minds; analyze[s] the whole of a character's mind and not just his or her inner speech; establish[s] through discourse analysis precisely how this is achieved in narratives; and show[s] how the novel can be seen as an interconnection of the embedded narratives, or dialogic consciousnesses, of its various characters. (*Fictional* 168, 154)

Considering the chosen narratives, this approach helps us to examine the central characters' mental functioning in their social as well as private contexts.

This approach, furthermore, helps reader in analysing the different existing perspectives within the fictional world. Because in Palmer's theory, any storyworld is considered to be aspectual in the sense that »its characters can only ever experience it from a particular perceptual and cognitive aspect at any one time« (*Fictional* 184). The narrative situations and events in McEwan's *AB*, *AT* and *CB* are presented strongly from different perspectives or they are »aspectual.« Within such a world, »The same object or event will be experienced under a different aspect by another character or by the same character at a different time« (Palmer, *Fictional* 187). Accordingly, in McEwan's narratives versions or simulations of the characters' embedded narratives exist inside the other characters' minds.

Thus, through the analysis of different embedded narrative, doubly embedded narratives and fully doubly embedded narratives[35] it is possible to find out the manner of fictional mental functioning and their similarities or differences from the other fictional minds. The approach, moreover, not only does take into consideration the characters' inner thoughts and states, it also situates characters in their public and social contexts wherein their

---

35 Palmer defines the term as following: »This occurs when the reader never meets a character directly, and he or she exists for the reader only through the doubly embedded narratives of other characters« (*Fictional* 235). Therefore, in such narratives the focalised character is fully absent from the storyworld. For example, in *AM* Molly does not exist in the storyworld, at the same time, she is present in the central characters' minds throughout the narrative.

outward aspects are delineated. As a result, Palmer finds the approach »valuable« for the following reasons:

> It is a detailed precise approach to the whole of a particular fictional mind that avoids the fragmentation of previous approaches; it views characters' minds not just in terms of the presentation of passive, private inner speech in the modes of direct or free indirect thought, but in terms of the narrator's positive role in presenting characters' social mental functioning, particularly in the mode of thought report; and it highlights the role of the reader, the process by which the reader constructs the plot by means of a series of provisional conjectures and hypotheses about the embedded narratives of characters. (*Fictional* 185)

This holistic nature of embedded narratives approach to fictional characters is what, according to Palmer, makes it different from the earlier narratological notions. That is so because, analysing the mental functioning of characters, the reader works in fact within two levels tying together »the microstructural level of specific mental events and particular actions with the macrostructural level of long-term plans and goals« (*Fictional* 183).

2.2.2 Fictional Minds and Theory of Intermental / Intramental Thought

Palmer's theory of fictional minds is a postclassical interdisciplinary approach to the presentation and analysis of fictional characters. Through applying an externalist perspective, Palmer expands the concept of fictional mind beyond the individual characters by connecting it to the context[36] of the other characters. Accordingly, his concept of fictional minds, more than being private, is social. Palmer's social minds theory, as Fludernik and Olson point out, »challenge[s] the Western philosophical tradition of locating identity and essence in isolated individual subjects« (12).

---

36 Palmer, however, uses a narrower sense of ›context‹ in his theory. When analysing a fictional mind he focuses on »both the context of the whole fictional mind during the analysis of a particular part of that mind and also on the social and physical context of the storyworld within which that mind functions« (*Fictional* 8). Therefore, regardless of the reader's social context, Palmer restricts his sense of ›context‹ to the represented textual context wherein the fictional mind operates. To understand the fictional mind in the fictional context; however, the reader uses his/her actual cognitive knowledge as (s)he uses the same cognitive tools to understand or communicate with other actual minds.

Palmer builds his theories about intermental/intramental thought and the social nature of the fictional characters' mental functioning based on Lev Vygotsky's (1896–1934) argument.[37] That is probably because of the influence of Vygotsky's »hypothesis« that, according to Herman, »had led to a broader interest in socially distributed cognition« (»Narrative Theory« 160). In Vygotsky's domain of theories on *ontogenesis* (the cognitive development of children), which stand in sheer contrast with those of Piaget's, egocentric speech succeeds the social one. In other words, it primarily functions based on the public and social nature of the speech. Vygotsky believed that »in the development of individuals, intramental thinking derives from shared, or intermental, thinking« (Herman, »Narrative Theory« 160). Vygotsky differentiates his own theory from Piaget's. In *Thought and Language* he observes that:

> The development of thought is, to Piaget, a story of gradual socialization of deeply intimate, personal, autistic mental states. Even social speech is represented as following, not preceding, egocentric speech. The hypothesis we propose reverses this course. [. . .] We consider that the total development runs as follows: the primary function of speech, in both children and adults, is communication, social contact. The earliest speech of the child is, therefore, essentially social. At a certain age, the social speech of the child is quite sharply divided into egocentric speech and communicative speech. [. . .] Egocentric speech emerges when the child transfers social, collaborative forms of behavior to the sphere of inner-personal psychic functions. [. . .] Egocentric speech, splintered off from general social speech, in time leads to inner speech, which serves both autistic and logical thinking. [. . .] Thus our schema of development—first social, then egocentric, and then inner speech—contrasts both with the traditional behaviorist schema—vocal speech, whisper, inner speech—and with Piaget's sequence—from nonverbal autistic thought, through egocentric thought and speech to socialized speech and logical thinking. [. . .] In our perception,

[37] Likewise, Herman points out the importance of Vygotsky to the later psychologists such as Jerome Bruner and Daniel Hutto who argued about storytelling as scaffolding for folk psychology. In the same way, Vygotsky's »account of psychological tools«, according to Herman, »has helped give impetus to recent work in cognitive science on narrative as a resource for sense making« (*Storytelling* 4). Moreover, despite Vygotsky's belated discovery in the West, in the 1980s, his theories are considered as one of the sources for the emanation of the so-called second cognitive revolution.

> the true direction of the development of thinking is not from the individual to the social, but from the social to the individual. (34–36)

For Vygotsky, it is the sociointeractional or sociocultural roots of personal thought that is substantial since children are considered as social beings from the very beginning. Any communicative event at that stage, nevertheless, occurs »as developing simultaneously on an »inter-« as well as an »intra-psychic plane« (Duncan 440), or on both planes—social and private. Vygotsky, moreover, as Palmer puts, »brought the notion of inner speech to the center of psychology« (*Fictional* 93). Succeeding private speech, inner speech is the child's »more individualized behavior« (Palmer, *Fictional* 149).

Considering the study of cognition, Vygotsky's argument on the social settings or »mediations of thought« (Herman, *Storytelling* 230) and its development from intermental functioning to intramental one in »children's cognitive development« (Wertsch 878) seems innovative in the history of psychology. Bringing »the notion of inner speech to the center of psychology« (Palmer, *Fictional* 93), Vygotsky, additionally, argued that:

> Enormous changes in the child's development occur when speech is socialized, when instead of turning to the experimenter with a plan for solving the problem, he turns to himself. In the latter case, speech that participates in solving the problem is converted from the category of intermental to intramental function. The child, organizing his own behavior according to a social type, applies to himself the same method of behavior that he applied earlier to the other person. (23)

Vygotsky considers intersubjectivity or the social aspect of thought as the basis upon which its intramental functioning develops. In other words, as Herman put, Vygotsky believed that »intramental capacities and predispositions arise from intermental coordination between self, other and world« (*Storytelling* 89) since according to Vygotsky:

> Every function in the child's cultural development appears twice: first, on the social level, and later, on the individual level; first between people (interpsychological), and then inside the child (intrapsychological). This applies equally to voluntary attention, to logical memory, and to the formation of concepts. All the higher functions originate as actual relations between human individuals. (qtd. in Zlatev 4)

Accordingly, as Herman states, intramental thought »derives from experiences of intermental functioning, or shared thinking, and social-constructionist accounts of human identity« (»Narrative: Cognitive« 456). Vygotsky, as well as Palmer, believes that cognition develops essentially from outside in. The emphasis on social mind and purposive thought triggered by Vygotsky and supported by the other Russian theorists (Palmer, *Fictional* 147), resonates in the subsequent researches on knowledge presentations. Thus, the social aspect of thought from Vygotsky's point of view, according to Palmer, seems threefold: »First, he saw that cognitive activity is social as well as individual. [. . .] Second, he stressed the importance of cultural, mediational tools for cognition. [. . .] Finally, Vygotsky realized the particular importance of the tool of language in this process« (*Fictional* 150–51). However, it seems that in Vygotsky's related theories the main discussion is not over the priority of social or personal aspect of thought but on their proceeding or succeeding. It is, nonetheless, certain that a developed human's thought functions both inter-personally and intra-personally being capable of working on either of the two at appropriate circumstances. Moreover, it is implied that a developed human's mind is generally functioning based on a balance between intermental and intramental thoughts. In other terms, the intersubjective communions as well as intermental thoughts complement the subjective experiences. Whenever the balance between the two is broken, either by too much egocentricism or by altruism, the person becomes unable to either establish or maintain the interpersonal relationships or the intermental thought. This is the problem with the central characters in *AM*, *AT* and *CB*.[38]

---

38 As it is shown in the following chapters, interpersonal relationships in *AM*, *AT* and *CB* are broken mainly because of the characters' too much egocentricism or persistence on personal perspective. Clive and Vernon in *AM* limit their perceptions of duty, ethics, enemy etc, to their own understanding or perspectives only. Likewise, in *CB*, Edward and Florence are unable to maintain the balance between their diverging perspectives which are affected both by the sociopolitical issues and the conventions of their time and those belonging to the past. In other words, they fail at finding a balance between their intramental thoughts. In *AT*, the emerging intermental unit between Cecilia and Robbie is broken by a third factor, Briony. In these

Following Vygotsky, Palmer also believes in »the social nature of thought and [. . .] the public nature of apparently private mental life« (*Fictional* 147). He considers human consciousness social and multiple. Furthermore, in Palmer's externalist approach to fictional minds, thought is basically considered »intermental« or »intersubjective first« before being »intramental« or »subjective first« (*Fictional* 5). Likewise, the central characters' thoughts in *AM, AT* and *CB* are both intermental and intramental. Nevertheless, during the narrative progression, their intramentality overcomes their intermental part. That is mainly caused by their social settings as much as by their personal characteristics. Therefore, *AM, AT* and *CB* can be read as representations of the fatal consequences of any imbalance between intermental and intramental orientations of thought. The characters' dissenting intramental thoughts and perceptions bring about their mutual calamities.

Consequently, Palmer builds his approach to fictional minds inclining towards one of the two different existing perspectives on the mind (*subjective first* and *intersubjective first*). He defines his approach as following:

> Mine [approach] is very much an intersubjective first approach to fictional minds, but not because I deny the importance of the subjective first approach. It is important to stress that both perspectives are equally valid, informative, and, indeed, necessary. The reason why this study favors the intersubjective first approach is that the subjective first position has become the dominant paradigm for the study of consciousness within narrative theory, and the bias contained in this book is intended to redress the balance a little. (*Fictional* 5)

This study, however, explores both the ways the established intermental units between and among the main fictional characters are broken in *AM, AT* and *CB*. And, it also explores the problems related with the construction of intermental units in them. To do that, the subjective and intersubjective factors are examined. Because, as implied by Palmer too, the outcome can

---

narratives, therefore, not only do they break their intermental thought or relationships, but also in their fully intramental phase they dissent completely which brings about their breakdown too. Taking into account these issues, *CB*, according to Childs, suggests a »gulf between generations and a turning point in social history« (»Contemporary« 31).

be more reliable when both approaches come together. As a result, this study argues that fictional minds' social situatedness delineates their mental functioning. Likewise, their own inner perceptions, beliefs, dispositions can reveal the manner of their thoughts. However, it is apparently their intramental thought that appears to orient their decisions. The ensuing imbalance, therefore, seems to be the main source of the deadly conflicts in the narratives.

Palmer considers the construction of intermental unit(s) or thought(s) as fundamental to the workings of fictional, as well as real, minds. According to him, they are »to be found in nearly all novels« (Palmer, *Social* 41). Palmer consequently defines intermental thought in comparison with intramental thought:

> *Intermental* [. . .] thinking is joint, group, shared, or collective, as opposed to *intramental*, or individual or private thought. It is also known as *socially distributed, situated,* or *extended cognition,* and also as *intersubjectivity*[39]. Intermental thought is a crucially important component of fictional narrative because, just as in real life, where much of our thinking is done in groups, much of the mental functioning that occurs in novels is done by large organizations, small groups, work colleagues, friends, families, couples, and other intermental units. (*Social* 41)

The stability of intermental units, nevertheless, is not certain or guaranteed because, as Palmer argues, »a large amount of the subject matter of novels is the formation, development, maintenance, modification, and breakdown of these intermental systems« (*Social* 41). Moreover, although intermental units, or »intermental cognitive systems,« as Palmer points out, are made up of individuals or individual thoughts but »the whole [. . .] is different from the sum of its parts« (*Social* 44) because it belongs to all rather than to any particular individual. To put it in other words, »intermental minds consist simply of individual minds pooling their resources and producing different results« (*Social* 50). Moreover, although intermental thought combines intramental thoughts, it is different from any of them. At the same

---

39 Opposed to subjectivity, it is defined as »*the sharing of experiential content* (*e.g., feelings, perceptions, thoughts, and linguistic meanings*) *among a plurality of subjects.* [...] the human mind is quintessentially a shared mind and that intersubjectivity is at the heart of what makes us human« (Zlatev 1–2).

time, it is »as beautiful and ugly, destructive and creative, exceptional and commonplace as intramental thought« (*Social* 44).

To study intermental activities of fictional minds, Palmer proposes what he calls a »basic typology« which includes »intermental encounters,« »small intermental units,« »medium-sized intermental units,« »large intermental units,« and »intermental minds« (*Social* 46–48). Nevertheless, as Zunshine points out, »No all works of fiction cultivate intermental units« (»Introduction« 20). The small intermental units at the onset of *AM* and *CB* and the emerging one in *AT* are transitory and prone to imbalance. As a result, the overall narratives, instead of cultivating intermental bonds, are presentations of the intermental breakdowns. Their main concern is to represent the destructive consequences of the breakdown of the intermental units—Clive's and Vernon's double murder at the end of *AM* as well as Florence's and Edward's separation before consummation of their marriage in *CB*.

2.2.3 Modes for Presenting Fictional Minds (Consciousness) in Fiction

The analysis of modes for fictional minds or consciousness presentation, according to Palmer, has been overshadowed by the established theories related with the modes for speech presentation. Theorists of the speech categories considered thought as verbal and hence preferred direct thought and FIT modes to the TR mode in the presentation and analysis of the fictional minds' functioning. The main logic behind such a preference, according to Palmer, refers to the flawed assumption of low degree of mediacy and hence high degrees of mimesis in their presentation of fictional thoughts. Nevertheless, based on Palmer's argument, the TR mode reveals the whole states of fictional minds. It delineates their inner speeches, latent states, mental events, mental actions etc. In addition, its linking function weaves together fictional minds' physical and social contexts with their private states presenting the whole mind in action[40]. Palmer's argument, nevertheless, does

40 Having acknowledged the importance of Palmer's »project of enlarging the category of fictional mind«, Brian McHale, nevertheless, points out the problem of Palmer's theory asserting that his emphasis on the analysis of the whole mind:

> is to turn nearly *everything* into a manifestation of fictional mind. The whole mind, according to Palmer, comprises not only the more or less discrete thoughts captured

not underestimate the importance of other two modes in presenting fictional minds mental functioning particularly their inner speeches. Instead, it attempts to compensate inattentiveness to TR mode in the earlier theories. Moreover, it intends to show that presentation of characters' mental events, physical actions and social contexts are as important to their consciousness presentation as their inner speeches (Palmer, *Fictional* 53–86).

»Thought and consciousness representation«[41] has been a seminal part of both narrative construction and narrative analysis. It has changed into one of the defining factors of narrativity[42] challenging even the traditionally central place of event in every narrative. In this case, with reference to Fludernik and Palmer, Semino also states that »Several narratologists have recently proposed that narrative generally should be defined not in terms of sequences of interconnected events, but rather in terms of the projection of the consciousness and subjective experiences of (fictional) individuals« (57). The analysis of modes of thought and consciousness representation in narrative is a crucial concern for the narratologists, especially for those working within cognitive perspective. That is so because in consciousness presenting passages of omniscient narratives, the narrator's voice is usually either merged with that of the character's, making his discourse coloured, or is replaced by it totally.

---

by the modes of consciousness representation, but also emotions, non-conscious states of mind, characters' long-term dispositions, and even their actions, and shades off into the »social mind« in which groups of characters participate. So capacious is the whole mind that it seems on the verge of coinciding with the *narrative as a whole;* »in essence,« Palmer writers, »narrative is the description of fictional mental functioning (*Fictional* 12). If narrative is essentially identical to mental functioning, one is tempted to wonder what, if anything, is left over. Is there anything in a narrative that is *not* mind? (119)

41 »This highly artificial device of direct access is considered by Cohn and others to be distinctive feature of fictional narrative. [...] It is also a very visible mark of the omniscient narrator of fiction« (Palmer, »Thought« 602).

42 »The set of properties characterizing NARRATIVE and distinguishing it from nonnnarrative; the formal and contextual features making a (narrative) text more or less narrative, as it were« (Prince, *A Dictionary* 65).

The change in the mode of narrative presentation contributes to its mimetic nature by producing an »illusion of immediacy of presentation« (Stanzel 7). Accordingly, the controversial term focalization[43] has been central to the discussions on narrative transmission. According to Gerard Genette, it dissolves the

> confusion between what I call here *mood* and *voice*, confusion between the question *who is the character whose point of view orients the narrative perspective?* and the very different question *who is the narrator?*—or, more simply, the question *who sees?* and the question *who speaks?*« (emphasis original, 86)

The confusion, however, does still exist because for some critics there does not seem to be a demarcating line between the narrator (teller) and character (perceiver or experiencer) since they are both authorial devices. S/he uses them to transmit the story material. The history of the debate over the priority of showing or telling techniques in narrative goes back to Plato's discussion on mimesis/diegesis[44] dichotomy. In narratology, this problem has

---

43 »The story is presented in the text through the mediation of some ›prism,‹ ›perspective,‹ ›angle of vision,‹ verbalised by the narrator though not necessarily his. Following Genette (1972), I call this mediation ›focalisation‹« (Rimmon-Kenan 73). Moreover, Jahn states that »In general, focalisation theory addresses the options and ranges of orientational restrictions of narrative presentation. [...] Perception, thought, recollection, and knowledge are often considered to be criterial features of focalisation« (»Windows« 241–243). The dominant focalisation mode in *AM, AT* and *CB* is, in Genette's term, is internal variable focalisation.

44 The two terms are seminal to the discussion of poetics from Plato to the theories related to narrative and in particular to the concepts of representation and imitation in the epic. The word *diegesis* came from Greek into English. It has two meanings. It refers to story. G. Genette (1980) uses this sense of the term to describe different narrative levels in his *Narrative Discourse* (24). *Diegesis* is also used to refer to the manner of narration or »indirect representation.« The latter sense of the word originated from the third Book in Plato's *Republic*. According to Plato, *diegesis* »is a mode where the poets speak in his or her own voice and renders the character's words summarily« (Shen 107). In this sense of the word, there is no authorial pretension to be someone else because the author speaks in his/her own voice without any attempt to even imply that anyone other than him/herself is speaking—it is pure narrative. This sense of the word is in opposition with that of *mimesis*—perfect imitation—Plato's another term. *Mimesis* refers to literary works like tragedy and comedy in which the author speaks through the characters, in other words »they pretend

been addressed under the terms of point of view and focalization respectively.

2.2.3.1 The Speech Categories, Thought Report and Free Indirect Thought

The confusion of the voices is more conspicuous in the case of third-person narratives where narratorial perspectives are mainly orienting the progression of the narrative. Some passages in such narratives are focalized through characters' perspectives. In other words, in some passages the narrative discourse is coloured with the characters' language and subjectivity. At the same time, a concurrent shift in the mode of narrative presentation takes place whenever there is a transformation in the reporting course of the events from the narrator's perspective to the character's one. The purpose of this technique is to give reader the impression of experiencing character immediately. Following that, the analysis and evaluation of the existing models for the presentation of fictional minds have been central to the discussions on literary characterization. For that purpose, different speech categories[45] have been used in narratology in order explain the modes fictional characters' mental functioning are presented in narrative. According to Palmer (*Fictional* 53–86), the main problem in this case is the fact that the same categories have equally been used for the analysis of both fictional speech and fictional thought presentation focusing primarily on *inner*

being someone else« (Schaeffer and Vultur 309). Plato prefers *diegesis* rather than *mimesis* because mimetic representation is only a copy of copy.

45 Palmer alludes to the problems of discussing speech category account as following: There is a wide range of models to choose from. They go from two speech categories, to the standard number of three, to Brian McHale's widely adopted seven-level model as contained in his influential article Free Indirect Discourse: A Survey of Recent Accounts«, and even to Monika Fludernik's particularly elaborate construct, which, in total, contains no fewer than thirty elements. Another problem, often referred to at this stage in the discussion, is that each category has several different names. Like Dorrit Cohn, I think that there are three fundamental categories to which, unlike her, I have given very simple names: direct thought, thought report, and free indirect thought. (*Fictional* 54)

speech[46]. Being unable to explain all aspects of mind, the speech category approach to fictional thought, according to Palmer:

> does not do justice to the complexity of the types of evidence for the workings of fictional minds that are available in narrative discourse; it pays little attention to states of mind such as beliefs, intentions, purposes, and dispositions; and it does not analyze the whole of the social mind in action. (*Fictional* 53)

As Palmer understands, the nature of fictional speech is different from that of the fictional thought wherein a »mind in action« with a wide range of mental parts is almost often presented. Therefore, a more comprehensive approach is needed for the analysis of the fictional thought. It should be able to delineate all mental aspects, including nonverbal ones, of the represented thought in the fiction.

The modes of consciousness representation, however, have gained variety of names and definitions by different critics. Referring to the modes for the analysis of thought and consciousness representation in classical narratology, the main problem that Palmer finds is the application of the same categories to both speech and thought. However, since they are not equal, the traditional models[47] used for the analysis of character's speeches cannot afford for the analysis of their thoughts. Palmer suggests »three fundamental categories« (*Fictional* 54), namely direct thought, TR and FIT.[48] He high-

---

46 »The highly verbalized flow of self-conscious thought« (Palmer, *Fictional* 53). In *AM*, *AT* and *CB* there are long passages of inner speeches (thoughts).

47 Palmer remarks that Dorrit Cohn's seminal work, *Transparent Minds* (1978), upon which he builds his own model too, »is the only full-length study solely devoted to thought presentation« (»Thought« 602).

48 Palmer (*Fictional*: 54–5 and »Thought« 602) describes the three categories as following:
1) Direct thought is the narrative convention that allows the narrator to present a verbal transcription that passes as the reproduction of the actual thoughts of a character (for example, »She thought, where am I?«). [...] Direct thought is also known as *quoted monologue* and *private speech* (and also *interior monologue* and *stream of consciousness*)

lights their differences by replacing speech with thought, Moreover, regarding the degrees of mediacy, diegesis and mimesis, Palmer puts TR higher than the other two. It seems to him that »it is the most diegetic and the most mediated category [. . .] presenting all areas of the mind including inner speech. [. . . it] is the most flexible and the most versatile category« (»Thought« 602–604). In contrast, the other two categories are mostly considered suitable for the presentation of fictional minds' inner speeches. The ability of TR, however, is to:

> link the thought processes of individual characters to their environment, and thereby demonstrate in very concrete and specific ways the social and active nature of thought as mental functioning. It is in thought report that the narrator is able to show explicitly how characters' minds operate in a social and physical context. (»Thought« 604)

Nonetheless, the reasons based on which Palmer puts higher emphasis on TR mode compared to FIT and direct thought modes do not seem totally convincing. Admitting that FIT is a »disputed« concept in terms of narrative mediacy, mimesis/diegesis opposition and its functions, Palmer seeks to

---

2) Thought report is the presentation of characters' thoughts in the narrator's discourse. It can range from the equivalent of indirect speech (for example: ›She wondered where she was‹) to highly condensed summary (for example: ›She thought of Paris‹). [...] It is the most flexible category and can be used for a number of purposes [...] One important feature is that it can present thought as mental action (for example, »She decided to walk.«). This mode is also known as *psychonarration, internal analysis, narratorial analysis, omniscient description, submerged speech,* and *narratized speech.*

3) Free indirect thought is most simply described as a combination of the other two categories. It combines the subjectivity and language of the character, as in direct thought, with the presentation of the narrator, as in thought report. For example: ›She stopped. Where the hell was she?‹ The second sentence is free indirect thought because it presents the subjectivity of the character (the narrator knows where the character is) and the language of the character (›Where the hell‹), but in the third-person (›she‹) and past tense (›was‹) of the narrator's discourse. [...] *Free indirect discourse* (that is, referring to both speech and thought) is also known as *free indirect style, le style indirect libre, erlebte Rede, narrated monologue, substitutionary speech, represented speech and thought, dual voice, narrated speech, immediate speech, simple indirect thought,* and *narrated thought.* (emphasis original)

subordinate it to TR although he truly acknowledges that, other than representing inner speech, it is also used to »represent some other areas of the mind« (*Fictional* 56 and »Thought« 603). FID has the potential to reveal some other aspects of the fictional minds than just inner speeches. Following that, in reporting consciousness, as Fludernik remarked, »free indirect discourse—next to psycho-narration—owns pride of place« (*The Fictions* 74). That is also the case in McEwan's later fiction where he, as highlighted by Hannah Courtney,

> favors narrated thought[49]. Narrated thought is not summary [as Palmer's thought report is generally characterized with]—it relays the step-by-step thought progressions of a character and so conveys finite detail of character consciousness; it also allows the voice of the character to subjectively color the narration, while aiding the flow of the narrative by keeping the narrator at the helm at all times. (186)

Thus, the analysed passages in this study are examined in terms of the three categories suggested by Palmer since, according to him, »in practice« the three categories »are usually found in combination with each other in an intricate and dense patchwork of effects« (»Thought« 603). Likewise, in case of the selected narratives, TR mode alone is not enough for the analysis of the fictional minds' thought presentation since the characterization emphasis in these narratives is primarily on the intramental, individual or private thought. Accordingly, FIT mode also turns out to be a helpful device for the interpretation purposes.

Moreover, the presentation of a mind in action or a social mind by FID is to some extent, if not as much as in the TR, feasible because in both cases the narrator controls the narration process continuously connecting or disconnecting him from his environment. In both cases, furthermore, the degree of mediacy and mimesis, compared to the direct thought, is lower since either the narrator indirectly summarises character's words or his representation of the character's thought and consciousness is *coloured* with the character's subjectivity and language. Accordingly, both categories seem adequate to the analysis of the character's thought and consciousness presentation in

---

49 Courtney's term is made by merging Cohn's »narrated monologue« with Palmer's »free indirect thought.«

narrative. However, in TR mode the narrator is seemingly free from the restraints of focalized character's language and subjectivity.

Palmer's approach to the presentation of thought and consciousness is interconnected with his theory of fictional minds that are considered to be active, social and contextual agents. Focusing on the interferences and intrusions of direct thought and FIT in typical fictional passages, the traditional speech categories do not account for the complexity of »the fictional mind acting in the context of other minds because fictional thought and real thought are like that« (Palmer, *Fictional* 53). They function within the social situations to which speech categories are mostly heedless.

According to Herman, »four dimensions constitute crucial concerns for postclassical approaches to the study of consciousness (re)presentation.« Herman believes that any approach to the thought and consciousness representation in narrative should consider,

> the construal or conceptualization of events from one or more perspectives in the storyworld; characters' inferences about their own and one another's minds; the use of discourse pertaining to emotions; and »qualia,« a term used by philosophers of mind to refer to the felt, subjective character of conscious experience. (»Cognition« 247–8)

Similarly, this study attempts to show how presentation of fictional minds' four dimensions—their perspectives (or aspectualities), inferences, (appropriate) discourses and qualia—reveals character's mental aspects and increases the narrativity level of the narratives. In this case, the following questions seem to be the primal questions in the chosen narratives: How the same event is conceptualised from different perspectives? (1) How the characters infer both their own and the other characters' thoughts? (2) How those emotions are represented? (3) And the way the felt experiences in the narratives are represented (4). Clive's mental responses to the same events are deadly different from that of Vernon's in *AM*. In the same way, Edward's and Florence's mutual misunderstandings, misreadings, flawed inferences, different beliefs and the felt mental experiences of those moments appear to be the fundamental narrative concerns in *CB*. Likewise, Briony's limited perspective towards some critical narrative moments bring about her deadly misunderstandings.

There are many passages in *AM, AT* and *CB* that are highly introspective representing the central characters' mental states. Herman's theory of the basic elements of narrative and the constituent characteristics of narrativity can provide us with efficient devices in order to analyse the central fictional minds. Accordingly, in the following part his related theories are discussed with an emphasis on his fourth basic narrative element, namely what is it like or qualia.

2.3 David Herman's Approach to Narrative and Narrativity

If Palmer's main concern is the analysis of the ways fictional minds operate within storyworlds as well as the ways readers experience them, Herman's area of investigation in his cognitive approach to narrative discourse is mostly concentrated on the fundamental elements of narrative. He analyses the ways narrative readers take for granted the represented world and understand or experience narrative using the worldmaking abilities[50] existing

[50] Herman connects this feature, or the way a narrative situates itself, to two sets of factors under two key terms: *narrativehood* and *narrativity*. The former refers to »what makes readers and listeners deem stories stories. [...] They undermine which event sequences qualify as narratives« (»Scripts« 1048). Herman's definition of the latter term is relatively the same as Prince's definition of it as the »formal and contextual features making a (narrative) text more or less narrative (64). Therefore, according to Herman, the contrast between the two terms is »the contrast between, on the one hand, the minimal conditions for narrative sequences and, on the other, the factors that allow narrative sequences to be more or less readily processed as narrative.« The »minimal conditions« necessary for *narrativehood* are linguistic, textual or semiotic features being capable of inciting narrative recipients to »activate certain kinds of world knowledge.« Similarly, narrative sequences with higher degrees of narrativity, compared with those with minimal narrativity, are interpreted more readily as stories because they are »readily configured into chronologically and causally organized wholes.« Accordingly, like narrativehood, narrativity has also got a cueing function for the recipients since it is »a function of the pattern of script-

in them. Or, in Herman's own words, his analysis focuses on the »interrelations among linguistic form, world knowledge and narrative structure« (»Scripts« 1048). All cognitive narratologists consider a crucial role for the narrative readers. Herman's theory derives from the researches in the field of language theory, cognitive science[51] and artificial intelligence concerning human generic knowledge structures and representations. He suggests that the readers' as well as the listeners' narrative processing occurs in a mind that »draws on a large but not infinite number of ›experiential repertoire,‹ of both static (schematic or framelike) and dynamic (scriptlike) types. Stored in the memory, previous experiences form structured repertoires of expectations about current and emergent experiences« (»Scripts« 1047)[52]. Follow-

activating cues in a sequence« (»Scripts« 1048). As he mentions in a note in his article, Herman's focus is not, however, the world knowledge structures but »standardized sequences of events« (»Scripts« 1058).

51 Herman claims that »narrative theory should be viewed as a subdomain of the cognitive sciences« (»Narratology«.

52 »*Schemata*«, writes William Florence Brewer in his entry article in MITCS, »are the psychological constructs that are postulated to account for the molar forms of human generic knowledge« (729). In other words, as Herman put, »it refers to memory patterns that humans use to interpret current experiences« (qtd. in »Scripts« 1047). Narrative readers use schemata to »make sense of events and descriptions by providing default background information for comprehension, as it is rare and often unnecessary for texts to contain all the detail required for them to be fully understood« (Emmott and Alexander 411). *Frames* are their synonym with the exception that the term was firstly introduced into the field of artificial intelligence; they are »knowledge structures that contain fixed structural information. They have slots that accept a range of values; each slot has a default value that is used if no value has been provided from the external world« (Brewer 729). In contrast, *scripts*, as a subclass of *schemata*, is a »description of how a sequence of events is expected to unfold.« Both, *frames* (stereotyped sequences of events) and *scripts* (stereotypic states of affairs or situations), refer to a set of expectations regarding the unfolding of sequence of events with the exception that »frames are used to represent a point in time. Scripts represent a sequence of events that take place in a time sequence« (qtd. in Herman, »Script« 1047). Schema theory has been used by Fludernik and Herman in order to redefine respectively narrativity and narrativehood (Emmott and Alexander 413–414). The very begging of the two novellas under consideration in this study anchor well to the readers' schemas/frames through presenting

ing that, any attempt to experience or understand fictional characters' mental functioning and behaviour should take into account the characters' experiential repertoire as it true for the real minds. Related to this discussion, Palmer also says, »as with all other aspects of the reading process, we bring our real-world cognitive frames to bear when we encounter fictional intermental units« (*Social* 49).

In his postclassical approach to narrative, Herman modifies the classical definition of narrative[53] by stating that other than the sequence of events, »Narrative also depends on how the form of a sequence is anchored in—or triggers a recipient to activate—knowledge about the world.« Based on Herman's theory, a narrative »is a certain way of reconciling emergent with prior knowledge« (»Scripts« 1048). It is worth telling that Herman's theory of narrative sequence passes through the history of the concept. Herman's theory of narrative originates from the ideas of the Francophone structuralists, especially from Roland Barthes narrative theory. According to Herman, they found Propp's, as well as the other Russian formalists', theory of story as insufficient. Propp paid attention to the linguistic and textual form of a story and its constituting parts. Emphasising on the role of functions, he believed that through following them readers accept the narrative sequence as a story. According to Herman, this approach did not appear a »sufficient condition for a story« to the structuralists. They, instead, considered not the form of the narrative sequence but the way its »form cues readers [. . .] to interpret the sequence as narrative« (»Scripts« 1050) as central to a narrative sequence. Therefore, besides the formal features of the narrative sequences, they paid attention to its context too. For example, Barthes emphasises on the role of narrative sequence as »a logical succession of nuclei [narrative hinges, or the elements without which a story would cease to be a story]

worldly well-known subjects, amity and animosity in *AM* and the newlyweds' floundering on their wedding night in *CB*. And along the narrative progression in many cases, the readers are able to fill in the gaps relying on their schemata or generic knowledge.

53 In classical narratology, according to Prince, a narrative was considered to be a representation of a succession of real or fictive events (*A Dictionary* 58–61). The debate on the meaning of narrative and its constituent elements, nevertheless, still continues.

bound together by a relation of solidarity« (qtd. in Herman, »Scripts« 1050). Furthermore, he underlines readers' acquired knowledge and experiences, or their narrative schemata, which enable them to interpret the other narrative sequences. The importance of the reader's experiences as script-providing mechanism, according to Herman, does also receive more attention in the recent developmental studies within the field of cognitive sciences and artificial intelligence (Herman, »Scripts« 1050–51).

Scripts provide chances for the reader in order to fill the blanks or gaps. Herman concludes that scripts enable readers to make inferences about the narrative situations and its participants. That is so because »the research on scripts suggests that it would be misguided to search for some purely formal property« that constitute a narrative. Referring to the short piece »Mary was invited to Jack's party. She wondered if he would like a kite,« Herman emphasises that what makes a narrative to be considered by the readers as narrative is instead »the relation between the (form of the) sequences and the party script that accounts for my [reader's] intuition« to consider this sequence as a story or at least part of a story. Thus, Herman reviews the continual changes of the concept of narrative from the centrality of event sequences to that of scripts. The latter cue the readers in order to »cocreate the story« (»Scripts« 1051).

All textual cues, nevertheless, should not be considered as capable of enticing readers' scripts and hence »definitive of a story,« because they are not equal concerning their tellability[54], which »attaches to configurations of facts« and narrativity, which refers to »sequences representing configurations of facts« (Herman, »Scripts« 1052). Herman, moreover, holds that »there is a direct proportion between a sequence's degree of narrativity and the range and complexity of the world knowledge set into play during the interpretation of (the form of) the given sequence« (»scripts« 1053). It means

---

54 Prince's synonym term is *reportability*, which refers to the qualities that »makes situations and events reportable, worthy of being told. Situations and events (are shown to be) extraordinary, wonderful; bizarre are reportable. A reportable assertion can be said to have the force of an exclamatory one, and narrators usually underline the reportability (TELLABILITY) of their assertions through evaluative devices« (*A Dictionary* 83).

that, textual markers such as spatiotemporal indexes, logiotemporal operators, grammar, noun phrases, morphology of the verbs, historical and geographical markers etc. cue in the recipients more experiential repertoires or scripts than the sequences with fewer ones. In other words, they are considered as sequences with higher degrees of narrativity. Thus, the more scripts-provoking elements in a text or the more its chances to be regarded as a story by its recipients, the more it provides thought experiment that anchor well in the recipient's world knowledge frames.

Nevertheless, the formal side of a narrative sequences which cues scripts is no longer considered as the only reason for its narrativity. Other than that, the content side of the narrative sequence or its discourse (*sujhet*) should also be taken into account because »narrativity is a function not of script use alone but also of a shifting constellation of formal and contextual factors« (Herman, »Scripts« 1053). Such a modification of narrativity takes into consideration intrasequential (or textual) events of a narrative as well as the intersequential (or contextual) features. Accordingly, from Herman's perspective, sequences are considered as stories because of »(1) the grammar of the language in which they are related, (2) standardised event sequences, among other sorts of experiential repertoires, and (3) other, prior sequences (and groups of sequences) mediating encounters with any particular string« (»Scripts« 1054). As it is obvious, the grammatical features of the text (1), its scripts-provoking strategies (2) and the strategies concerning knowledge about the intersequential or generic relationships (3) seem indispensable for accepting a narrative sequence as a narrative or story. Herman, however, revises his theory of narrativity in his later studies (*Story Logic, Basic* and *Storytelling*). Therefore, in order to explore *AM, AT* and *CB* narratives in terms their narrativity degrees[55], Herman's definition of narrative and narrativity should be examined more clearly. Following that, a synopsis of the

55 Because it seems that the event sequences in these narratives cue strongly the reader's world knowledge scripts. Such issues are related to Herman's (1997) theories concerning cognitive approach to narrative that he believes should »study how interpreters of stories are able to activate relevant kinds of knowledge with or without

related discussion, from Prince to Fludernik, is given in the following pages in order to explain clearly Herman's characteristics for narrativity of a narrative in the next section.

Prince binds narrativity primarily to the recounting of events that occur at different times. This event presentation in time sequence, however, does not in itself determine the narrativity degrees of any concerned narrative. Besides that, there should also be (a) considerable conflict(s) presented through the narrative events which bring(s) about a »fundamental change« of state or situation between the opening and the ending parts of a narrative. Because of that, narrative middle is as important for Prince as narrative opening and ending since the change takes place in the middle. Moreover, that change, whatever it is, acts as the »point of narrative« towards which all the constituent elements are oriented or the general »narrative orientation« is aligned. The events should also be particular or »individualized« besides rendering a »certainty« or »assurance« in the overall narrative. Prince, moreover, points out the importance of context in the concept of narrativity in order to highlight the importance of narrative audience or its reader. From this perspective, the concept of narrativity and its degrees are variable and dynamic since one particular narrative may well anchor to the experiential or cognitive tools of a reader more than to those of any other reader. Following that, other than the necessary constituent elements within the narrative text, the presented sequential events and situations should be related to human beings or be meaningful in terms of a humanised universe. To put the same concept in other words, the presented sequential events should be valuable from human perspective (*Narratology* 145–161). Or, »the degree of narrativity of a given narrative,« as Prince illustrates in his dictionary,

> depends party on the extent to which that narrative fulfills a perceiver's desire by presenting oriented temporal wholes [. . .] involving a conflict, consisting of discrete,

---

explicit textual cues to guide them. At the same time, it should investigate how narratives, through their forms as well as their themes, work to privilege some world models over others« (1057).

specific and positive situations and events, and meaningful in terms of a human(ized) project and world. (65)

Prince, furthermore, points out some other textual features such as disnarrated and embedded narratives as the influential factors in a narrative's narrativity.[56] Nevertheless, in Prince's view, its definition is variable, subjective and relational.

Monika Fludernik has also tried to redefine narrativity. While reviewing Prince's conception of the term, states that »Prince's definition [. . .] veers off into a number of tangents that trace this slippage from what narrative ›is‹ (with essential narrative ›features‹ attached) to what it ›does‹ to the receiver, and to the establishment of a scale of features that increase a text's narrativity.« Narrativity, however, is mainly »*a function of narrative texts and centres on experientiality of an anthropomorphic nature*[57] (emphasis original) (*Towards*

---

56 Likewise, in *AM, AT* and *CB* the intermittent embedded narratives of the central characters contribute to their narrativitiy.

57 Pointing out what he calls the »weakness of Fludernik's model«, Caracciolo attempts to redefine the concept of experientiality arguing that »Her [Fludernik's] insistence on a mimetic and representational view of experientiality minimises the importance of the experiencing consciousnesses that are really involved in storytelling—quite simply, the story producer's and the recipients'« (»Notes« 177). Therefore, according to him, although experience is one main part of narrative but experientilaity cannot be reduced to the representation of (character's) experience, or, as he states, »It is one thing to say that narrative is at various levels involved in human experience, and reflects its fundamental embodiment. It is another thing to say that narrativity consists in the representation of experience« (»Notes« 177). Accordingly, Caracciolo thinks that »the experientiality of texts (and, in particular, of stories) should be extricated from representational talk; it depends, above all, on the way they can affect the experiential background of those who produce and receive them« (»Notes« 183). Thus, Caracciolo, drawing on Wolfgang Iser's reader response theory, considers reader's experience, past and present, as another important condition for experientiality stating that »The basic idea behind my approach to the experientiality of narrative is that our engagement with stories is inseparable from our experiential background. [...] all stories are enmeshed in an experiential background, which enables readers to understand ›what is at stake‹ in the representation of a set of events and existents« (»Notes« 185–186). Accordingly, building on Herman's argument that experientiality can be thought of as »the impact of narrated situations and events on an experiencing consciousness« (qtd. in Caracciolo, »Notes« 182),

234, 19). Therefore, according to Fludernik, »experientiality—conceived of as the representation of the experience of characters—is the necessary and sufficient condition for there being narrative« (Caracciolo, »Notes« 178). Furthermore, »arguing that narrativity and the representation of experience are, in fact, the same thing« (Caracciolo, »Notes« 177), Fludernik places emphasis on the cognitive aspects of narrative and hence considers mediation of human experientiality as the essential quality of narrativity. She believes that narrativity is »not a quality inhering in a text, but rather an attribute imposed on the text by the reader who interprets the text as narrative, thus *narrativizing* the text« (qtd. in Abbott 320). This is possible through a feature that Fludernik calls »the most basic to experientiality«—*embodiment*. It »evokes all the parameters of a real-life schema of existence which always has to be situated in a specific time and space frame, and the motivational and experiential aspects of human actionality likewise relate to the knowledge about one's physical presence in the world« (»Towards« 22).

Accordingly, readers draw on their real life knowledge and experiences or frames and scripts in order to process the sequences of narrative events and situations within a storyworld. Hence, the narrativization process, as Fludernik puts, »enables readers to recognize as narrative those kinds of texts that appear to be non-narrative. [. . .] Such interpretative strategies serve to naturalize texts in the direction of natural paradigms« (*Towards* 33). Thus, the narrative critic, analyst, interpreter or reader applies an interdisciplinary approach to its understanding since s/he drives from diversity of sources such as cognitive sciences, linguistics and narratology in order to understand both how the story is narrated or told in narrative and what it

---

Caracciolo proposes his own definition of experientiality stating that »The experiential ›feel‹ that results from the impact a story has on its recipients is what I propose to call ›experientiality‹« (»Notes« 186). This definition of experientiality is closer to the hypothesis of the present study too because it includes the representation of the impact of narrative events and situations on the central characters in the selected narratives —Clive and Vernon in *AM*, Edward and Florence in *CB* and Briony in *AT*. In addition to that, it takes into account the impact of those events on the reader's experiential background and the dialogic discourse between the two. Storytelling in this hypothesis, therefore, becomes a group project encompassing the producer, the character and the reader.

is all about. In this way, as it is in CN, the »non-natural mind reading« is possible »within a natural frame« (Fludernik, *Towards* 128). In omniscient narrations, according to Fludernik, where consciousness of the fictional characters is mostly concerned, the readers draw on their »natural frame of EXPERIENCING« in the process of experiencing narrative. Thus, drawing on Florence. K. Stanzel's model of the third person omniscient narration or »figural or reflectoral narrative,« Fludernik highlights the role of readers' experiential repertoire in reading both real minds and fictional minds,

> From the all-knowing narrator who interferes less and less with the fictional personae [. . .] telling can be dispensed with, readers simply orient themselves to a position within the fictional world; they are no longer constrained to experience the story as something that happened to another person and which they must relate to their own life by means of a conscious effort of empathy and understanding. Figural or reflectoral narrative allows them, instead, to experience the fictional world from within, as if looking out at it from the protagonist's consciousness. Such a reading experience is structured in terms of the natural frame of EXPERIENCING, which includes the experiences of perception, sentiment and cognition. Real-life parameters are transcended. Instead of merely observing and guessing at other people's experiences, frames naturally available only for one's own experience become accessible for application to a third person. (*Towards* 35)

Fludernik redefines narrativity not in terms of action sequences but in terms of »experientiality« defined as ›the presence of a human protagonist and her experience of events as they impinge on her situation or activities‹ (22).[58] In agreement with her theory, Palmer holds that »even the most apparently simple reading process involves a number of complex cognitive operations« on the part of narrative reader who employs his/her »real-world knowledge [. . .] for narrative comprehension« (*Social* 54). Similarly, in McEwan's *AM*, *AT* and *CB*, the central concern of the fictional worlds seems to be the representation of the fictional characters' consciousness and more particularly the impact of narrative events and situations on their mental functioning. Furthermore, the characters' motivations, beliefs, dispositions, feelings and

58 In this case, Fludernik holds that »In my model there can therefore be narratives without plot, but there cannot be any narratives without a human (anthropomorphic) experiencer of some sort at some narrative level« (*Towards* 9).

the impact of narrative actions and situations on their thought or subjectivity are both constructed and reconstructed based on their experiential repertoire. This study follows that definition of experientiality that refers to the textual representation of experience.[59]

In a similar manner to Fludernik, Herman also grounds his theory of narrativity on human experience. In other words, from Herman's perspective, the more a narrative anchors on the readers' real world experiences and knowledge or frames and scripts the higher its narrativity is. Herman's theory, nevertheless, differs from Fludernik's in the sense that he considers experientiality not as the only salient quality of a narrative in order to be considered as narrative but as one of the »roles« of »narrative participants.« Therefore, according to Herman, »the role of Experiencer is just one participant role made possible the narrative system. That system allows different preference rankings for the role of experiencer to be matched with different narrative genres« (*Story* 169). Moreover, from Herman's perspective, narrativity refers to some qualities that distinguish narratives from non-narratives making the sequences of events worthy of telling, it is:

> A scalar predicate: a story can be more or less prototypically story-like. Maximal narrativity can be correlated with sequences whose presentation features a proportional blending of »canonicity and breach,« expectation and transgression of expectation. Conversely, a story's narrativity decreases the more its telling verges on pure stereotypicality, at one end of the spectrum, or on a wholesale particularity that cannot help but stymie and amaze, at the other end. (*Story* 91)

Herman, furthermore, compares narrativity with narrativehood of a narrative referring to the minimal conditions of the event sequences of a narrative. In other words, the characteristics of a narrative event sequences that make them different from the non-narrative sequences or qualify them as narrative sequences. Likewise, narrativity, as Herman perceives it, refers to those qualities that allow such event sequences to be perceived as narratives, the qualities based on which the narrative reader or audience takes a

---

59 As Caracciolo summarizes, »experientiality lends itself to two interpretations: it can refer to the textual representation of experience, but it also hints at the experiences undergone by the recipients of narrative« (»Experientiality«).

narrative as narrative. Accordingly, Herman proposes, »narrativity is a function of the more or less richly patterned distribution of script-activating cues in a sequence. Both too many and too few script-activating cues diminish narrativity« (*Story* 91).

Herman extends and refines Prince's and Fludernik's theories of narrativity respectively. He goes beyond event sequencing to the connection between narrative events and the perceiver's mental processing of them or the ability of presented sequences of events or formal components to »cue« some »scripts« in the perceiver's mind through making a connection between the presented events and the perceiver's real life knowledge, experiences or models. That is so, because, as Herman puts, people read »by naturalizing, and they naturalize by using scripts« (*Story* 106).[60]Accordingly, the relationship between scripts and stories is the most considerable factor, form Herman's perspective, concerning narrativity of a narrative because »scripts and stories are in some sense mutually constitutive; recipients' ability to process a narrative depends on the way it anchors itself in—but also plays itself off—knowledge representation of various sorts« (*Story* 13). In this case, Herman states that:

> All other things being equal, then, the greater the number (and diversity) of the experiential repertoires set into play during the processing of sequence S, and the more that S nonetheless deviates from or militates against expectations about what was likely to occur or be done, the more narrativity will the processor be likely to ascribe to S. (*Story* 92)

Herman also compares, as well as binds, the term narrativity to »tellability« or »reportability« proposing that »whereas both predicates are scaler tellability attaches to configurations of facts and narrativity to sequences representing configuration of facts« (*Story* 100). Of the variables associated with degrees of narrativity, Herman as Prince does, points out the importance of contextual factors, besides textual constituents, arguing »my experiment has indicated that a sequence's degree of narrativity is a function not of a script use alone but also of a shifting constellation of a formal and contextual (in

---

60 This statement is similar to Fludernik's concept of natural narratology.

particular cognitive) factors« (*Story* 104). Accordingly, Herman's proposal to narratologists and narrative interpreters is that they

> should study how interpreters of stories are able to activate kinds of knowledge with or without explicit textual cues to guide them. As the same time, researchers should investigate how literary narratives, through their forms as well as their themes, work to privilege some world models over others. (*Story* 113)

Having revised his theories related with narrative and narrativity, Herman thus defines four elements—situatedness, event sequencing, worldmaking/world disruption[61], and what it's like (or qualia)[62]—as the basic elements for a narrative in order to be considered as narrative or the way they »constitute conditions for *narrativity* or what makes a story (interpretable as) a story.« Situatedness or situating stories refers to »a mode of representation that is situated in—must be interpreted in light of—a specific discourse context or occasion for telling.« Situatedness refers to those textual features and communicative contexts that are considered necessary for telling and comprehending stories. In other words, it is in fact »the grounding of stories in specific discourse contexts or occasions of telling.« Herman, thus, analyses this element in relation to the discussions concerning narrative levels—story, narration and text. Likewise, under the second basic element, event sequencing, Herman tries to define *narrating* in comparison with *describing* and *explaining*. Following that, his definition of the term event sequencing

---

61 Herman grounds the second part of his third basic narrative element, world disruption, on Todorov's discussion of narratives progression. Todorov, according to Herman, argued that »narratives characteristically follow a trajectory leading from an initial state of equilibrium, through a phase of disequilibrium, to an endpoint at which equilibrium is restored (on a different footing) because of intermediary events« (*Basic* 96).

62 Herman considers these elements as the result of his *emic* and *etic* approach to narrative study. His approach takes into account those elements »oriented to as basic by participants engaged in storytelling practices (=emic).« At the same time, they are »imposed on the data from without (=etic)« as a part of the analysis system (3). Moreover, considering it as a central part of neuronovel, Gaedtke defines qualia as following: »the (first-person) feelings of phenomenal experience and the question of their integration within a (third-person) materialist, neuroscientific account of the mind« (185).

refers to his argument that »narrative representations cue interpreters to draw inferences about a structured time-course of particularized events.« In other words, he connects the richness of the sequences of particularised events scattered through different times within the presented storyworld to the narrativity of a narrative as compared to other non-narrative texts. That is so, because the more a narrative presents various particular events in varying spatiotemporal sequences the more it is able anchor itself on the reader's real world experiences and knowledge. Accordingly, Herman follows two purposes under his discussion of event sequencing and the next two basic elements—worldmaking/world disruption, and what it's like—in order to capture »critical properties of narrative viewed as a type of text as well as a cognitive structure.« Moreover, Herman's next binary basic element, worldmaking/world disruption, refers to the ways narratives construct the plausible, possible or believable worlds »with the referential, world-creating potential.« He states that »The events represented in narrative are such that they introduce some sort of disruption or disequilibrium into a storyworld involving human or human-like agents, whether that world is presented as actual or fictional, realistic or fantastic, remembered or dreamed, etc.« Under the third element, Herman tries to explore the narrative ways of world making and disruption using both the textual and cognitive features. In order to do that, he firstly defines storyworld as »the world evoked implicitly as well as explicitly by a narrative [. . .] Storyworlds are global mental representations enabling interpreters to frame inferences about the situations, characters, and occurrences either explicitly mentioned in or implied by a narrative text or discourse.« Accordingly, he examines narrative beginnings as well as the WHAT, WHERE and WHEN dimensions of storyworlds in order to show the ways narratives make worlds. In addition, Herman also shows that as far as the narrative progression takes place through its worldmaking techniques, it also goes forward through noncanonical events and situations. In other words, »the way stories prototypically represent not just a narrative world but also world disruption, that is, events introducing disequilibrium or noncanonical situations into that world—as experienced by human or human-like agents.« Finally, under the fourth and last basic element, Herman considers a narrative's what it's like or qualia feature as a determining factor for its narrativity. In that case, he believes that narratives are no more than consciousness representations and the impact of narrative events on conscious awareness. Aas Herman argues, »narrative is centrally concerned with qualia, a term used by philosophers of mind to refer to the sense of »what it is like« for someone or something to have a particular experience.« Thus, Herman binds the representation of mental experience in narrative to the degrees a narrative includes narrativity (*Basic*: x, 37, 35, 75, 706, 106, 105, 106, 133, 137).

As it is already mentioned, in the present study Herman's last basic narrative element, what it's like or qualia, along with Palmer's theories related with fictional minds will act as the background for the analysis of the selected narratives. Therefore, in the next part his concept of what it's like or qualia is explored in detail in order to display the connections between Herman's term and McEwan's representation of human conscious awareness or experientiality in the chosen narratives.

2.3.1 What It's Like or Qualia

Representation of experiencing consciousness[63], according to Herman, is central for all kinds of narratives as well as a key factor of narrativity. This,

63 Characters in *AM*, *AT* and *CB* are primarily presented as experiencing narrative events and situations in particular moments of their lives. This technique is not apart from McEwan's general understanding of a novelist's principle role. According to him, a novelist »gives you a full sense of what it is to be someone else. What he is in effect doing, is milking the human instinct for what psychologists call a theory of mind, which explores our innate tendency to construct an understanding of what others are thinking« (Ridley vii). Likewise, experiencing events and situations that are in flux throughout the narrative, is fundamental to the operation of fictional minds in the selected narratives. The central characters in *AM* undergo some experiences related mainly with the complete disruption of the intermental unit between themselves. Likewise, in *CB* the newlyweds experience some intense moments of intramental dissents that lead them to their separation. Therefore, these characters are anthropomorphic images of human beings since, according to Nicklas, McEwan's:

characters do not appear as puppets standing in for large ideas and ideologies but they experience their lives as though they were the final human being on earth—only in special moments or with hindsight do they realize that they belong to a

however, does not mean that the other basic elements should be subordinated to this one. Instead, it implies »representation of what it's like to experience disruptive events in a storyworld« (*Basic* 137) is an important basic element of narrative. This idea, nevertheless, differs from Fludernik's concept of narrativity for which human experientiality is both central and sufficient whereas for Herman it is only one of the four basic elements or, as he puts, »capturing what it's like to experience storyworld events constitutes a critical property of but not a sufficient condition for narrative« (*Basic* 139). At the same time, Herman continues his argument, a narrative is impossible without representation of experientiality, even if for minimum degrees: »the absence of the element of what it's like from a text or a representation is tantamount to zero-degree narrativity—even if one or more of the elements of situatedness, event sequencing, and worldmaking/world disruption is in play« (*Basic* 142). Herman uses the concept of qualia or what it's like to be someone or something in order to re-contextualise Fludernik's anti Aristotelian[64] concept of experientiality. Qualia, which comes from philosophy of mind, according to Herman, »are felt, subjective properties of mental states« or »states of felt, subjective (or first-person) awareness attendant upon consciousness) (*Basic* 143, 145). Herman, moreover, not only considers qualia as a basis and condition for narrative but, in a reciprocal manner, he also considers narrative as a basis and condition of conscious experience itself (Basic 143–160). Nevertheless, for both theorists, the impact of disrupting events on fictional minds besides the consciousness representation should be at the centre of any narrative. For example, from Fludernik's perspective,

> Experientiality in narrative as reflected in narrativity can therefore be said to combine a number of cognitively relevant factors, most importantly those of the presence of a human protagonist and her experience of events as they impinge on her situation or activities. The most crucial factor is that of the protagonist's emotional and physical reaction to this constellation, which introduces a basic dynamic feature into the

group or nation. The collective memory is at the bottom of their experience but they have to go through their experience by themselves. (12)

64 Aristotle emphasised on plot while Fludernik emphasises on experientiality as the most important element of narrative.

> structure. Second, since humans are conscious thinking beings, (narrative) experientiality always implies—and sometimes emphatically foregrounds—the protagonist's consciousness. (*Towards* 22):

Furthermore, based on Herman, the events and situations that cause disequilibrium within narratives affect fictional minds both diachronically, in temporal dimensions, and synchronically, simultaneously varying perspectives. Because, as Herman says, »more than just representing minds, stories emulate through their temporal and perspectival configuration the what-it's-like dimension of conscious awareness itself« (*Basic* 157). Moreover, narrative, Herman argues, is a »mode of representation tailor-made for gauging the felt quality of lived experiences.« This element, however, like Herman's other three basic elements of narrative, »operates in a gradient or more or less manner« (*Basic* 138), meaning that the more the impact of narrative events on the consciousness awareness of the fictional minds are represented within a narrative the more narrative it is. Herman also extends the importance of consciousness experiencing or conscious awareness representation beyond modernist psychological novels to all types of narratives. He considers it a fundamental element of narrative in general no just the constituent element of psychological or figural narratives. That said, it should also be noted that the dominant mode of representation in *AM, AT* and *CB* is figural narration although the narratives are primarily designed in authorial mode. That is so, because in quite a lot passages the third person narrators are immediately replaced by the experiencing characters or »there is in effect a blending of first-person and third-person narration: a third-person or heterodiegetic narrator recounts events filtered through the perspective or focalizing perceptions of a reflector figure, that is, a particularized centre of consciousness« (Herman, *Basic* 140). The use of representational techniques such as FIT, moreover, foregrounds representation of the impact of narrative events and situations on the fictional minds experiencing them and hence what it's like or the qualia aspect of their consciousness. Similarly, McEwan *AM, AT* and *CB* uses this technique, FIT mode, a lot along with the other modes in order to provide unmediated or direct access to the qualia of the fictional minds. The experiencers within these worlds, moreover, act out as the »default role-assignment for protagonists« (Herman, *Basic* 142) meaning that their consciousness is foregrounded in the narratives. Thus, the narrative readers or audiences »adopt a particular interpretive stance toward the text as a whole« (Herman, *Basic* 148) based on the represented perspectives. For example, in *AM* the interaction of Clive's perspective with that of Vernon's signify their double efforts to minimise the felt experiences or qualia of each other. Embedding each other's narrative in their own narratives, they misconstrue each other's minds. In other words, *AM* narrative advances fundamentally through Clive-Vernon mutual mental ascriptions to themselves and to each other. McEwan's narrative is similar to Herman's concept of the term,

> narrative allows for critical and reflexive engagement with competing accounts based on different strategies for ascription. Just as stories, and stories alone, afford an environment in which versions of what it was like to experience situations and events can be comparatively evaluated, likewise narrative provides a discourse context in which different accounts of someone's mind can be proposed, tested against other versions, and modified or abandoned as necessary—based on the goodness-of-fit between the ascribed mental states and the whole pattern of the person's experiences, conduct, and demeanor. (*Basic* 159)

In the same way, the competing interpretive stances or accounts of Edward and Florence in *CB* indicate the different impacts of same situations and events on them. From this perspective, *AM*, *CB* and the first part of *AT* and are more narratives or they are narratives with high degrees of narrativity because narrative, according to Herman, generally

> allows for more or less direct, explicit reflection on—for critical and reflexive engagement with—competing accounts of the world-as-experienced. Arguably, narrative is unique in this respect: stories, and stories alone, afford an environment in which versions of what it was like to experience situations and events can be juxtaposed, comparatively evaluated, and then factored into further accounts of the world (or *a* world). (*Basic* 150–151)

In McEwan's narratives the representation of fictional minds' repository of qualia besides presentation of the other aspects of their mental states such as beliefs, emotions, wishes, dreams, memories, plans and goals, decisions etc. allows readers to enter into the characters' consciousness. That makes it possible for the reader to evaluate their stances comparatively in order to find a general interpretive stance for the general or frame narrative. Accordingly, these narratives both display the characters' quails and mental states, and show the way(s) the others are focalized through the focalizer-characters' perspectives. That seems so because »narrative bears crucially on one's relation with one's own as well as others' minds [. . .] narrative can be viewed as the fundamental resource used to construct explanations of others' behaviour in terms of assumptions or hypotheses about their minds« (Herman, *Basic* 157–159).

The three following discussion chapters explore McEwan's *AM*, *AT* (the first part) and *CB* in terms of the key theoretical concepts discussed in this chapter. They explore some aspects of central fictional minds in terms of intermental/intramental thought as revealed in their embedded and doubly embedded narratives and the dominant modes of their consciousness representation. The chapters, furthermore, examine the impact of narrative events and situations on the characters' consciousness or narrativization of what it's like for them to undergo some experiences or its qualia. These questions are generally central to the novella genre too—»a focus on one or two characters, an emphasis on interiorised experience, and a plot that hinges on a moment of crisis in which the essential nature of the characters' experience is revealed to themselves and/or to the reader« (Head, »*On Chesil Beach*« 118). Therefore, this study explores the manner of central characters' mental functioning, their embedded narratives, the modes used for their consciousness representation. Characters or individuals, as in CN, are fundamental to the selected narratives where the primary purpose in the representation of narrative situations and events seems to be the examination of their impacts on fictional minds. That is so because »Both of these short novels present dramatic conflicts between individuals that reflect on the moral blind spots of their times—greed, ambition, egotism, gender inequality—all of which are products of a concentration of on the self to the detriment of others« (Wells, *Ian McEwan* 96).

Chapter three explores *AM* focusing on Clive's and Vernon's manner of thoughts or mental functioning, their modes of discourse, their varying perspectives and the different impact of some shared events and situations on their consciousness or the what it's like aspect of their embedded narratives.

Chapter four analyses McEwan's *AT* in terms of the impact of Briony's intramentally functioning mind on the small intermental unit between Cecilia and Robbie. Likewise, chapter five examines McEwan's *CB* focusing on Edward's and Florence's totally different manner of thought, their consciousness representation and their strongly doubly embedded narratives along with the impact of the shared disrupting events on their consciousness. The fictional worlds in these narratives are mirrored primarily through the consciousness of the four reflector characters. Each of them, according to Jahn, »Wholly unaware of both his/her own intradiegetic status and the part s/he plays in the extradiegetic universe comprising narrator and narratee, the reflector's consciousness nonetheless *mirrors* the world *for* these higher-level agents and thus metaphorically functions as a window him- or herself (»Windows« 252). Moreover, *AM, AT* and *CB* are brilliant examples of internal focalization[65] or internally focalized narrations in which readers are simultaneously allowed to »experience the fictional world through the consciousness of a character« (Caracciolo, »Fictional« 43).

---

65 »A text is internally focalized when it implements stylistic and representational strategies that invite readers to construe the storyworld ›as perceived and registered (recorded, represented, encoded, modeled and stored) by some mind ... which is a member of this world‹ (Margolin). In short, internal focalisation creates a tension between the audience's imaginative access to the storyworld and the mental processes they attribute to a character on the basis of textual cues« (Caracciolo, »Phenomenological« 63).

3. *Amsterdam*

3.1 Intramental Characterization and Consciousness Presentation: *AM*

> Imagining what it is like to be someone other than yourself is at the core of our humanity. It is the essence of compassion, and it is the beginning of morality. (»Only Love« 2001)

The present chapter explores fictional minds within the storyworld of *AM* in terms of their intramental dissents, the impact of some momentous fictional events and situations on their mental functioning as well as the representational modes used for the presentation of characters' consciousness. The chapter firstly examines Clive's and Vernon's embedded and double embedded narratives focusing on the converging and diverging nature of their thoughts. The former characteristic, which depends heavily on their old days as inferred from the narration, constructs the intermental aspect of their friendship. The latter one, however, which derives from the intramental aspect of their mental functioning, brings the deadly imbalance to their intermental or joint activities, cooperation or relationship. The narrative analysis, firstly, reveals that the diverging nature of Clive-Vernon's doubly embedded narratives is the dominant aspect in *AM*. Therefore, the intramental dissents between the two friends, which lead in their final annihilation, are examined. The chapter, secondly, explores the impact of fictional events and situations on the central characters' consciousness. It studies the manner in which these characters undergo certain experiences within the represented world or the qualia nature of their narratives. Besides that, the methods or modes used for the presentation of their consciousness are also examined.

AM was published in 1998. In five parts, it recounts the disintegration or ending process of an old friendship between an eminent composer, Clive Linely, and a famous newspaper editor, Vernon Halliday, in the mid-1990s.

It highlights »an escalating conflict[66] between two friends [...] both of whom are ruthlessly self-promoting« (Wells, *Ian McEwan* 84). According to Malcolm, it is »part psychological novel and part social satire« (194). The narrative mostly focuses on the presentation of the impact of the dissenting conflicts on central characters', particularly Clive's, consciousness. According to Ingersoll,

> The narrative focuses on Clive's consciousness so extensively that in the end his entrapment in the isolate's hell of solipsism may come as a major shock to readers. Unlike Vernon who is motivated by shabby self-aggrandizement, Clive has the luxury of longer reader sympathy, one suspects, because his obsessive aspirations are culturally legitimated through his art. (»City of Endings« 128)

The novel, moreover, »begins dramatically with an ending: the cremation of Molly lane's remains« (Ingersoll, »City of Endings« 125). She is absent from the storyworld but her fully doubly embedded narratives are present everywhere in the frame narrative particularly in the consciousness of the two focal friends. She is, in other words, »the dynamic centre of the novelistic narrative« being »somehow able to smooth away interpersonal uneasiness« (Tsai 9). Her »glittering funeral« (Kohn 93) at the beginning of the narrative is remarkable since, as Wells put, »With her death, the world depicted in *Amsterdam* loses the benign ›feminine‹ principle of caring for others« (*Ian McEwan* 86). Furthermore, according to Schwalm, »In *Amsterdam,* empathy as a projection of oneself into the minds of others operates on various levels of plot and narration« (175). At the beginning of narrative, while Molly's crematorium ceremony is advancing, her two former lovers, Clive and Vernon, are talking about their memories of her, the immediate nature of her death, and her other two lovers—George Lane, her husband, and Julian Garmony, the right-wing foreign secretary. In the earlier parts, the two friends are intermentally despising Molly's other two lovers. They, furthermore, agree to make a pact of euthanasia in case of being afflicted by a fatal disease like Molly's. Their later perceptions and ensuing actions, however, deadly affect their friendship since they both have »delusions of grandeur

66 Kohn emphasises that »The conflict between vice and virtue is [...] a never-ending one in McEwan's *Amsterdam*« (100).

of the Ego« (Nicklas, 13). First of all, they disagree about Vernon's decision to defame Garmony through publishing his transvestite photographs with Molly in his newspaper, *The Judge*. He pretends to do it in order to prevent Garmony from running for the leadership. Their second confrontation arises over Clive's decision on a row between a woman and a man, later identified as the Lakeland rapist. There, Clive avoids doing his moral duty under the pretext of being absorbed in his genuinely artistic creation at that moment. As a result of such disagreements or confrontations, Clive's and Vernon's intermental friendship finally ends in their mutual murder since »Each friend understands the ›sinister direction‹ the other has taken for the ›salvation‹ of his career, warns him of the dangers, but these ›parting gift[s‹] are ignored« (Kohn 93). Moreover, according to Wells,

> Their pact to help each other in the event of incapacitation, reached after Molly's illness, was intended as a gesture of true friendship; instead, it becomes their method of revenge against one another that leads paradoxically to their own deaths, as they trick each other into agreeing to euthanasia in Amsterdam. (*Ian McEwan* 91)

The two moral disagreements exacerbate considerably the already diverging rift in the two friends' intermentality. They finally change their conventionalised cooperation into an unfair competition.

The events in *AM*, accordingly, are unfolding while the two friends' strong aspectuality control the narrative's main orientation. Clive's and Vernon's different moral understandings besides their intermental as well as intramental preferences bring forth the fatal imbalance in their relationship. As a result, while mutually misusing their euthanasia pact[67], they finally poison each other in the city Amsterdam. Despite that, Clive-Vernon relationship is, according to Ingersoll, »complicated [. . .] by the knowledge of each that the other has also been Molly's lover, just as they both know that the husband George is also aware of his dead wife's former lovers«

---

[67] Dana Catrinescu argues that they »poison each other out of revenge, having forgotten their pact. But, in fact, the fact that they kill each other is euthanasia performed at the proper moment, because Clive is already sick and no longer capable to create music and Vernon is finished as a public figure. The symptoms of their involution are evident from the beginning of the novel.«

(»City of Endings« 126). This knowledge, nevertheless, acts as a potential force in the backdrop of their relationship leading them towards the catastrophic subsequent intramental dissents when their perspectives regarding self (private), other (public), moral duty etc. vary completely. At the same time, their egocentrism does not allow them to imagine, let alone embody, the other position. In other words, they find themselves unable to go beyond their own perspectives. However, Childs insists that »Most reviewers of *Amsterdam* were positive, seeing this short novel as an exquisite social satire or moral fable« (*The Fiction* 118). By the same token, *AM*, according to Malcolm, »is anything but benign and optimistic. It is a dark and sour account of contemporary Britain (or part of it)« (189).

Being a »quintessentially ›scriptible‹ novel« (Kohn 89)[68], *AM* is mostly a narrative of subjectivity since it is strongly focalized through Clive's and Vernon's internal perspectives. It is also about the differences between their inner perceptions and outer behaviours. As Nicholas Lezard put, »the book's deeper subject matter: deception, both of others and of the self« (qtd. in Childs, *The* 125). This does not mean that the omniscient narrator's presence or comments are not obvious in the narrative. Rather, whenever the central characters' perceptions about their own thoughts and actions and those of the others are concerned, the narrator's discourse seems to be replaced by the character's discourse or subjectivity. At the same time, occasionally in the background other times directly, »The narrator expresses himself in educated and authoritative [. . .] language« (Malcolm 191). The omniscient narrator's principal role in *AM* seems to be organizing the relationship between the diegetic level and the extradiegetic one. As Schwalm says: »While on the diegetic level the authorial plan of deliberate intersubjective asymmetry goes out of control, the extradiegetic narrator has composed a perfectly arranged scenario which coolly displays the emotional, cognitive, and moral shortcomings of his characters« (176).

---

68 Robert E. Kohn calls *AM* a scriptible novel, »Because the title of the novel is itself a city, and because the novel conjures up particular works of literature that convey holiness and connote an inner, spiritual center.« These particular works, according to Kohn, are the works of W. H. Auden, James Joyce, Allen Ginsberg and Shakespeare (90).

The first part of narrative, composed of two chapters, is focalized mostly through Clive's perspective concentrating on the aftermath of Molly's death on him. Thus, whenever the narrative turns into the characters' perceptions and evaluations of their own actions and those of the others, the narrator leaves floor over for the character and the narrative events are represented through the reflecting character's consciousness or mental functioning. The nature of characters' thoughts in terms of intermentality and intramentality turns out to be growingly in subjective-first manner. It is because of these characteristics that the narrative, according to Malcolm, is considered to be a »thoroughly sour account of human shabbiness and frailty without a single moment of redemption.« Having pointed out the significance of social satire as well as the political and historical dimensions of the narrative, Malcolm concludes that »Yet the focus in this novel, too, is on the present and on certain psychological states« (6).

Moreover, the critical readings of *AM* generally point out the significance of morality and the *other* in this narrative. Clive's and Vernon's moral decisions and their aspectual evaluations of each other's actions are generally interpreted as the central concerns in *AM*. They are presented as being at war with themselves and at the same time with the other characters. As far as they seem to be controlled by their rational or controllable thoughts and actions, they are also controlled by their irrationally oriented thoughts and desires which invigorate their dissents. Self-centeredness and misrecognition of the other lie at the heart of their ethical problems, which, as put by Tsai, seems to be criticised in the narrative:

> McEwan criticizes the enclosure of selves and the inability to engage with others ethically most conspicuously through the portrayals of Clive and Vernon: the former fails to rescue a woman about to be raped in order to grasp an inspiration for his symphony while the latter publishes the pictures showing Garmony in female attire in *The Judge*, a paper which he edits and is currently in decline. (3)

Tsai, moreover, believes that Clive's and Vernon's moral concerns are in the control of their »narcissistic« selves,

> McEwan appears to foreground Clive and Vernon as interpreters of the other: both are in a position to construct what one can know about the world, but the commanding niche they entertain, nevertheless, accompanies moral responsibilities. Somehow, their approach to the other implies and mirrors their narcissistic images. (15)

Critics, however, do not consider the characters' propensity to be self-centred in *AM* apart from the socio-cultural standards of the storytime. For example, according to Head, »*Amsterdam* engages with the literary consequences of Thatcherism, [. . .] especially with the era of entrepreneurial self-promotion« (»*On Chesil Beach*« 116). The nature of the relationship between the two friends, however, reveals more than that.

The centrality of irrational self in narrative, according to Malcolm, is not unique to *AM*, but McEwan generally »is very concerned with the role of the irrational in his characters' lives. From the early short stories the reader sees characters driven by desires and emotions that they cannot control or really analyse themselves« (14). The central characters' »irrational« thoughts and actions, furthermore, refer to their self-centred or »egoistic« inclinations as »Garmony has uncontrollable transvestite desires that destroy his career, while Clive is an egoist who cannot place a woman's life above his own artistic aims. Vernon's case is more complex, but even he is driven by a desire for success that makes him deaf to rational argument« (Malcolm 15). Nevertheless, these characters, particularly Clive and Vernon, endeavour to frame their »egoistic« and somehow »irrational« thoughts and actions within a strongly aspectual moral understanding. In other words, they turn »each into the cruel analyst of the other's moral depravity« (Ingersoll, »City of Endings« 133). While hiking in the Lake District, Clive is represented as thinking that his only »moral duty« is to focus on his music rather than to meddle in a row scene in which a woman may be in danger. Vernon, however, accuses Clive of ignoring his moral duty and putting his self-interest higher than his human duties. Likewise, Vernon »constructs himself as a liberal warrior« (Ingersoll, »City of Endings« 127). Clive is unable to persuade him to stop blackmailing Garmony. He accuses him of being an egotistic person ignoring the impact of his actions on another person's (Garmony's) real life. Their moral perspectives, accordingly, are totally opposing each other. As Malcolm holds in this case, »One of the principal concerns of the McEwan critic must be the moral perspective of his texts. [. . .] Overall, McEwan's career shows a trajectory from quite extreme moral relativism toward a rather clear moral focus« (15). Moreover, according to Tsai, both Clive and Vernon »are criticized by McEwan for their pursuit of self-interest encouraged under Thatcherism« (11).

Considering the moral perspectives within *AM* storyworld, a strong aspectuality is shown without presenting any central moral standing against which the presented moral understandings can be weighed. However, throughout the narrative, the two friends, Clive and Vernon, undergo »processes of defining and re-defining friendship and the tempting of ethical limits.« Accordingly, as stated by Tsai, »the dialectic between friendliness and animosity« (5, 9) is the narrative dynamic in *AM*. As a result, the reader is presented with different moral interpretations of the same issues. At the end of the narrative,

> Clive and Vernon are punished for their stupidity and moral baseness, as is the hypocritical Garmony. But George, who is equally corrupt, wins out in the end and sets off to start an affair with Vernon's widow. The whole world of the novel (largely restricted, let it be noted, to men) is morally corrupt, but there is no real voice of honesty or honor to provide a moral standard within the novel. (Malcolm, 17)

The friendship between »the two friends are determined to abide by their promises, because they loathe each other for betraying their friendship and causing the subsequent frustration of each other's ambitions (Tsai 16). Moreover, in spite of their loyalty to their promises—reciprocal euthanasia—their double murder at the end of the narrative, according to Schwalm, »exhibits both friends in a kind of parody of intersubjectuive reciprocity. Cold-heartedly anticipating and calculating the actions of the other, they both fail to recognize their opposite's equally nasty schemes« (176). Since the two old friends cannot agree with each other, as well as with the others, to maintain their friendship in spite of their disagreements, their self-centeredness together with their intramental dissents and »reciprocal misrecognition« (Schwalm 176) lead them to their annihilation.

In three parts, the present chapter examines the construction, workings or operation and presentation of the central fictional minds in *AM*. Through the slow analyses of the of characters' embedded and doubly imbedded narratives, the chapter attempts to show the ways their intermental, shared or intersubjective first minds are replaced by intramental, private or subjective first minds. It turns out that their disagreements or dissents over some shared issues destroy the fragile balance both in their social life and in their private perceptions. Such non-canonised disrupting events, ultimately, bring about Clive's and Vernon's total destruction at the end. Concurrently, the impact of the narrative events and situations on their experiencing minds or consciousness is examined in order to portray the way(s) Clive and Vernon experience the deteriorating situations differently.

3.2 The Passage from Intermental to Intramenal Minds: Clive Linely's and Vernon Halliday's (Doubly) Embedded Narratives

In the early part of the narrative, Clive and Vernon are represented as intermental minds with joint actions. Molly's death and the ensuing events, however, change their thoughts of each other and hence their friendship. Palmer argues that »a large amount of the subject matter of novels is the formation, development, and breakdown of the(se) intermental systems.« He defines them as »joint, group, shared, or collective thought as opposed to *intramental,* or individual or private thought« (»Social Minds in Little« 28). Further, Palmer considers fictional minds' mental functioning or cognitive activity as the primary concern of narrative. He holds that »Narrative is in essence the presentation of fictional mental functioning« (2004: 188). Likewise, Herman regards the presentation of characters' cognitive activity as the fundamental function of narrative. As a consequence, he considers qualia or »what it is like for them [characters] to have or undergo experiences from a particular vantage-point on the storyworld« (*Basic* 152) as the forth basic element of narrative which is the most important one too. Accordingly, this part examines the formation and breakdown of intermental units between Clive and Vernon in *AM*. It also explores representational modes of the impact of narrative events and situations on the primal experiencing minds.

At the beginning of *AM*, the omniscient narrator provides a summary of Molly Lane's sudden disease and her ensuing death colouring it with Clive's and Vernon's perspectives. Clive's intermental unit with Vernon is obvious from their shared thoughts regarding Molly, her husband George and one of her lovers, Julian Garmony, the Foreign Secretary. In the early part of the narrative, we encounter »two old friends [Clive and Vernon]« who have some shared, joint or intermental communions. Looking at Molly's husband, George, for example, they both share the same thoughts. The narrative, in TR mode and focalized through their perspectives, shows

> Her death had raised him from general contempt. [. . .] Refusing to consign her to a home, he had cared for her with his own hands. [. . .] He vetted her visitors. Clive and Vernon were strictly rationed because they were considered to make her excitable and, afterward, depressed about her condition [. . .] Clive and Vernon, however, continued to enjoy loathing him. (*AM* 5)

They »loathe« George only because he was an obstacle on their way to the attracting Molly. In other words, they loath him since he did not support them in their self-centred plans keeping them away from his own wife. Presentations of their extremely egoistic expectations, therefore, are the shared manner of their thoughts' functioning in the early parts of the narrative. Likewise, they are intermental considering Garmony since they both take him as an enemy although Vernon is much more confident than Clive in this case. For example, when Clive is asked to go to Garmony in Molly's crematorium ceremony, Vernon warns him: »›Hey, Linley. No talking to the enemy!‹« Clive's unvoiced reflection shows their difference in this case although his discourse is closely overlapped with the narrator's: »The enemy indeed. What had attracted her?« (*AM* 13). The unvoiced manner of the initial conflicts, nevertheless, changes into open confrontations in the later scenes.

Their internal perceptions of each other, however, are unlike their utterances in the early parts. Clive's question »Did you ever learn anything from her?« brings about Vernon's conservative answer: »I can never remember sex.« Clive's judgment of what Vernon says, nonetheless, implies a growing rift in their already established intermental unit: »Clive assumed this was an evasion and decided against any confidences of his own.« The rift in their intermental relationship, moreover, is enhanced by Vernon's succeeding disagreement with Clive. For example, in the following conversation when

Clive confides in him by telling his private thought, Vernon's reaction is ironic:

> [Clive] »You know, I should have married her. When she started to go under, I would have killed her with a pillow or something and saved her from everyone's pity.« Vernon was laughing [. . .] »Easily said. I can just see you writing exercise yard anthems for the cons, like what's her name, the suffragette.« (*AM* 8)

Vernon's theory of mind about Clive reveals his certainty about Clive's preference of his music over any other person or thing. This, moreover, implies the level or significance of Clive's music from Vernon's perspective. Based on Vernon's statement, Clive writes »exercise yard anthems for the cons.« The teleological contribution of such negative perceptions to the general progression of the frame narrative turns out to be more meaningful in later parts. The more narrative advances, the more Clive becomes concerned either with his music or with the critics' admonishing evaluations of it. Nevertheless, the two friends knowingly continue with their bitter double criticisms. Their relentless pursuit of solipsism, bilateral misunderstandings and intramental dissenting decisions in the course of narrative finally break down the already established intermental unit between them.

The process of intermental breakdown between the two friends is also enhanced by their different thoughts towards Julian Garmony, the foreign secretary and one of Molly's close or private friends. In the funeral scene, when Clive is summoned by Garmony to talk to him, Vernon warns him: »Hey, Linely. No talking to the enemy!« (*AM* 13) Vernon's internal ironic assessment of the word »enemy,« indicates their different perspectives on an issue which is crucial to their friendship. That finally will bring about their firstly proclaimed diverging thoughts in case of Vernon's greedy insistence on publishing Molly-Garmony photographs:

> The enemy indeed. What had attracted her? [. . .] He [Garmony] had made a life in the political marketplace with an unexceptional stall of xenophobic and punitive opinions. Vernon's explanation had always been simple: high-ranking bastard, hot in the sack. But she could have found that anywhere. There must also have been the hidden talent that had got him to where he was and even now was driving him to challenge the PM for his job. (*AM* 13)

Clive's inner thought reveals his theory of mind regarding Garmony. It is different from that of Vernon's. Clive does not change his idea about Garmony-Molly photographs in the later scenes. His perceptions concerning Garmony suggest the ability or capacity of his theory of mind as well. He tries to consider the issue from Molly's perspective. Therefore, his mind has more tendency towards intermentality than that of Vernon's despite the fact that in both cases the construction of an intermental unit with Garmony seems untenable since they both consider him as a rival. Vernon pretends his egocentric action to be for the profit of public. The more Clive remains beside Garmony the more he wants to leave him. As revealed in the scene focalized through his perspective in the dual-voiced statement, he feels that »there was still a little more to be wrung from the famous composer's presence« (*AM* 15). It is dual voice because seemingly the narrator's discourse is combined with the character's subjectivity rendering their ironic perceptions of the situation. Clive is, however, unable to read Garmony's mind from his statements:

> [1] More followed in similar style [Garmony's talking] as Clive gazed on, no sign of his [Clive's] growing distaste showing in his expression. [2] Garmony, too, was his generation. High office had eroded his ability to talk levelly with a stranger. Perhaps that was what he offered her in bed, the thrill of the impersonal. A man twitching in front of mirrors. [3] But surely she preferred emotional warmth. Lie still, look at me, really look at me. [4] Perhaps it was nothing more than a mistake, Molly and Garmony. Either way, Clive now found it unbearable. (*AM* 17)

Clive endeavours to hide his real thoughts and feeling from Garmony [2]. Binding Garmony to his generation, Clive, moreover, ascribes to him »impersonality« inflicted on him by his office. In this way, he criticises Garmony's social context for bestowing him such characteristic [2]. He, nevertheless, reconstructs his theory coming to the thought that Molly should have wanted something more than impersonality from Garmony, something like »emotional warmth« [3]. That thought, however, infuriates Clive in a way that he finds Molly-Garmony' emotional relationship »a mistake« and therefore »unbearable.« This sense of abhorrence and loathing, nevertheless, will not take him to an agreement with Vernon in terms of disgracing Garmony through publishing his transvestite photographs with Molly. Despite that,

Clive shows his restlessness by asking an unrelated question to the context: »›I was wondering,‹ Clive said to Molly's ex-lover, ›whether you're still in favour of hanging‹.« This issue had in fact been raised by Vernon's paper in order to stain Garmony's public fame and position before the general election. Garmony answers Clive by reminding him of a story once Molly told him:

> [Garmony:] »The very last time I saw Molly she told me you were impotent and always had been.«
> [Clive:] »Complete nonsense. She never said that.«
> [Garmony:] »Of course you're bound to deny it. Thing is, we could discuss it out loud in front of the gentlemen over there, or you could get off my case and make a pleasant farewell. That is to say, fuck off.« (*AM* 20)

In spite of the fact that, more than any other person, Clive is aware of himself as a man on the verge of impotence,[69] this story irritates him since it is metaphorically narrated by Garmony. The fact, nevertheless, is that Clive's monopolistic sense of Molly is questioned here. There are plethora of opposite references to her by Vernon, Garmony and also George which all show her as a certain source of their shared intermental units. Despite that and relying on his personal intermental experiences with her, Clive, unlike Vernon, respects her actions and decisions. This is obvious from his retrospective reflection on that scene: »then the foreign secretary did an extraordinary thing that quite destroyed Clive's theory about the effects of public office[70] and that in retrospect he was forced to admire« (*AM* 16). Garmony's ironic farewell words at the end of chapter one, however, appears to be much more intermental: »To air differences and remain friends, the essence of civilized existence, don't you think?« (*AM* 21). Unlike Garmony's recommendation, Clive and Vernon are not able to remain friends despite their differences. That seems to be a key factor in constructing intermental relationships as well. To respect differences means both to recognise the other person's pres-

---

69 We are told that »he had failed to meet two deadlines—the millennium itself was still years away« (McEwan, *AM* 22).

70 It refers to Clive's earlier conjecture about Garmony: »High office had eroded his ability to talk levelly with a stranger« (McEwan, *AM* 19).

ence or existence and to respect their different perceptions of the shared issues. This demonstrates the ability to take into account the other possibilities even though disagreeing about them. What exacerbates the breaking down process of Clive's and Vernon's intermental friendship throughout the narrative is in fact the lack of any assent in their intramental perspectives about Molly, Garmony and George. Their moral, professional and humane duties are also uncompromising.

The intermental relationship between Vernon and Clive is not broken until their first confrontation. This happens when Vernon shows Clive Molly-Garmony's three photographs right after the injunction against publishing the photos is declared. For example, when Clive calls Vernon and says, »I need to talk to you about something,« we are told, »there was a heaviness in his old friend's tone that made Vernon reluctant to put him off. All the same, he tried halfheartedly« (*AM* 42). Although that day is a »hectic day« for Vernon and he should visit George in order to buy the photographs, he accepts his friend's request with reluctance. However, right after their conversation, he regrets his indeterminacy about his only intimate friend. This scene sparks in Vernon's mind a brief picture of their entire friendship. Clive, Vernon finds out, has helped him much in his difficult times. This sympathetic scene, however, is Vernon's last true intermental feelings towards Clive:

> He had a few seconds after the call to wonder about Clive's manner. So pressing in a lugubrious way, and rather formal. Clearly something terrible had happened, and he began to feel embarrassed by his ungenerous response. Clive had been a true friend when Vernon's second marriage came apart, and he had encouraged him to go for the editorship when everybody else thought he was wasting his time. Four years ago, when Vernon was laid up with a rare viral infection of the spine, Clive had visited almost every day, bringing books, music, videos, and champagne. And in 1987, when Vernon was out of a job for several months, Clive had lent him ten thousand pounds. Two years later, Vernon discovered by accident that Clive had borrowed the money from his bank. And now, in his friend's moment of need, Vernon was behaving like a swine. (*AM* 42–43)

The impact of his friend's request and his reluctance to accept it, therefore, entices in Vernon's mind a reassessment process. He finds his own behaviour inappropriate towards Clive's helps and kindness throughout the past years. Moreover, the qualia or what it's like aspect of this passage, as shown in FIT mode, displays the deeper nature of their friendship. Nevertheless, despite his awareness of being »ungenerous,« or »behaving like a swine« towards his old friend, Vernon's conservative intramental ambitions push him away from the intermental thought they once shared.

Likewise, Clive's life course leads him towards his propensity to intramental thoughts and actions. His private life during the past years as well as his professional difficulties all establish Clive's propensity towards intramental dissents. We are told that »Over several years Clive seemed to race through two childless marriages relatively unscathed. [. . .] The years and all the successes had narrowed his life to its higher purpose; he was becoming not quite zealous, but cagey, about his privacy. [. . .] The open house [Clive's] was no more« (*AM* 46–47). Such inclination towards his privacy finally directs Clive to his »cagey« state. Accordingly, when Vernon shows him the photographs and recounts the story of injunction, in TR mode we are told that Clive »showed no curiosity about the photographs and the injunction and seemed to be only half listening« (*AM* 48). Nevertheless, Clive confides in Vernon his intimate request, »help me to die [. . .] Just as we might have helped Molly if we'd been able.« Vernon's answer to his close friend's request is careful and calculated, »Well, look, it's quite a thing you're asking me. It needs some thought« (*AM* 49). Such double feelings of intimacy will never recur in their future interactions:

> Both men accepted that the nature of the request, its intimacy and self-conscious reflection on their friendship, had created, for the moment, an uncomfortable emotional proximity, which was best dealt with by their parting without another word, Vernon walking quickly up the street in search of a taxi and Clive going back up the stairs to his piano. (*AM* 50)

The narrator's TR in this passage displays the impact of Clive's proposal on Vernon's consciousness and its reciprocal effects on his own mind. They are represented as experiencing »emotional proximity,« however, its »uncomfortable« nature forces them to leave each other for a while. The converging or intermental reactions to the same situation, moreover, indicate the deep level of their engagement. It is even more displayed when Vernon, after meeting George, scribbles a note and pushes it through the front door of Clive's house, »Yes, on one condition only: that you'd do the same for me« (*AM* 57). The teleological implications of this pact, however, will change their intermental friendship as well as their fate.

In a flashback mode in chapter III part II (pp. 68–90), the narrative focuses on the night Clive and Vernon had their first serious confrontation. Clive is reported as being not interested in Vernon's narrativizations of *The Judge* related events: »Clive had no idea what Vernon was talking about, but he said nothing« (*AM* 69). Vernon's reasoning for the publication of Molly-Garmony's three photographs does not persuade Clive as he asks him, »Tell me this. Do you think it's wrong in principle for men to dress up in women's clothes?« (*AM* 73). While he does not intend to get involved in that issue, Vernon expects him to do so. Nearly at the end of their argument, Vernon complains: »I came round hoping for your support. Or at the least, a sympathetic hearing. I didn't expect your fucking abuse« (*AM* 74). Clive, however, turns Vernon's expectation down consciously: »He was watching hungrily, waiting for a reaction, and it was partly to conceal his thoughts that Clive continued to gaze into the picture« (*AM* 70). In this scene Clive is represented as a mind reader of both Vernon's and Molly's intentions. At the same time, he tries not to betray his inferences and mental states to Vernon:

> [1] What he felt first was simple relief, for Molly. A puzzle had been solved. [2] This was what had drawn her to Garmony—the secret life, his vulnerability, [3] the trust that must have bound them closer. [4] Good old Molly. She would have been creative and playful, urging him on, taking him further into the dreams that the House of Commons could not fulfil, and he would have known that he could rely on her. [5] If she had been ill in some other kind of way, she would have taken care to destroy these pictures. (*AM* 70)

The reporting mode in this passage moves from TR to direct thought mode revealing Clive's states of mind full of conjectures and judgments. He is happy to find out the reasons of Garmony's attraction to Molly [1]. Based on his inferences, the pleasure of a »secret life.« Garmony's weakness, and a trust bond between them are what made Molly-Garmony friendship possible [2]. What is defining to his later actions and his friendship with Vernon is his determinacy to respect their mutual »trust« [3]. He is able to imagine the scope of Molly's profound impact on Garmony and his trust in her. It is based on such a conception that *the narrator relates that Clive knows that Garmony thinks that he could* »rely on her.«[71] This is a compelling mind reading ability which takes place based on outward behaviours [4]. Clive, moreover, is able to imagine that if Molly had chance before her death, she would have »destroyed« the photographs. Therefore, since he thinks to be aware of her real intentions concerning the pictures, he becomes more determined to respect her trust. Clive's reflections concerning the second picture reveal even more mind reading ability:

> [1] They should have been ridiculous, these photographs, they were ridiculous, but Clive was somewhat awed. [2] We knew so little about each other. We lay mostly submerged, like ice floes, with our visible social selves projecting only cool and white. [3] Here was a rare sight below the waves, of a man's privacy and turmoil, of his dignity upended by the overpowering necessity of pure fantasy, pure thought, by the irreducible human element-mind. (*AM* 71)

---

71 This is the positive form of Lisa Zunshine's model of embedded minds' cognitive load where »We are keeping track, that is, of the two or three most immediate mind-readings (as in »now X doesn't know that Y knows what X does«) and not of the whole series (as in »X doesn't know that Y knows that X knows that Y knows that X knows that Y knows what X does«)« (*Why We Read Fiction* 31). Moreover, it is related to Bal's discussion of the hierarchy in a narrative text. According to him, »Narrative communication is considered as a locutionary act.« Moreover, it is »considered as a triple message, in which each level is defined by a *subject*, its *activity* and the *result* of this activity, and in which each activity has an object, its content, which is the next level. In other words, the narrator speaks the text whose content is the narrative; the focalizer presents the narrative, whose content is the history; the history is acted out by the actors.« Accordingly, Bal proposes five possible narrative situations among which number one, »X relates that Y sees that Z does (N[narrator] ≠Florence[focalizer]≠A[actor])«, and number four, »X relates that Y sees that Y' does (N≠Florence=A)«, are the characteristics of »the so-called realist novel, where the principal character is occasionally allowed to present events from »his point of view« (»Notes« 44–45). The selected novels are realistic novels in which sometimes the first possibility, (N≠Florence≠A), is true when the narrator, or who tells, focalizer, or who sees, and the actor, or who does or experience, are not equal. While in many other defining scenes, the focalizer and the actor refer to the same character. In other words, the experiencing person is the same as the focalizing one although the activity and the result are related by the narrator who is not equal with the other two.

Clive in this scene is »awed« not by the ridiculousness of the photographs but mainly by what they suggest [1]. The second picture makes him to review his relationship with Molly. He finds out how little they knew each other and how unaware they were of each other's deeper self below their visible, public or social selves [2]. Comparably, when he thinks about the relationship between Molly and Garmony, he finds it a relationship not between two social selves but between two private selves. He even ascribes this ideal relationship to Molly's mental power, which was able to visualise it through fantasy and imagination [3]. Such broodings, provoked by three pictures, bring a change in his attitude towards Garmony: »For the first time Clive considered what it might be like to feel kindly toward Garmony. It was Molly who had made it possible« (*AM* 71). The reason of this change is Clive's ability to build an intermnental bond with Molly and hence evaluate her relationship with Garmony based on that. Through such passages, he is represented as being able to put himself in somebody else's (Molly's) place and imagining the occasions and events from her perspective. As a result of such ability, Clive upends Vernon's expectations. When he is shown all the three photographs: »He said, ›So you're fighting to keep them out of the paper.‹ It was part tease, part mischief, as well as a wish to delay voicing his thoughts« (*AM* 72). His controlled and directed articulation here varies greatly from Vernon's expectation in terms of the pictures and Garmony. Despite that, he evades from any straight answer. When Vernon emphasises, he shares his thought with him but he hides the main part of his objection:

> ›My idea is to publish next week. What do you think?‹
> Clive tilted back on his chair and clasped his hands behind his head. ›I think,‹ he said carefully, ›your staff is right. It's a really terrible idea.‹
> ›Meaning?‹
> ›It'll ruin him.‹
> ›Dead right it will.‹
> ›I mean, personally.‹
> ›Yup.‹
> There was a stalled silence. So many objections came crowding in on Clive that they seemed to cancel each other out. (*AM* 72)

Garmony, who was once their joint distaste or »pure poison, [. . .] Vile, [...and] Terrible for the country« (*AM* 73), has now changed into the basis of their disagreement. He is also one of the two major factors behind their two deadly conflicts in the storyworld. Flexibility in Clive's perception happens because, while he is pondering on the pictures, he reaches an intermental bond with Molly. This brings about his ability to consider Garmony's case from her perspective. In other words, going beyond the restrictions of his own perspective, Clive imagines the bond between them from Molly's perspective. Compared to that, Vernon is considering the case only from his own benefit-seeking perspective. As a result, he puts his career benefits and personal advantages higher than those of the others, including Molly's. The ability to read the other's mind and infer the content of their mental functioning lies at the heart of intermentality. This is the main lack in the confrontation scene between Clive and Vernon. Such paucity primarily derives from their inability to read each other's mind or to put oneself in each other's place. Besides that, they have different understandings of moral act. What Vernon considers as the right act—publishing the photographs in his newspaper *The Judge* and disgracing Garmony—is an immoral act from Clive's perspective. Not only does he consider the events from his own perspective, but also he evaluates them from the others' perspectives. Clive also attempts to encourage Vernon in order to evaluate the Garmony issue from the other aspects too. He reminds him of his own mistakes:

> You yourself were once an apologist for the sexual revolution. You stood up for gays. [. . .] You stood up for plays and films that people wanted to ban. Only last year you spoke up for those cretins who were in court for hammering nails through their balls. [. . .] Isn't this the kind of sexual expression you're so keen to defend? What exactly is Garmony's crime that needs to be exposed? (*AM* 73)

According to Clive, what Vernon considers as »Garmony's crime,« does derive from his own personal intentions since, more than Garmony, he committed mistakes in his past life. As Clive suggests, if he can take into account his own mistakes and be able to evaluate the issue from Garmony's perspective, he can forgive him as he forgives himself in the similar situations. Although Vernon takes Garmony's false or »transvestite« cloth as standing for

»His hypocrisy« (*AM* 73), Clive, as well as the reader, knows that Vernon's enmity of Garmony is based on his own hypocrisy. That is so because to save his newspaper, he should get his »hands dirty.« He also asks his colleagues in *The Judge* to do so: »›If we're going to save this paper,‹ Vernon liked to say at the morning editorial conference, ›you're all going to have to get your hands dirty‹« (*AM* 33). Therefore, Clive is aware that Vernon's intention to stay in *The Judge* as its editor and his dislike of Garmony are his main reasons for his insistence on publishing Molly-Garmony photographs. Likewise, according to Wells, Vernon's »real motivations are completely self-serving« (*Ian McEwan* 90). As Clive states in the following passage, George stimulates Vernon to despise Garmony because he was his wife's, Molly's, beloved:

> You know what this is really about? You're doing George's work. He's setting you on. You're being used, Vernon, and I'm surprised you can't see through it. He hates Garmony for his affair with Molly. If he had something on me or you, he'd use that too. [. . .] I don't think you're being straight with me. What is it you really object to about this? (*AM* 74–75)

The last rhetorical question is directed at what Vernon is trying to hide. Clive here reads Vernon's mind from his actions and questions his aspectuality concerning Garmony. His judgment is not based on his own feelings towards Garmony; rather, it is based on Molly's preferences. Although he does not like Garmony, his intersubjective first principle forces him, instead of backing up his closest friend, to support those who »trusted« and »respected« each other. Therefore, Clive's intermental bond with Molly and through that his flexibility towards Garmony has no other reason than his tendency to intermentality:

> Because of Molly. We don't like Garmony, but she did. He trusted her, and she respected his trust. It was something private between them. These are her pictures, nothing to do with me or you or your readers. She would have hated what you're doing. Frankly, you're betraying her. (*AM* 75)

Clive's aspectuality and intermental thought here, however, is not the general trend of his thought. He, for example, cannot imagine himself in Vernon's place as Vernon accuses him: »You know nothing, Clive. You live a privileged life and you know fuck-all about anything« (*AM* 119). More than anything else, Vernon needs a story to save his newspaper. Otherwise, he will be sacked. Therefore, he grabs to whatever at hand in order to stand upright. Their main difference, however, seems to derive from their different understanding of morality. After his return to London, Clive himself is accused of ignoring his »moral duty« (*AM* 119) in terms of not saving a woman while he was hiking in the rocks. Their mutual accuses show the breach in their friendship or already established intermental unit. When Vernon says: »There are certain things more important than symphonies. They're called people.« Clive accuses him on the same basis: »And are these people as important as circulation figures, Vernon?« (*AM* 119–120) Their different understandings of the same issues, thus, reveal their strong aspectualities and hence their intramental or subjective first characters.

Having found everything related with publishing Molly-Garmony photographs agreeable, Vernon is finally able to find out the disturbing thought that has been violating his »successes« and hence his happiness for a long time: »But for this one little thing he would be hugging himself, he would be dancing on the desk. It was rather like this morning, when he had lain in bed contemplating his successes, denied full happiness by the single fact of Clive's disapproval.« In his reported broodings, he finds out the reason for his restlessness at last: »there he had it. Clive. The moment he thought of his friend's name, it came back to him. He went across the room toward the phone. It was simple, and possibly outrageous.« From Vernon's perspective, Clive could have entered the row and hence save the woman's life because, according to him, it was »simple« to do so. Since Clive did not act as Vernon expects it should had happened, he finds Clive's action »outrageous.« As a result of these internal calculations, Vernon calls Clive in order to check the information. Once more, he hears through the line the »protracted, clattering pick-up, the sound of bedclothes, the cracked voice.« This triggers some conjectures persuading him that his friend is simply doing nothing: »It was past four o'clock, so what was it with Clive, lying there all day like a depressed teenager?« (*AM* 117) Vernon is aware that Clive is doing nothing and mutually Clive knows the he is right but at the same time, he does not want to acknowledge it. When Vernon asks Clive to go to the police station and inform them about what he saw in the rocks, he reminds him that it is his »moral duty« (*AM* 119) to do so. This enforcement, however, brings forth the appearance of their strong aspectuality, which finally leads to the deadly rift in their already diverging intermentality. Clive's aggressive response and Vernon's equal answer indicate the real depth of the imbalance in their relationship:

> [Clive]: »You're telling me my moral duty? You? Of all people?«
> [Vernon]: »Meaning these photographs. Meaning crapping on Molly's grave.« (*AM* 119)

Following such mutual charges, Clive and Vernon pour out their carefully kept inner thoughts. The contribution of this scene to the general plot of the narrative is considerable since it is influential on their intermental unit. They equally accuse each other for ignoring the other people by putting their self-interests higher than them. Vernon accuses Clive of being unable to understand the other people and of pursuing his own goals since he is from a different social class. Similarly, Clive accuses Vernon of not doing »journalism« but pursuing people restlessly from his own office:

> Vernon cut in. »You know nothing, Clive. You live a privileged life and you know fuck-all about anything.«
> »Meaning hounding a man from office. Meaning gutter journalism. How can you live with yourself?«
> »You can bluster all you want. You're losing your grip. If you won't go to the police, I'll phone them myself and tell them what you saw. Accessory to an attempted rape-« »Have you gone mad? How dare you threaten me!«
> »There are certain things more important than symphonies. They're called people.«
> »And are these people as important as circulation figures, Vernon?«
> »Go to the police.«
> »Fuck off.«
> »No. You fuck off.« (*AM* 119–120)

Clive and Vernon, therefore, both attempt to display their perspectives reasonable. However, they never get rid of their unmatched and »self-absorbed« (Malcolm, 2002: 194) interpretations of their shared subjects. Vernon accuses Clive for ignoring his moral duty and »While Vernon's high dungeon seems reasonable, it conceals the fact that he ignored Clive's earlier attempt to describe what he had witnessed because he was preoccupied with his plans to publish the photos of Garmony's transvestism« (Wells *Ian McEwan* 89). This dialogue, moreover, can be taken as an obvious sign for the irreversible nature of the growing imbalance in their friendship. At the same time, the reader's experiential repertoire gathered from Clive's and Vernon's embedded narratives indicate the degree they both think and act intramentally.

Moreover, Clive and Vernon ascribe the same adjectives to each other. Although the conflicting issues are the same for both friends, their too much personal or intramental interpretation of the shared issues, however, brings about the deadly imbalance in their friendship. The incomplete nature of the two old friends' interpretations of the shared issues is revealed by the narrator's explanatory comment on the disastrous point the two friends have reached. Ascribing the possibilities of misreading to language itself, the omniscient narrator highlights the limited nature of the two friends' perspectives reminding us that:

> [1] What Clive had intended on Thursday and posted on Friday was, You deserve to be sacked. What Vernon was bound to understand on Tuesday in the aftermath of his dismissal was, You deserve to be sacked. Had the card arrived on Monday, he might have read it differently. [2] This was the comic nature of their fate; a first-class stamp would have served both men well. [3] On the other hand, perhaps no other outcomes were available to them, and this was the nature of their tragedy. [4] If so, Vernon was bound to consolidate his bitterness as the day wore on and to reflect, rather opportunistically, on the pact the two men had made not so long ago and the awesome responsibilities it laid upon him. For clearly Clive had lost his reason and something had to be done. [5] This resolve was bolstered by Vernon's sense that at a time when the world was treating him badly, when his life was in ruins, no one was treating him worse than his old friend, and that this was unforgivable. And insane. [6] It can happen sometimes, with those who brood on an injustice, that a taste for revenge can usefully combine with a sense of obligation. (*AM* 148–149)

The first part in the above passage [1] indicates the relationship between time and meaning or interpretation. It argues that the same statement in Clive's letter, »You deserve to be sacked,« could have been interpreted totally differently in different times. This, the narrator continues his comment, shows both the comic [2] and, at the same time, tragic [3] nature of the two old friends' fates. Clive could have sent the letter by a first-class stamp. That simple action could have changed Vernon's interpretation of his words. Their situation, moreover, is tragic because they could possibly have done nothing to their fate since they were ›bound‹ to it. The narrator expands the second possibility based on which Vernon starts thinking about the contract he had made with Clive [4]. He uses it as a pretext to »revenge« himself on his friend [5]. The narrator's comment in part [6], nevertheless, shows how the two friends' perceptions of obligation for doing something against what they consider as »injustice,« are afflicted with their personal desires. To put the same point in other words, it points out the manner they both pretend to be concerned primarily with »justice« while they are in fact following their own personal or intramental goals.

Molly's four former lovers gather for the second and last time towards the end of narrative after the two old friends' »mutual murder« (*AM* 177) took place. Julian Garmony, from Clive's part, and George Lane, form Vernon's, have come to Amsterdam in order to »escort the coffins back to England« (*AM* 175). The narrator's TR of their feelings and perceptions concerning each other and the dead ones reveals the diverging orientations of their thoughts. It turns out that there is no sign of intermentality between them: »Lane did not know how much Garmony knew. Garmony in turn was uncertain about Lane's attitude to his affair with Molly. Lane did not know whether Garmony realised just how much he, George, despised him« (*AM* 174). When Garmony asks George whether, as it is rumoured, it was he who sold his transvestite photographs with Molly to Vernon, his negative answer triggers some thought in Garmony's mind: »If Lane was lying, he did it well. If he wasn't, then Linley and all his works be damned« (*AM* 175). The narrative ending focuses on the presentation of George's subjectivity. It highlights his content inner feelings about the fates of Molly's former lovers:

> Garmony beaten down, and trussed up nicely by his lying wife's denials of his affair at her press conference, and now Vernon out of the way, and Clive. All in all, things hadn't turned out so badly on the former-lovers front. This surely would be a good time to start thinking about a memorial service for Molly. (*AM* 178)

George is elated because he finds the »former-lovers front« out of his way at last. In this way, the narrative seemingly rewards George because of the fact that for a long time he had been humiliated by his wife's extremely intramental persistence on her relationship with them.

Through the *AM* narrative, therefore, the initial intermentality between Clive and Vernon changes into intramental dissents leading to their enmity and total breakdown. Presentation of the sequences of events leading to their breakdown delineates their mutual inability and reluctance to take into account the perspective(s) of the other(s). Accordingly, among the other shared subjects, they measure the moral duty, friendship, love, enmity, private and public interests only by their perspectival criterions without going beyond their intramental beliefs. Therefore, through their embedded and doubly embedded narratives we are presented the impact of some private and social issues on their mental functioning. Clive is concerned about his own advancement in music as far as Vernon is haunted with his professional promotions. The breakdown of their initial intermental unit, thus, derives mainly from their personal weaknesses since according to Victoria Gaydosik, »Vernon's great weakness is his failure to imagine what he has not witnessed. [. . .] In contrast, Clive's great weakness is his inability to witness and remember the ordinary events of quotidian life in his devotion to the inspired moment« (16–17). Their personal concerns bring about their deadly dissents. Their analyses, by the help of Palmer's and Herman's terminologies, delineates the intramental propensities deeply embedded in their consciousness.

3.3 The (Im)Balance between Intermental and Intramental Thoughts: Representation of the Impact of Narrative Events and Situations on Clive Linely's Mind

Clive's embedded narratives reveal a mind that is primarily concerned with music. It is more important for him than his close or intimate friend(s). They represent the impact of the external or public factors on the operation of his mind which is moulded by them. Furthermore, they display how his intramental desires develop the deadly rift between him and his close friend,

Vernon. Feeling compelled to offer his sympathy to George in the crematorium ceremony, Clive in the following scene, reported in FIT [1 and 2] and TR [3 and 4] modes, assesses Molly-George relationship. The passage also reveals Molly's importance to Clive as he envisages her face in his »cellos in mirror image.« The affinity between his music and Molly continues until Clive's death. It is as if she is part of his music through which he expresses his repressed (sexual) desires,

> [1] Soon it would seem rude not to go over and say something to George. [2] He got her finally, when she couldn't recognise her own face in the mirror. He could do nothing about her affairs, but in the end she was entirely his. [3] Clive was losing the sensation in his feet, and as he stamped them the rhythm gave him back the ten-note falling figure, ritardando, a cor anglais, and rising softly against it, contrapuntally, cellos in mirror image. Her face in it. [4] The end. (*AM* 6)

Clive in this passage is represented as being concerned about the social understandings or interpretations of his actions. For example, he thinks that if he does not go to George and say something about his wife's, Molly's, death to him, he will take it as his rudeness [1]. Clive also reviews George's relationship with Molly. Based on his perception, they never had any intermental unit in their shared life. Molly's beauty and George's money were the only factors in holding them together in the same house. However, George's desire to possess and control her was realised only after her disease. Clive, furthermore, is reminded of Molly after some notes strike his consciousness [3]. The last word, »The end,« however, offers, according to Ingersoll, »a masterpiece of irony because as it turns out this is not »the end« at all but the beginning of the end, just as it is literally the beginning of the narrative« (»City of Endings« 127).

In the early pages, the narrative almost often proceeds between the time of narration and the time of story. It is triggered by Clive's and Vernon's intermittent questions that tie them to their shared memories.[72] When Vernon asks Clive, »She was a lovely girl. Remember the snooker table?« he

---

[72] It should be noted that in *AM*, the word »memory« has a plethora of repetition which does not seem unrelated to the importance of characters' experiences on their present actions.

replies with a repetition »A lovely girl« (*AM* 6). The question, however, changes the course of narrative chronotope, or narrative time and space, to twenty years earlier. Molly had danced on a snooker table in a group of friends in 1978. This analepsis or flashback, embedded between their dialogues, shows their intermental minds regarding their shared but now-dead friend Molly. In addition, it incites more memories in Clive's mind restoring their shared moments. The passage, reported in both FIT and direct speech modes, invites us to experience immediately what Clive re-experiences subjectively,

> [1] She had looked right at him when she pretended to bite the apple, and smiled raunchily through her chomping, with one hand on a jutting hip, like a music hall parody of a tart. [. . .] She taught him sexual stealth, the occasional necessity of stillness. [2] Lie still, like this, look at me, really look at me. We're a time bomb. [3] He was almost thirty, by today's standards a late developer. (*AM* 7)

Clive's nostalgic recollections of the past in this passage reveal his unuttered thoughts about Molly's impact on him. The considerable part of such influence is, however, mostly sexual as it is obvious from the narrator's word choices in order to render Clive's subjectivity—»she smiled raunchily;« »jutting hip« [1]. The passage, furthermore, shows Molly's power on Clive as she could calm him down or control him. As it is clear from Molly's direct speech [2], she is presented as being able to have Clive do whatever she wants. The next part [3], however, in TR mode shows Clive as a »late developer« who did not understand anything about Molly's sexual behaviour then. Their relationship, nevertheless, would change into a more intermental one after a while when,

> she was no longer a girl by then, no longer his lover. They were companionable, too wry with each other to be passionate, and they liked to be free to talk about their affairs. She was like a sister, judging his women with far more generosity that he ever allowed her men. Otherwise they talked music or food. (*AM* 20)

Their »companionship« continues with more intermental connections until Molly's disease and finally her death. After that, Clive finds himself without any intermental bonds with anybody including his closest friend, Vernon. The inception of the breakdown in their intermental unit, however, seems to be mostly motivated by Clive's growing inclination towards misanthropic introspections. His centrifugal character is shown in the following passage:

> So many faces Clive had never seen by daylight, and looking terrible, like cadavers jerked upright to welcome the newly dead. Invigorated by this jolt of misanthropy, he moved sleekly through the din, ignored his name when it was called, withdrew his elbow when it was plucked, [. . .] Clive heard a voice cry out, but for the moment no one could escape the centripetal power of a social event. (*AM* 9)

Clive's ability to read George's mind indicates his capacity of theory of mind in entering into other people's minds. However, it is heavily shown in the aspectual manner from his own viewpoint disregarding George's perspective. In accordance with the perspectival change, from external to internal, the mode of narrative representation also changes from direct speech [1] into direct thought [2] mode introducing the reader into what Courtney calls as »the finite detail of character's consciousness« (186):

> [1] At last Clive was gripping George's hand in a reasonable display of sincerity.
> »It was a wonderful service.«
> »It was very kind of you to come.«
> [2] Her death had ennobled him. The quiet gravity really wasn't his style at all, which had always been both needy and dour; anxious to be liked, but incapable of taking friendliness for granted. A burden of the hugely rich. (*AM* 9)

Clive ascribes some characteristics to George and binds them to his richness at last. His judgments, furthermore, are intramental perceptions since they are unlike George's own perspectives. They are, nevertheless, congruent with the overall presentation of George's character in the narrative. The narrative readers primarily gets to know him through Clive's and Vernon's intermental and intramental perceptions.

All Molly's admirers, including George, try to be sure of a shared, joint and intermental bond between themselves and her. Despite that, the more their memories are unfolded, the more they find out the real breach in their supposed intermental unit with her. From their past stories with Molly, it is astonishingly revealed that Molly had had an intramental life. Although she had many relationships, she belonged to none of her admirers. In his passing conversation with one Hart Pullman, Clive gets infuriated when he finds out that the man had also met Molly: »Statutory rape, then. Three years before him. She never told him about Hart Pullman. And didn't she come to the premier of Rage? Didn't she come to the restaurant afterward? He couldn't remember. Not a fucking thing« (*AM* 10–11). Pullman's infuriating story haunts Clive for a while when he hums »Hart Pullman and the teenage Molly« (*AM* 11). His detailed evaluation of the story, moreover, indicates Molly's utmost importance to him to the extent that his carefully preserved egotism does not let him share Molly with anybody even in the past. In a subjective-first manner, he holds to be the only one [1] who truly understood her in past and misses her at present:

> [1] He felt himself to be the only one who really missed Molly. [2] Perhaps if he'd married her he would have been worse than George, and wouldn't even have tolerated this gathering. Nor her helplessness. [3] Tipping from the little squarish brown plastic bottle thirty sleeping pills into his palm. The pestle and mortar, a tumbler of scotch. Three tablespoons of yellow white sludge. She looked at him when she took it, as if she knew. With his left hand he cupped her chin to catch the spill. He held her while she slept, and then all through the night. (*AM* 11)

Clive is comparing himself with George in a sympathetic way deeply understanding his difficult position as Molly's husband [2]. Despite the social nature of his thought,[73] his self-centeredness persuades him to imagine Molly's euthanasia in order to prevent her »helplessness« [3]. His imaginary, unrivalled cognitive unit with her, based on his conjectures, lead her to the conclusion that »Nobody else was missing her« (*AM* 11).

One of the several reasons for Clive's carefully kept distance from all Molly-related issues is his self-communion character. Clive pays great respect to his introspective, centrifugal self. That is shown from his yearning for seclusion in »the warmth of his studio« as well as his longing »to be home« in order to work on the »final pages« of the symphony (*AM* 14). According to Wells, »Clive, with some exceptions, strongly dislikes other human beings and prefers to retreat to artistic solitude« (*Ian McEwan* 87).

---

[73] His consciousness is concerned with the other characters' thoughts. He even imagines how the represented narrative situations would appear from the other perspectives. Despite that, his mental decisions are basically individualistic or intramental.

Nourished by his now-fading-way music ability and at the same time irritated by the »bureaucratic intrusion« of the deadline, Clive still yearns for »his creative independence« (*AM* 18). His nostalgic yearning, moreover, is for a self-contained, self-absorbed and self-concerned existence. It turns out that he finally is not able to fulfil creating original symphony notes as he reiteratively claims doing that. This tendency is intensified with Molly's sudden death. It is indicated in Clive's dramatic broodings, rendered in FIT mode, in his room: »Molly was ashes. He would work through the night and sleep until lunch. There wasn't really much else to do. Make something, and die. [. . .] Almost right, almost the truth. They [notes] suggested a dry yearning for something out of reach. Someone« (*AM* 19). Clive is increasingly concerned with his name after his death. Since his work is the only way for him to be able to do so, he struggles in order to create something original or »the truth.« However, as Ingersoll points out, this »truth« »is represented as the end of a pursuit with subtle sexual overtones« (»City of Endings« 128). Moreover, his music is a »dry yearning« for Molly and ironically for what he intends to (re)create. Nonetheless, the »yearning to climb« and arrive at the missing finale is what Clive, as well as the commissioning committee members, considers to be »a concluding melody, a valediction, a recognizable melody of piercing beauty that would transcend its unfashionability and seem both to mourn the passing century and all its senseless cruelty and to celebrate its brilliant inventiveness.« His perceptions, furthermore, rendered in FIT mode, signifies the supposedly revealing characteristic of his would-be melody: »Long after the excitement of the first performance was over, long after the millennial celebrations, the fireworks and analyses and potted histories, were done with, this irresistible melody would remain as the dead century's elegy« (*AM* 20). Ironically, the melody will turn out to be primarily a dead man's, Clive's, elegy revealing his departed self as far as a »dead century's melody.« We are told that the whole modernist project in music was »orthodoxy taught in the colleges« during seventies and its advocates were »reactionaries.« Clive's reaction to the project, given in his manifesto, Recalling Beauty, was also dualistic being »attach and apologia« at the same time (*AM* 21).

Although Clive iteratively pretends to be »satisfied« because of his continual progression in the melody, he is at the same time »apprehensive.« It takes some time for him to come out of such dualistic feelings. When »He had reached the core, and felt burdened. He turned out the lamps and walked down to his bedroom. He had no preliminary sketch of an idea, not a scrap, not even a hunch, and he would not find it by sitting at the piano and frowning hard. It could come only in its own time« (*AM* 24). His mental efforts, moreover, to find a way out of his precarious situation persuade him to make a decision to go to the Lake District so that he might find an inspiration there. That thought, however, does not firstly make him happy or relieved. With »tormenting fantasies« (*AM* 26), Clive is comparing his own situation with that of Molly:

> Anxieties about work transmuted into the baser metal of simple night fear: illness and death, abstractions that soon found their focus in the sensation he still felt in his left hand. [. . .] Wasn't this the kind of sensation Molly had had when she went to hail that cab by the Dorchester? He had no mate, no wife, no George, to care for him, and perhaps that was a mercy. [. . .] The nursing home, the TV in the dayroom, bingo, and the old men with their fags, and piss and dribbling. [. . .] They could manage your descent, but they couldn't prevent it. Stay away then, monitor your own decline; then, when it was no longer possible to work, or to live with dignity, finish it yourself. But how could he stop himself passing that point, the one Molly had reached so quickly, when he would be too helpless, too disoriented, too stupid to kill himself? (*AM* 25)

Clive's perspective is the controlling device in this passage. It is coloured by his momentary disappointed mood. The time of narration also changes into future following Clive's imaginary account of his life after his possible disease. The presentational mode, moreover, is a combination of direct thought and FIT modes. This immediate representation of Clive's consciousness seems to transfer his felt mental experiences or what it's like to undergo such a constraining situation more easily. After taking a sleeping pill, Clive, nevertheless, restores his fluctuating benign thoughts immediately: »Still massaging his hand, he mothered himself with sensible thoughts. His hand had been in the cold, that was all, and he was overtired. His proper business in life was to work, to finish a symphony by finding its lyrical summit. What had oppressed him an hour before was now his solace« (*AM* 26). Clive's imaginations concerning his would-be trip to the rocks, moreover, help him temporarily forget his inability to finalise the symphony as well as the pain in his left hand which is, according to Wells, a »symbol of his moral impairments« (*Ian McEwan* 87).

Clive thinks long and hard about the fact that as far as he stays in his studio in London, the melody notes will not come to him. He »hopes that by escaping from London to the countryside he can seclude himself in a landscape [. . .] and receive inspiration for his symphony from the sublime experience of nature« (Wells, *Ian McEwan* 88).[74] In doing so, he »wants to separate himself from the others« (Catrinescu 201). Nevertheless, his state of mind, presented through FIT mode, does not demonstrate a revelation about his future. It is deeply entangled with the repetitive actions that occupy his time:

> [1] As Clive had predicted, the melody was elusive as long as he remained in London, in his studio. [2] Each day he made attempts, little sketches, bold stabs, but he produced nothing but quotations, thinly or well disguised, of his own work. [3] Nothing sprang free in its own idiom, with its own authority, to offer the element of surprise that would be the guarantee of originality. [4] Each day, after abandoning the attempt, he committed himself to easier, duller tasks, like fleshing out orchestrations, rewriting messy pages of manuscript, and elaborating on a sliding resolution of minor chords that marked the opening of the slow movement. (*AM* 61)

The fact that Clive now finds music notes »elusive« [1] reveals his unproductive thought. Through making himself busy doing only secondary things, he pretends or »disguises« [2] to produce notes. The fact that there is no sense of »authority« and »guarantee of originality« in his work [3] adds to Clive's restlessness and introvert inclinations. Despite that, Clive pretends to be still producing [4]. However, he is either unaware of his own abilities as well as helplessness or he takes this state as a transient period replaceable with the creative part of his self as soon as he takes a short trip to the Lake District. The teleological effects of these states in the narrative

74 Wells, moreover, holds that »Through the passage set in the Lake District, McEwan draws a clear distinction between Clive and the Romantic poets who found inspiration there« (*Ian McEwan* 88).

plot, however, are highlighted dramatically when Clive is advancing more into desperation and repetition in the later pages.

Clive is aware of the public or social nature of his action. He tries to align his outward behaviour with the social expectations and norms. For example, as an artist and unlike some of his friends, he loathes using »the license of the free artistic spirit« as the »genius card« for what he considers as »bad behaviour« (*AM* 61–62). Instead, as we are told, »a mask for mediocrity was Clive's view.« That is, however, the same mask Clive wears consciously in order to hide his true mental states, »he told no one was stalled in his work. Instead, he said he was off on a short walking holiday. In fact, he didn't regard himself as blocked at all« (*AM* 62). Through his own actions, he pretends both to the others and to himself. Nevertheless, as a traditional musician, Clive provides »internalized textual reflections on aesthetic theory and practice and the ethical role of artists in society« (Wells, *Ian McEwan* 87). Finally, he sets out to the Lake District after having his »major disagreement with Vernon« which is »for the first time in his life« (*AM* 62).[75] The aftereffects of this confrontation accompany Clive along his trip to the District. As at the beginning, he is filled with »a dark mood« (*AM* 62). The narrator elaborates on this mood first through reporting Clive's physical actions, »unevenness in his stride« and the changes of his internal or thought mood. When Clive finds a »flattened black mass of chewing gum embedded deep in the zigzag tread of the sole,« the narrator's report dissolves into the character's subjectivity. As a result, the reader is left alone with the character's perceptions revealing the impact of the past events, the presents situations and the future expectations on his consciousness: »How appalling, the intimate contact with the contents of a stranger's mouth, the bottomless vulgarity of people who chewed gum and who let it fall from their lips where they stood.« Clive is appalled by the »bottomless vulgarity« of the strangers who threw gum after chewing it. Such a harsh criticism is in line with the same

75 The confrontation scene, Part III, chapter II (pp. 68–75), is recounted in a proleptic or flash-forward mode. In the story level, as in an abstract manner it is perceived by the reader, Clive sets out to his trip after having his confrontation with Vernon. However, McEwan disturbs the chronological event sequences in the discourse level of narrative.

»dark mood« that Clive ascribes to Vernon after their confrontation. The mood, furthermore, affects Clive's interpretation of the outside scene. On his way to the Lake District, he is looking out from the train window: »When at last he directed his attention out of the window, a familiar misanthropy had settled on him and he saw in the built landscape sliding by nothing but ugliness and pointless activity« (*AM* 63). What is more considerable in this TR is the familiarity of Clive's misanthropy. Since in this part, Part III/chapter II (pp. 68–75), narrative events and situations are mainly focalized from Clive's perspective, the reported misanthropy, therefore, seems to be the latent dispositions of his mind. The outward world, therefore, cues the repressed antisocial states and dispositions in Clive's mind. As shown in the later scene, still looking outside from the window, Clive is contemplating deeply on human beings' civilization: »It looked like a raucous dinner party the morning after. No one would have wished it this way, but no one had been asked. Nobody planned it, nobody wanted it, but most people had to live in it« (*AM* 63–64). When the vulgar scenes disappear, Clive's morose mood dissolves into a vibrant one.

Clive's trip from the city to the countryside, therefore, is in fact a trip into Clive's mind. The reader shares Clive's perceptions of the human beings, his assessment of the relationship with Vernon and Molly and above all his engagement with music. Or, it is a trip from »bottomless vulgarity« to the »beginnings of beauty« (*AM* 63, 64). The main source of such a bleak mental state at the beginning, however, refers back to the confrontation scene which reiterates itself in many occasions in Clive's consciousness. It, furthermore, provides a situation that invigorates Vernon's doubly embedded narrative in Clive's mind. He rethinks their relationship:

> [1] If anyone was to blame, it was Vernon. [2] Clive had traveled this line often in the past and had never felt bleak about the view. [3] He couldn't put it down to chewing gum or a mislaid pen. [4] Their row of the evening before was still sounding in his ears, [5] and he worried that the echoes would pursue him into the mountains and destroy his peace. [6] And it was hardly just a clash of voices he still carried with him, [7] it was growing dismay at his friend's behavior, and a gathering sense that he had never really known Vernon at all. (*AM* 64)

Recounted in FIT mode, the above passage presents Clive as re-experiencing his confrontation with Vernon. It also reveals its impact on his consciousness. Clive ascribes all the »blame« to Vernon since he is the only reason for his present bleak mood [1]. Moreover, based on his experiential repertoire, this »bleak« mental state is a new state [2] for which neither the chewing gum nor the lost pen [3] can in fact be blamed. Clive considers his »row« with Vernon as its fundamental reason [4]. The worrying part of their confrontation for Clive is its possible teleological impact on his concentrations and hence artistic productivity in the Rocks. In other words, he is worried about its »echoes« [5]. Besides the row scene memories or its »clash of voices.« Clive is also concerned with the growing dismay in Vernon's behaviour. He growingly feels that he neither does know Vernon nor he did in the past. Clive's speculations include also his »intimate request of his friend« in order to help him die easily if necessary [1]. Nevertheless, the more he reconsiders this request, the more his diverging friendship with Vernon becomes clear. The scope of the problem, furthermore, goes beyond the confrontation experience,

> [1] What a mistake that had been, especially now that the sensation in his left hand had vanished completely. Just a foolish anxiety brought on by Molly's funeral. One of those occasional bouts of fearing death. But how vulnerable he had made himself that night. It was no comfort that Vernon had asked the same for himself; all it had cost him was a scribbled note pushed through the door. [2] And perhaps that was typical of a certain [. . .] imbalance in their friendship that had always been there and that Clive had been aware of somewhere in his heart and had always pushed away, disliking himself for unworthy thoughts. Until now. Yes, a certain lopsidedness in their friendship, which, if he cared to consider, made last night's confrontation less surprising. (*AM* 64–65)

The narrator's comment in TR mode [2] reveals the hidden history of the »imbalance« in their relationship although Clive repressed it from his own consciousness. The extremely aspectual nature of his speculations, nevertheless, shows the degree he thinks intramentally ignoring the other possibilities or the other side's, Vernon's, perspective. For example, he thinks that Vernon is unaware of his kindness, helps and supports to him. In other words, the confrontation makes him reconsider his friendship with Vernon:

> [1] Put most crudely, what did he, Clive, really derive from this friendship? He had given, but what had he ever received? [2] What bound them? They had Molly in common, [3] there were the accumulated years and the habits of friendship, but there was really nothing at its center, nothing for Clive. [4] A generous explanation for the imbalance might have evoked Vernon's passivity and self-absorption. [5] Now, after last night, Clive was inclined to see these as merely elements of a larger fact—Vernon's lack of principle. (*AM* 65–66)

Clive's strongly aspectual re-evaluation of the past shows him regretting his relationship with Vernon. He weighs their mutual contribution to their friendship [1]. He draws the conclusion that Molly was their only shared interest [2]. Therefore, he finds nothing worthwhile in their friendship since it has changed into a habit with an empty core [3]. Parts [4] and [5], given in TR mode from the narrator's perspective, shows ironically the aspectuality of Clive's perceptions. Part [4] reveals Clive's lack of generosity in explaining the imbalance in their friendship. He ascribe it to »Vernon's lack of principle« [5]. Such reports, all in all, reveal a growing and irretrievable imbalance in Clive-Vernon friendship. Their teleological impact on the advancement of the frame narrative plot becomes more highlighted towards the last pages bringing about their double murder. Like an actual human being, Clive explores the possible reasons of Vernon's actions and based on his findings, he makes decisions. Clive's mind, therefore, (re)constructs not only his past perceptions but also the future ones too:

> [1] But Clive stared ahead at the empty seat opposite, lost to the self-punishing convolutions of his fervent social accounting, unknowingly bending and colouring the past through the prism of his unhappiness. [2] Other thoughts Cliverted him occasionally, and for periods he read, but this was the theme of his northward journey, the long and studied redefinition of a friendship. (*AM* 66)

Clive's inclination to »Clivert« both the past and present situations is suggestive of his unconscious tendency to put his side higher than that of Vernon's. This is the burgeoning of a defining imbalance in their already established intermental friendship. It is, however, unconscious because Clive is reported as »unknowingly [. . .] coloring the past« [1]. Therefore, he is unaware of his own mental states too. That accelerates his advancement towards pure intramentality in the later scenes. Clive yields to »color« his past friendship with Vernon with his present perceptions. That changes into the central theme of his journey which is labelled as »redefinition of a friendship« [2]. The passage moreover, discloses Clive's mind in action. He is struggling with an ongoing conflict between the private, unknown part of his personality and the social or public side of that. The passage displays Clive's mental functioning as being trapped between his memories and his plans and aspirations. Thus, the more Clive reflects on his deadly »confrontation« (*AM* 66, 62) with Vernon, the more Vernon's doubly embedded narratives seem detached and bleak within Clive's »brooding« mind. When Clive continues his broodings in the Lakeland hotel, his mental obsessions are revealed with more aspects:

> [1] He read for an hour and then lay in darkness, listening to the swollen crashing beck, knowing that his subject was bound to return and that it would be better to indulge it now than take it with him on his walk the next day. [2] It wasn't the disillusionment that forced itself on him now. There were his memories of the conversation, and then something beyond-what had been said, and then what he would like to have said to Vernon now that he had had hours to reflect. [3] It was remembering, and it was also fantasising: he imagined a drama in which he gave himself all the best lines, resonant lines of sad reasonableness whose indictments were all the more severe and unanswerable for their compression and emotional restraint. (*AM* 67)

Clive knowingly gives himself totally to Vernon's thought. In this way, he hopes to read the different aspects of Vernon's mind. Doing that, he might be able to redefine his friendship before setting out to the rocks where he is looking forward to restoring his music creativity and originality [1]. His momentary concern, however, does not derive from his artistic »disillusionment«; rather, it descends from the memories of the confrontation scene. Clive pushes that occasion into its edges. The more he »reflects« upon that, the more he gives himself the best lines. He overinterprets the experience by going »beyond« the issues they argued about. Such intramental inferences, however, will affect his later decisions and perceptions [2]. The intention to go »beyond,« moreover, allows Clive to delve into fantasy. Rather than operating based on what really happened, it functions mostly based on his intramental (re)construction of the experience [3]. This passage, therefore, is highly aspectual. As it is shown and reported in TR mode, it reveals the direction towards which Clive's mental functioning is heading.

Recounting the details of Clive's purposeful trip to Lakeland, the narrator extends his embedded narratives in chapter three (pp. 76–90). It is the only part in the narrative, which is strongly focalized through Clive's perspective mostly using internal focalization and FIT modes. It reveals Clive's intramental inclinations as reflected in his thoughts and actions in different situations. This becomes more apparent to the reader when Clive's encountering experience with a row scene in the rocks is narrated. Clive in this chapter is presented as desiring to write »the key element of his finale,« The narrator's TRs, »He felt optimistic. [. . .] He knew exactly what he wanted« (*AM* 76), reveal Clive's determination and austere obsession with the missing symphonic finale he hopes to find in the rocks through »serendipitous inspiration« (Kohn, 93). Nevertheless, as it is hinted in the next sentence, »He was working backward really, sensing that the theme lay in fragments and hints in what he had already written.« After its unrealised performance in Amsterdam, critics will highlight Clive's artistic regressing trend as the main drawback of his Millennial Symphony.[76] Clive strongly hopes to find his elusive notes through »an act of inspired synthesis« as well as through »the exalted nature of his mission, and of his ambition. Beethoven« (*AM* 76). Nevertheless, while he is presented as pushing against his own latent sensation of artistic emptiness, he is decided to repress such feelings at the same time.

Clive's mental functioning is presented in all his embedded narratives as being intermittently concerned with Molly, Vernon and his own affairs including his ability to write original notes or to finish the assigned symphony. Nevertheless, when he is hiking in the Lake District, he endeavours

---

76 Although Clive pretends to be original and creative, his supporters granted for him »the term »archconservative«, while his critics preferred »throwback.« However, they »agreed that along with Schubert and McCartney, Linley could write a melody.« At the same time, their ascriptions imply the repetitive nature of Clive's work. He, nevertheless, denies such terms: »He regarded himself as Vaughan Williams's heir, and considered terms like »conservative« irrelevant, a mistaken borrowing from the political vocabulary« (McEwan, *AM* 21).

to avoid any thought other than writing the final notes for his symphony. He feels »optimistic« in the early moments of his trip; nevertheless, the more he goes inside the rocks, the more he turns inwards: »he felt, despite his optimism, the unease of outdoor solitude wrap itself around him. He drifted helplessly into a daydream, an elaborate story about someone hiding behind a rock, waiting to kill him.« This TR suggests the imbalance in Clive's mental functioning, his unconscious disillusionment as well as his artistic draining. However, his conscious self is persisting in the contrary. Clive struggles against the malign feelings he was encompassed by at the beginning of his trip. For example, although the solitude and the »colossal emptiness« of the mountains frighten him, still »There was always a reluctance to be overcome« by such feelings. Clive's mental functioning here derives from his experiential repertoires in the old days. He is aware of the malign states inside his mind. He also knows that he can fight them based on his own experiences. Therefore, he prefers »the language of threat« in the rocks to that of the social life: »It was an act of will, a tussle with instinct, to keep walking away from the nearest people, from shelter, warmth, and help« (*AM* 77). Clive's artistic tendency stands beyond his social bonds and needs. In other words, it is a highly intramental functioning. While he is hiking in the rocks, such a mental state orients Clive's evaluation of a suspicious scene in the tarn.

While walking in the rocks, Clive's mind is reported as experiencing a major conflict. The sensation to go on hiking or not resonates in his mind. It discloses the degree of indeterminacy in his thoughts. His final reasoning to continue the trip, however, suggests his determinacy to »be set free«:

> [1] His shrinking spirit and all his basic inclinations told him that it was foolish and unnecessary to keep on, that he was making a mistake. [2] Clive kept on because the shrinking and apprehension were precisely the conditions, the sickness, from which he sought release, and proof that his daily grind, crouching over that piano for hours every day, had reduced him to a cringing state. He would be large again, and unafraid. There was no threat here, [. . .] There were dangers, of course, but only the usual ones, [. . .] [3] Managing these would restore him to a sense of control. [4] Soon human meaning would be bleached from the rocks, the landscape would assume its beauty and draw him in; the unimaginable age of the mountains and the fine mesh

> of living things that lay across them would remind him that he was part of this order and insignificant within it, and he would be set free. (*AM* 77–78)

The extradiegetic narrator's mediatory function is closer to zero in this passage. Instead, the central character's internal perceptions orient the textual information. FIT reports, particularly in [2] and [3], closely convey the process of his unvoiced calculations. Moreover, Clive's two conflicting voices, in [1] and [2], articulate his different positions. However, he decides to »control« his internal state in order to achieve his goal [3]. The last part is more concerned with the teleological outcomes of his trip reporting Clive's dreams and desires [4]. The passage all in all shows Clive entrapped by his past doubts, his future goals as well as his fragile present determination. The passage is also significant in its contributions to Clive's embedded narratives. It shows the latent inclinations of his mind, which call him for passivity and intramentality. It also reveals Clive's conscious determination to pursue intermentality. Although Clive pretends to be careless about his own malign thoughts, his »basic inclinations« or the sensation of his »shrinking spirit«; however, such feelings accompany him in the rocks. As Clive understands, they delay his »beneficial process« (*AM* 78). The narrator's TR does also reveal some other aspects of Clive's mental functioning. It socialises Clive's malign inclinations or entangles them with the other minds:

> He had been walking for an hour and a half and was still eyeing certain boulders ahead for what they might conceal, still regarding the sombre face of rock and grass at the end of the valley with vague dread, and still pestered by fragments of his conversation with Vernon. (*AM* 78)

Clive's feeling of being »pestered,« does not solely refer to his intrapersonal inclinations, it also extends to his interpersonal concerns. Although he evades admitting it, Clive's continuing consciousness frame relentlessly pursues Vernon's thought being haunted by its echoes. As a result of such bleak sensations, therefore, Clive's revelation-seeking trip course changes into a blank horizon. His ontological predicament is enticed with the »open spaces« in the rocks but, to immortalise himself, Clive endeavours to »control« them:

> The open spaces that were meant to belittle his cares were belittling everything; endeavour seemed pointless. Symphonies especially: feeble blasts, bombast, doomed attempts to build a mountain in sound. Passionate striving. And for what? Money. Respect. Immortality. A way of denying the randomness that spawned us and of holding off the fear of death. (*AM* 78)

The reporting voice of this passage is so close to the simultaneously focalizer-focalized character that their differentiation is nearly impossible.

The stubborn side of Clive's character compels him to ignore the dual feelings residing in his mind: »He didn't really feel like a hand-over-hand scramble, but neither did he like the possibility that he might be giving in to weakness, or to age.« Therefore, Clive's struggle with his »torpor« state or his desire to »jolt« out of it goads him to choose scrambling. At the same time, he is aware that his physical power may fail him because of his age. Disregarding it, Clive ignores such possibility: »It bothered him that his pulse was so rapid so soon and that he was pausing for breath every three or four minutes« (*AM* 79). Through persistence, he attempts to take »advantage of his solitude« so that he might be free from the other's presence. As he hopes, that will finally enable him to write the final missing notes for his symphony. However, the narrator's involvement in the situation reveals Clive's tragic predicament. He is unaware of his own situation. Unlike his optimism, although while ascending the rocks he could make jokes with someone else there in his solitude, they could also make »humiliations of growing older.« Nevertheless, Clive did not have any strong social bonds to stop him from preferring solitude: »But these days he had no close friends in England who shared his compulsion. [...He] cursed his friends for their dullness, their lack of appetite for life. They had let him down. No one knew where he was, and no one cared« (*AM* 80). In other words, when Clive finds out that his social aspect has weakened, he gets upset. At the same time, he is aware of the conflict between his desire to concentrate on sounds in order to produce music and his inclination to be among people. When Clive reaches the col, his mental state changes at last. The narrator's TR does not reveal the real reason(s) of such a difficult change. That shows the degree of Clive's invisible mental dispositions not only to the narrator but also to Clive himself:

> [1] More debilitating thoughts pursued him as he climbed toward the col, [. . .] it began to happen at last, he began to feel good. [2] Perhaps it was no more than the effect of endorphins released by muscular exertion, [3] or because he had simply found a rhythm. [4] Or it might have been because this was a cherished moment in mountain walking, when one reached a col. (*AM* 80)

Whatever the reason(s) of the change may be, neither Clive nor the reader can be sure of that. However, referring to Clive's embedded narratives, the reader might consider one of the recounted possibilities ([2], [3] and [4]) in the passage as the main reason for Clive's change. For example, the reader already knows for certain about Clive's internal dilemma concerning continuing or discounting his trip in the rocks. S/he also knows that, repressing his dissuading inclinations, Clive chooses to continue the trip although he is not sure of attaining his goal. Accordingly, the change in his mental state either derives from his physiological activities, which lead to Clive's unconscious celebration of rising to a peak and conquest of it, [2] and [4], or it really derives from his realization of the lost notes [3]. Therefore, the reader, as narrator does, can only draw some inferences about Clive's mental functioning. That knowledge, however, does not directly come from Clive's perceptions instead it is deuced from Clive's actions.

The more Clive advances in the rocks, the more his mental functioning becomes apparent. Along his hiking path, either a continuous chain of some clashing thoughts begins to flow in his mind or some external events incite his internal reflections. However, Clive's intramental perceptions in the rocks prevent him from making connections with external situations. In one of the scenes when Clive observes a »solitary hiker in blue,« he begins making inferences about her. They are, however, not mostly about the woman but about what she cues in Clive's mind. The scene reminds him of his own state as he imagines himself »in the role of her man.« Moreover, it provokes or »prompts« Clive's experiential repertoire reviving his repressed feelings:

> As he approached he saw that it was a woman, which prompted Clive to cast himself in the role of her man, in the assignation she seemed so keen to reach: waiting for her by a lonely tarn, calling her name as she approached, taking from his pack the champagne and two silver flutes, and going toward her. [...] Clive had never had a lover, or even a wife, who liked hiking. (*AM* 81)

The intramental side of the represented situation in this passage is that Clive does not perceive the solitary woman, or the woman in blue, for her own sake but for what she cues in his mind. She is forgotten among the personal memories her appearance entices in Clive's mind. Clive, for example, does not even ask himself what a solitary woman can be doing in such a secluded area with the dangers that might threaten her life. Instead, he humorously extends his dreams about the scene. He imagines the woman as his beloved rushing for their rendezvous. His interpretation, furthermore, reveals the degree of his intramental approach to the narrative situations and events. The narrator's TR account of the situation does also reveal the character's internal broodings. More importantly, it delineates Clive's mental functioning binding it to his actions and surroundings. When Clive restores his consciousness, once more he considers the woman as a barrier to his views. To avoid that, he decides to linger so that he might have all the view to himself: »He stopped to let her go in order to have the great upland field to himself« (*AM* 81).

Clive's self-persuasions, concerning his physical and mental states, increase after his ascending the col. His encounter with the woman in blue and what she arose in his mind do not affect Clive's advancement in benign thoughts. The conflict, nevertheless, continues inside his mind although he is reported as »[1] feeling that there was not really so much physical difference between him and his thirty-year-old self after all, and that it was not sinew but spirit that had held him back. [2] How strong his legs felt now that his mood had improved!« (*AM* 82). The narrator's TR mode in this text reveals Clive's internal feelings and perceptions [1]. Changing the mode of narration into FIT in [2], the text, moreover, discloses Clive's thoughts more closely. It portrays his exclamations arising from the internal refreshment he has found after ascending to the col. Clive's strong aspectuality affects both his goals and his re-evaluation of the past events. Following that, he intends to have benign thoughts. He is reported as thinking:

> [1] about his life and situation in fresh terms, gladdening himself with recollections of recent small successes. [. . .] [2] Clive thought of his work in totality, of how varied and rich it seemed whenever he was able to raise his head and take the long perspective, how it represented in abstract a whole history of his lifetime. And still so much

> to do. [3] He thought affectionately about the people in his life. Perhaps he had been too hard on Vernon, who was only trying to save his newspaper and protect the country from Garmony's harsh policies. He would phone Vernon this evening. Their friendship was too important to be lost to one isolated dispute. They could surely agree to differ and continue to be friends. (*AM* 82–83)

Clive is concerned with the past and prospect of his artistic work [1 and 2]. Besides that, he is concentrated upon his intermental friend, Vernon, and their friendship [3]. Clive, however, de-familiarises his own ordinary situations and events to align them with his intention of having »benign thoughts.« For example, he uses ›fresh terms« [1], he considers his past work as »rich« in its »totality« as well as his prospect as hopeful [2] and finally he re-evaluates his confrontation with Vernon. Contrary to the reasoning based on which he opposed Vernon in terms of publishing Molly-Garmony's photographs, Clive's thoughts here are completely different. This time he evaluates the situation not from Garmony's perspective but from Vernon's aspect. Clive, furthermore, accepts the differences among people [3]. Nevertheless, this mood, to have benign thoughts with fresh terms, is very fragile. For example, when Clive sees a large group of schoolchildren near the tarn in the rocks, his malign thoughts restore easily as if following the change in landscape:

> Instantly the landscape was transformed, tamed, reduced to a trampled beauty spot. Without giving himself time to dwell on old themes of his, the idiocy and visual pollution of Day-Glo anoraks, or why people were compelled to go about in such brutally large groups, he turned away to his right, toward Alien Crags, and the moment the party was out of sight he was restored to his good mood. (*AM* 83)

Therefore, Clive does not make any intermental bonds with anybody while hiking in the rocks. Even more, he avoids joining any »groups« which, according to him, act brutally. That is because Clive wants to maintain his concentration in order to finalise his symphony notes. Finally, he thinks the right moment has come:

> [1] It finally happened, just as he had hoped it would: he was relishing his solitude, he was happy in his body, his mind was contentedly elsewhere, when he heard the music he had been looking for, or at least he heard a clue to its form. [2] It came as a gift. [3] A large grey bird flew up with a loud alarm call as he approached. As it

> gained height and wheeled away over the valley, it gave out a piping sound on three notes, which he recognised as the inversion of a line he had already scored for a piccolo. [4] How elegant, how simple. (*AM* 84)

As the TR mode reveals in [1], Clive's body and mind are at last happy and content. Despite that, his mind is reported as being »elsewhere« the moment »he heard the music.« Furthermore, Clive's recognition of the birdcall as a »gift« [2] is the FIT report of his misreading of the sound. Clive here is represented as plunging into the music the bird emanates. This experience is not unlike Clarissa Dalloway's experience. At the beginning of Woolf's novel, *Mrs Dalloway*, she is reported as plunging into the past feelings. Molly Hoff's (2009) interpretation of Clarissa's exclamatory words, »What a lark! What a plunge!«, appears to resemble the signification of Clive's words, »How elegant, how simple« [4]. Hoff states that, »This exclamation again is a marker of figural subjectivity, the character and the narrator sharing in the duties« (11). By the same token, the state of Clive's subjectivity is revealed in this exclamatory statement. Even the birdcall, however, does not resonate a completely benign or pleasant tune in Clive's mind since »There was a glow of a tantalising afterimage and the fading call of a sad little tune. This synesthesia was a torment« (*AM* 84). Clive's perception or interpretation of the tune, nevertheless, becomes optimistic when, after reaching »the top of the angled rock slab,« he gets ready to write it down, »It wasn't entirely sad. There was merriness there too, an optimistic resolve against the odds. Courage.« The optimistic perspective finds a »resolve against the odds« based on which Clive's mind was mainly functioning from the early moments of his hiking. Clive's gaiety, however, does not last long. The moment he wants to »scribble out the fragments« (*AM* 84), he hears the murmur of a voice. Clive reluctantly looks at its source. He sees the woman in blue. She has just reminded him of his own beloved waiting in a rendezvous with him. This scene demonstrates Clive's preference between intermental and intramental thought. He should either intervene in the dispute between the woman in blue, who is in danger, and a man or concentrate on his work scribbling down the notes enlivened in his mind by the birdcall:

> Facing her and talking in a low, constant drone was a man who was certainly not dressed for rambling. [. . .] A hill farmer possibly, or a friend who disdained hiking and all the gear who had come up to meet her. The very assignation Clive had imagined. [. . .] They were arguing a marital row. (*AM* 85–86)

Clive's inferences about the man and his relationship with the woman in blue are far from the man's true identity and the nature of his relationship with the woman. This is so because Clive does not even pretend to give the scene a real thought. Instead, his strongly aspectual evaluation of the scene restricts his interpretation to personal benefits:

> This stark surprise, these vivid figures among the rocks, seemed to be there for his benefit alone. It was as if they were actors striking up a tableau whose meaning he was supposed to guess, as if they were not quite serious, only pretending not to know that he was watching. Whatever they were about, Clive's immediate thought was as clear as a neon sign: I am not here. He ducked down and continued with his notes. [. . .] He ignored the woman's voice when he heard it. Already it was hard to capture what had seemed so clear a minute before. For a while he floundered, and then he had it again, that overlaid quality, so obvious when it was before him, so elusive the moment his attention relaxed. He was crossing out notes as fast as he was setting them down, but when he heard the woman's voice rise to a sudden shout, his hand froze. He knew it was a mistake, he knew he should have kept writing, but once again he peered over the rock. (*AM* 85–86)

Clive attempts to read »the vivid figures[›]« mentality. He ascribes them mental states. At the same time, he imposes his own intentions. To put the same point in other words, Clive develops a theory of mind by imagining that according to them he should make out the »tableau« they form. Invalidating his previous inferences, however, Clive intends not to meddle in their row. As a result, avoiding the scene instantly, he wants to overcome his floundering so that he might register the »elusive« notes. Despite that, Clive cannot take over his own curiosity about the scene. Still, he ponders over the consequences of his entering into their argument when he finds out the couple arguing. As represented in the following passage, the possibilities in his mind are cancelling each other:

> [1] Was he really going to intervene? [2] He imagined running down there. The point at which he reached them was when the possibilities would branch: the man might run off; the woman would be grateful, and together they could descend to the main

> road by Seatoller. Even this least probable of outcomes would destroy his fragile inspiration. The man was more likely to redirect his aggression at Clive while the woman looked on, helpless. Or gratified, for that was possible too; they might be closely bound, they might both turn on him for presuming to interfere. (*AM* 86–87)

Clive's subjectivity and language in this passage are mixed with the past tense and third person pronoun, which are the characteristics of FIT mode. According to Palmer, it »combines the subjectivity and the language of the character with the discourse of the narrator« (*Fictional* 56). Although the narrator knows whether Clive is going to intervene in the row or not from the very beginning, still it transfers the character's discourse as it appeared in the character's mind [1]. Furthermore, Clive's latent decisiveness is revealed in the possibilities he is reviewing [2]. He is reluctant to intervene in the row because he fears that it will destroy his »fragile inspiration.« Thus, he gently inclines towards thinking that both man and woman are against his interference. Accordingly, Clive »fails to overcome his egoistic concerns. [. . .] Clive's self-centredness is indeed so strong that he is not prepared to engage with real others« (Schwalm 175).

The embarrassing revelation of Clive's intramentality comes with his statement »Their fate, his fate.« Differentiating between himself and the others, Clive puts his artistic fate higher than the man's and particularly the woman's fates. At the same time, he is aware that her life is in danger and she may need his help. The teleological contribution of this scene to the narrative plot is also considerable. In this case, Vernon will criticise Clive for his ignorance of anthropomorphic values. Clive, however, thinks that if he interfere in the row, »Something precious, a little jewel, was rolling away from him« (*AM* 87). As a result, Clive finds himself in a life-threatening situation. Nevertheless, he pretends to be fairly concerned about the woman. The reader, however, knows that he is primarily concerned about his symphony, fate, reputation and immortality. Clive weighs the consequences of two possibilities—the notes he was going to scribble down after the birdcall and the necessity of intervening in the row. To justify his passivity towards the row, Clive allows for exaggeration in his evaluation of what he was going to write down before being interrupted by the row scene:

> He did not doubt that what he half heard could bear the weight. In its simplicity lay all the authority of a lifetime's work. He also had no doubt that it was not a piece of music that was simply waiting to be discovered; what he had been doing, until interrupted, was creating it, forging it out of the call of a bird, taking advantage of the alert passivity of an engaged creating mind. (*AM* 87)

Clive's TR reveals the unacknowledged intention behind his decision. He thinks that what he was about to do before being interrupted, was not discovering something already existing but creating or forging it. By drawing on his frame of Clive's embedded narratives, the narrative reader, however, is aware of Clive's inability to do so. The reader's inferences in this case, moreover, is enhanced by the critics' evaluation of Clive's symphony after his death. Clive pretends to do original work »taking advantage of the alert passivity of an engaged creating mind« (*AM* 87). Finally, Clive's decision to avoid the row and instead concentrate on his »creation« process is mainly reported in FIT mode:

> [1] What was clear now was the pressure of choice: he should either go down and protect the woman, if she needed protection, or he should creep away round the side of Glaramara to find a sheltered place to continue his work, if it was not already lost. He could not remain here doing nothing. [. . .] [2] She made a sudden pleading whimpering sound, and [3] Clive knew exactly what it was he had to do. Even as he was easing himself back down the slope, he understood that his hesitation had been a sham. [4] He had decided at the very moment he was interrupted. (*AM* 87–88)

Clive's thought is presented as mental action. He is pretending to be able to choose between two situations [1]. Furthermore, although his subjectivity prevails in this passage, the narrator's language presents his discourse. Therefore, »if the character's subjectivity is present but not the character's language, then the passage should be regarded as free indirect thought« (Palmer, 2004: 56). Clive is hearing the woman's scared voice [2]. Drawing on his knowledge repertoire and experience, he knows well what he should and is expected to do, in such a situation. At the same time, he is aware of his pretentious behaviour. Part [4], shows Clive's mind in action in TR mode. It reveals that from the very beginning Clive had made his decision not to meddle in the row between the man and the woman in blue. His subsequent thoughts and actions were merely pretentions. Therefore, Clive pretends to be someone other than he really is. Moreover, he is not able to make an intermental mind. His intramental ambitions do not allow himself to do so with the woman. He is so concerned with his goals and plans that he ignores the other minds. The falsity of Clive's aspectuality, furthermore, becomes more apparent when, after fleeing away from the row scene, he finds himself unable to forge or create the final notes of his symphony. As he was haunted by Vernon's thoughts for a long time after their confrontation, Clive is now obsessed with the row scene and his decision to flee from it:

> [1] Twenty minutes later he found a flat-topped rock to use as a table and stood hunched over his scribble. [2] There was almost nothing there now. He was trying to call it back, but his concentration was being broken by another voice, the insistent, interior voice of self-justification: whatever it might have involved-violence, or the threat of violence, or his embarrassed apologies, or, ultimately, a statement to the police if he had approached the couple, a pivotal moment in his career would have been destroyed. [2] The melody could not have survived the psychic flurry. [. . .] how easily he could have missed them. [4] It was as if he weren't there. He wasn't there. He was in his music. His fate, their fate, separate paths. It was not his business. This was his business, and it wasn't easy, and he wasn't asking for anyone's help. At last he managed to calm himself and begin to work his way back. (*AM* 88–89)

Finally, Clive, full of hope, sits down in a secluded part in order to scribble down the final notes for his symphony [1]. Still, when he finds himself enmeshed in the row scene, Clive begins self-justifications implying that his decision to flee from the scene was the only right decision he could make. Further, the narrator's TR mode brings together the character's past decision, its impacts on the present state of his mental functioning and its possible consequences in his future. Clive, for example, although passively, thinks of »a statement to the police.« The teleological importance of this possibility becomes more apparent when Vernon, after Clive's returning to London and his confiding of the Lakeland experience to him, accuses Clive of disregarding his moral duty more by not reporting the event to the police [2]. Part [3] shows the primacy of melody or music to any other thing from Clive's perspective. Moreover, Clive's assessment of the couple and himself becomes more intramental in part [4], recounted in FIT mode. This portrays

Clive as a needless or self-contained person. He is contained in himself. After such broodings, Clive, finally, »crouched above his writing.« Moreover, feeling that »He got what he wanted from the Lake District« (*AM* 89) and loaded with a kind of »creative excitement,« Clive leaves the mountains ardently. As Clive's subjectivity is presented while he was leaving the mountains, he »wanted the anonymity of the city again, and the confinement of his studio, and, he had been thinking about this scrupulously, surely it was excitement that made him feel this way, not shame« (*AM* 90). Clive's inclination to be in the »confinement of his studio« signifies his tendency to intramental existence. He wishes to be away from any interruptions or as Dana Catrinescu says, Clive »shuts himself up in the studio. Apparently doing so in order to finish his symphony, Clive abandons himself to the disease which is starting to grow inside him, paralyzing his mind, will, actions.« Furthermore, the ironic statement, »surely it was excitement that made him feel this way, not shame,« reveals the breach between the character's discourse and that of the narrator. The narrator knows that Clive is ashamed of his passivity in the row scene although he evades acknowledging it.

Moreover, Clive's perception of his own mental capabilities in terms of music is inconsistent with the other characters' perceptions. In this case, Clive's thought is counterfactual again. For example, it is ironically stated that »with London already heading noisily for work,« Clive's »creative turmoil finally smothered by exhaustion« (*AM* 133). His pretension is, however, two sided—towards the others and himself. For example, while going to his bedroom, Clive »looked back at the rich, the beautiful chaos that surrounded his toils« (*AM* 133). In a similar manner to Vernon's, the reader's interpretation of Clive's »chaos« and »toils« in the studio signifies not Clive's creativity but his time-wasting in the studio. Nevertheless, Clive is represented as being at war within himself. Although he keeps it a secret, Clive imagines himself as a »genius.« In this way, he levels himself with his countrymen geniuses such as Shakespeare, Darwin and Newton. He desires to be his country's Beethoven[77] (*AM* 133). Clive's mental states about his oeuvre, in general, and about the melody he is working on—the millennium

---

77 Or as Malcolm states, he is »seeing himself as a latter-day Beethoven« (194).

symphony—in particular, suggest his intramental subjectivity. In a »near hallucinatory state« (*AM* 134), Clive considers himself to be a »genius« producing a »masterpiece.« The reader, however, already knows that such perceptions are in continuation with Clive's strongly self-centred broodings on his artistic originality while hiking in the Lake District. Such overwhelming feelings push Clive more towards intramentality:

> When he had this suspicion about himself, and it had happened three or four times since he had returned from the Lake District, the world grew large and still. [. . .] Reminding him of how things had looked to him once in his youth when he had taken mescaline: bloated with volume, poised with benign significance. (*AM* 133–134)

Clive is represented as being continuously haunted by his experience in the rocks. Nevertheless, cuing »his youth« feelings, its after-effects are destructive to his character. It shows him as if »he had taken mescaline« since it gives him the wrong perception of benign significance. Clive as a »genius,« however, is stuck in his creation not being able to complete the symphony while he is only one week away from the last »looming deadline.« It is »stalking him like a beast and closing in« (*AM* 151, 134). Finally, this »ridiculous« pressure incites Clive to scribble the last notes: »He complained, but in his heart he was untouched by the pressure, for this was how he needed to be working, lost to the mighty effort of bringing his work to its awesome finale« (*AM* 135). When he feels that his work is almost done except that he should »go back several pages in the score to the clamorous restatement and vary the harmonies perhaps, or even the melody itself« (*AM* 136), Vernon's »disorienting« (*AM* 137) calling takes place. It destroys Clive's happy thoughts. The variation, according to him, was going to be the »crucial feature« of his work delineating »the future's unknowability« and hence prompting »insecurity in the listener« (*AM* 136). Nevertheless, Clive concentrates on »the important change to the restatement« (*AM* 136). Compared to his music, the other issues are considered to be only »subplots«:

> The call [Vernon's] was reassuring. Clive had been meaning to get in touch since he returned, but his work had swept him away, and Garmony, the photographs, and *The Judge* seemed to him like subplots in a barely remembered movie. All he knew

> was that he did not wish to be quarrelling with anyone, least of all one of his oldest friends. (*AM* 136)

His dreams and goals are, however, violated when Vernon calls him for the second time asking »to go to the police now and tell them what you saw.« Acting in shock, Vernon's request »jolted Clive into the truth. He emerged from a tunnel into clarity« (*AM* 137). The words exchanged between the two old friends and their protracted reflection and recollections on them signify the growing imbalance between their shared unit. Coming after the major conflict over Molly-Garmony's transvestite photographs, their conflict over Clive's passivity in the Lakeland finally brings about the total breakdown of their intermental unit. Clive's inclination to lose himself in divisive thoughts, instead of any attempt to save their friendship through self-control, indicates his cardinal importance for intramentality. It is portrayed in his relentless pursuit of the final notes:

> Clive allowed a full flood of hot indignation to bathe him, and when Vernon outrageously threatened to go to the police himself, Clive gasped and kicked the bedclothes clear and stood in his socks by the bedside table for the concluding barter of abuse. Vernon hung up on him, just as he was about to hang up on Vernon. (*AM* 137)

The more Clive drinks gin and tonic, he waters his anger through brooding about Vernon's words and accusations. As a result, he frames a threatening letter addressing his old friend. As we are told, he:

> [1] thought bitterly of the outrage. The outrage of it! [2] He was framing the letter he would like to send to [3] this scum he had mistaken for a friend. Him, with his loathsome daily round, his sordid cynical scheming mind, the wheedling sponging hypocritical passive-aggressive. [4] Vermin Halliday, who knew nothing of what it was to create, because he'd never made anything good in his life and was eaten up with hatred for those who could. [5] His poky suburban squeamishness was what passed for a moral stand, and meanwhile he was up to the elbows in shit, in fact he had verily pitched his tent on excrement, and to advance his squalid interests he was happy to debase Molly's memory and ruin a vulnerable fool like Garmony and call up the hate codes of the yellow press and all along pretend to himself and tell anyone who would listen-and this was what took the breath away-that he was doing his duty, that he was in the service of some high ideal. [6] He was mad, he was sick, he didn't deserve to exist! (*AM* 137–138)

The first sentence in this passage shows Clive's conscious intention to expand his malign thoughts about Vernon [1]. He is thinking about writing a letter to him [2] but the adjectives [3] he uses to describe his old friend notify the degrees of his hate for Vernon. Given in free indirect mode, his thoughts reveal the strong rift in their friendship since they are widely different in terms of moral duty and Garmony's case. The narrator is recounting fundamentally Clive's subjectivity but in terms of language, it is difficult to say whether it belongs to the character or the narrator. However, some of the words, mostly adjectives Clive uses in order to describe his friend Vernon, appear to belong to the character. In part [4] Clive is comparing himself with Vernon. He belittles his old friend in thinking that he is unable to create anything artistic. He accuses him of envying those who are capable of doing so. Following that, Clive finds a connection between Vernon's perspective and his class or his »poky suburban squeamishness« [5] based on which, according to live, he is advancing his ideal morality. Clive, furthermore, thinks that, from Vernon's perspective, whatever seems to be necessary in order to reach at that ideal morality is justified. He also accuses Vernon of being unaware of his actions because in pursuing his »squalid interests,« he seems to be in »shit« or part of »excrement.« Accordingly, based on Clive's reasoning [6], Vernon »deserves not to exist.« The teleological contribution of this scene to Clive's later actions seems to be fundamental to the frame narrative. His later decision to poison his friend through a carefully arranged plot is mainly based on his recollections of such reasoning. In the same way, Clive will ascribe his failure in completing his symphony to Vernon's communication of the Lake District news to the police.

Accordingly, Clive calms himself down by writing a short letter, which he considers to be a »masterpiece of restraint« (*AM* 140), to Vernon: »Your threat appalls me. So does your journalism. You deserve to be sacked.« However, he does not send him the letter until Friday. Having done that, Clive recollects his earlier thoughts. He exaggerates his creativity, which he believes will bring him immortality. The restoration of such benign thoughts and his comparisons between himself and Vernon continue in his imagined future too. Therefore, his thought that Vernon does not »deserve to exist« (*AM* 138) is supported by his self-admiring conception that, unlike

Vernon, he will immortally exist in his music: »There would come a time when nothing would remain of Vermin Halliday, but what would remain of Clive Linley would be his music. Work, quiet, determined, triumphant work, then would be a kind of revenge« (*AM* 138–139). Thus, Clive hopes working on »one inspired modification« upon which the integrity of his symphony depends will act as a »revenge« to what he considers as Vernon's insults. The narrator, nevertheless, informs us that Vernon is not the only cause for Clive's helplessness in completing the symphony, as he himself believes it to be so. Clive's own »belligerence« in addition to the alcoholic drinks that intoxicate him, are also driving him to his sluggish state »hearing and seeing only the bright hurdy-gurdy carousel of his twirling thoughts.« Furthermore, despite his optimistic prospects, Clive is unable to avoid his experiential repertoire: »they came again. The outrage! The police! Poor Molly! Sanctimonious bastard! Call that a moral position? Up to his neck in shit! The outrage. And what about Molly?« (*AM* 139) Clive, nevertheless, continues drinking »to his success« in his entire professional life ascribing, in his drunkenness, his present failure feelings to Vernon's »betrayals.« Even after some hours when he becomes sober, Clive cannot get rid of the recollections of Vernon's words as we are told that he »lay there for hours, open-eyed in the dark, exhausted, desiccated, and alert, once more forced to attend helplessly to his carousel. Neck in shit? Moral position! Molly?« Furthermore, in his hallucinations between intoxication and sobriety, Clive is represented as having »dreams of crossing a desert on hands and knees, carrying the Tare's only grand piano« (*AM* 140). In the same way, some moments later Clive is finding himself unable to »cross« the desert in his creation since he is not able to apply the needed »modification« to the symphony notes. He is taken to Manchester in order to »identify« the rapist. Clive ascribes his present stall to Vernon's words on phone since they set in motion Clive's queasy feelings and perceptions; nevertheless, he is aware of the role of something personal in this case:

> He knew the roll, the creative spree, was over. It was not simply that he was tired and hung over. As soon as he sat at the piano and tried out a couple of approaches to the variation, he found that not only this passage but the whole movement had died on him suddenly it was ashes in his mouth. He didn't dare think too hard about

> the symphony itself. [. . .] The work was stalled. What had been a luscious fruit was now a dry twig. (*AM* 140–141)

The above passage reports in comprehensive form the orienting dispositions of Clive's mental functioning. He is represented as being frightened by his own inability to complete his symphony finding himself a »dry« fountain. Clive's embedded narratives also show the slippery nature of his artistic inspiration triggered by a birdcall in the Lake District. Despite that, he does not acknowledge his own role in not being able to do the »significant variation« (*AM* 142) in the symphony notes. Clive, however, is persistent in his goals. In order to find a way out of his present situation, or to ›clear his head« (*AM* 140), and post Vernon's letter, Clive goes out. When he buys Friday's *Judge*, its front page is shocking to him:

> [1] But the front page was an embarrassment, not because, or not only because, a man had been caught out in a delicate private moment, but because the paper had worked itself up into such a lather about it and brought to bear such powerful resources. As if some criminal political conspiracy had been uncovered, or a corpse under the table in the Foreign Office. [2] So unworldly, so misjudged, so uncool. It was inept too in the ways it tried so hard to be cruel. [. . .] [3] Again the thought recurred: not only was Vernon loathsome, he had to be mad. But that wouldn't stop Clive loathing him. (*AM* 141)

Although Clive finds both *The Judge* and Garmony's actions equally as an »embarrassment,« still he reprimands *The Judge* for its unremitting covering of Garmony's case. Such thoughts, however, derive from the mental state he has recently achieved after his helplessness in his creation. Clive's mental frames, loaded with his experiences with Vernon, propels him to consider Vernon's action as »misjudged [. . .] cruel.« He does not think that Vernon's action was because of Garmony. Equally, he is not concerned about the implications of his old friends' transvestite photographs with Molly. At this moment, he ascribes everything to Vernon's selfishness. These perceptions make Clive »loath« Vernon more. Accumulations of such feelings, moreover, make Clive more confident not only to break all his intermental ties with Vernon but also to seek »revenge on him. Thus, there is no longer »happy thought« to lead Clive to benign prospects. When he enters into his studio in order to work on his still incomplete symphony,

> Its squalor oppressed him, and when he sat in front of his manuscript, the handwriting of a younger, more confident and gifted man, he blamed Vernon for the fact that he could not work, and his anger redoubled. His concentration had been shattered. By an idiot. It was becoming clear that he had been denied his masterpiece, the summit of a lifetime's work. [. . .] Now the proof, the very signature of genius had been spoiled, and greatness had been snatched away. For Clive knew that he would never again attempt a composition on such a scale; he was too weary, too emptied out, too old. [. . .] Every idea he had was dull. He shouldn't be let near this symphony; he was not worthy of his own creation. (*AM* 142–143)

Therefore, Clive is not separable from his work. The moment he finds out he is no longer able to »create« any music, he feels both mentally and emotionally non-existent. Clive, furthermore, is represented as being fairly tough on Vernon as he is on himself. He is in fact negating his »weary,« »emptied,« and »too old« self by refuting his »sanctimonious« (*AM* 139) friend. The moment Clive gets to know Vernon's resignation on Tuesday, he returns to his previous self. Justifying his friendship obligations, he exempts himself: »It was grimly satisfying to have his own views of Vernon's conduct confirmed. He had done his duty by Vernon, he had tried to warn him, but Vernon wouldn't listen.« After reading the »three scathing indictments« (*AM* 143) against Vernon, Clive's mental states ironically change and once more he finds himself »feeling better.« He imagines his merry life after the symphony's successful premier in Amsterdam. Following that, his sense of creativity returns:

> He was aware that his finger was tapping the radiator to the beat of some new rhythm, and he imagined a shift of mood, of key, and a note sustained over changing harmonies and a savage kettledrum pulse. He turned and hurried from the room. He had an idea, a quarter of an idea, and before it went he had to get to the piano. (*AM* 144)

The restored hope, however, does not last long since Clive's past does not allow him to be free. When »he was about to crack the variation,« the police call. Following that, leaving the symphony unfinished, Clive is obliged to go with the police in order to »nail a suspect« (*AM* 144). His memory, nevertheless, is shown to fail there too.

Clive's misanthropic disposition shows itself once more when he is in Manchester airport. It firstly appears in Molly's crematorium ceremony at the beginning of the narrative when Clive wants to offer his condolences to Molly's husband, George. On his way towards him, Clive's flow of thoughts indicates the degree of his »misanthropy«:

> So many faces Clive had never seen by daylight, and looking terrible, like cadavers jerked upright to welcome the newly dead. Invigorated by this jolt of misanthropy, he moved sleekly through the din, ignored his name when it was called, withdrew his elbow when it was plucked, and kept on going toward where George stood. (*AM* 9)

This aspect of his mental functioning is the general disposition of Clive's mind at the moment. It is in contradiction with the other social minds. The more he finds himself unable to create a new symphony, the more his misanthropy shows itself in his behaviour. In other words, the beginning point of his communication is his art. When he fails in his music, he also fails in his human relationships. The nature of his world perspectives and relationships follow the changing state of his literary mind and its fluctuating nature impacts them deeply. One of the aspects of his »familiar misanthropy« (*AM* 63) returns to him when he is in Manchester airport. Looking outside from a window,

> through gaps in the fog he could see other airliners waiting competitively in ragged, converging lines, something brooding and loutish in their forms: slit eyes beneath small brains, stunted, encumbered arms, upraised and blackened arseholes. Creatures like this could never care about each other. (*AM* 150)

Clive's actions also represent his mental dispositions. For example, he is disappointedly certain that Vernon does not care about him. Therefore, discrediting the pact they already made, he justifies his preparations for his intended crime in Amsterdam. It brightens his mood when in his prospects he finds everything as he expects: »All in all, given what he'd been through and the ordeals that lay ahead, and the certainty that events now were sure to accelerate giddily, he didn't feel so bad« (*AM* 150). His lack of awareness about the social realities, however, is suggested when Clive observes some natural, but to him intolerable, scenes in the police station. For example, when he sees a constable with split lip, we are told that »No one seemed much bothered, not even the policeman with the split lip, but Clive put a restraining hand over his leaping heart and was obliged to sit down« (*AM* 152). Such scenes imply Clive's distance from real life, actual people and their social problems. As a result of his self-contained existence, he finds the police officials' welcoming full of »courtesy and even deference.« He even gets shocked perceiving »They seemed to like him, these policemen, and Clive wondered if there were not certain qualities he had never known he possessed, a level manner, quiet charm, authority perhaps« (*AM* 153). Clive's self-assessments are, however, prone to exaggerations. For example, as his confrontations with Vernon portray, he strongly believes that his perspective is the only one ever possible. When he is asked to identify the suspect in the police station, the narrator's summary of Clive's action reveals the general tendency of his thought as well:

> Straight away he saw his man, third from the right, the one with the long thin face and the telltale cloth cap. What a relief. When they went back inside, one of the detectives gripped Clive's arm and squeezed, but said nothing. Around him was an atmosphere of suppressed rejoicing, and everyone liked him even more. They were working together as a team now, and Clive had accepted his role as a key prosecution witness. Later on there was a second parade, and this time half the men had cloth caps and all had long thin faces. But Clive wasn't fooled and found his man right at the end, without a cap. Back indoors he was told by the detectives that this second line up was not so important. In fact, for administrative reasons they might even discount it completely. (*AM* 154)

The officers know that Clive is wrong but, to be polite, they do not mention it. However, both Clive and the main officer are intermentally aware of each other's thoughts without uttering anything: »he noticed that the policeman in the driver's seat was the very man he had picked out of the line the second time. But neither Clive nor the driver found it necessary to comment on the fact as they shook hands« (*AM* 154). Clive's experience in the police station reveals the weakness of his memory from the narrator's perspective. He seems to be unaware of his mental powers. It is possibly because of this disposition that Clive thinks highly of his judgments about Vernon's actions as well as about his own music. Accordingly, according to Schwalm, »Clive's perception of others, including their response to him, is repeatedly revealed to be erroneous, particularly in the case of his statement at the police station when he fails to identify the suspect« (176).

Before the big day of performance in Amsterdam, Clive is spirited thinking of the place as a »tolerant, open minded, grown up sort of place« (*AM* 155). This cheerful thought, however, does not last long when he is reminded of his symphony and Vernon:

> [1] He thought about Vernon, and the symphony. [2] Was the work ruined, or simply flawed? [3] Perhaps not flawed so much as sullied, and in ways that only he could understand. Ruinously cheated of its greatest moment. [4] He dreaded the premiere. [5] He could tell himself now, in all tortuous sincerity, that in making his various arrangements on Vernon's behalf, he, Clive, was doing no more than honouring his word. That Vernon should want a reconciliation and should therefore want to come to Amsterdam was surely more than a coincidence or a neat convenience. Somewhere in his blackened, unbalanced heart he had accepted his fate. He was delivering himself up to Clive. (*AM* 155–156)

Clive builds a strong relationship between Vernon and his symphony [1]. The direct thought [2] represents Clive as acknowledging for the first time the incomplete, »ruined« or »flawed« nature of his symphony. Despite that, he still thinks that the only person who can recognise the flawed nature of his symphony is himself. This perception, however, turns out to be wrong by the evaluation of symphony's director and the critics. Furthermore, although Clive persuades himself that no other person can recognise the problem in his symphony, the TR [4] shows an inner sense of fear about its first performance. However, such an underestimated problem in the symphony finally takes Clive to justify his own preparations for his amnicide [5]. Ironically, Clive thinks that, based on Vernon's behaviour, it is now obligatory for him to keep his promises in terms of helping Vernon to die soon. Vernon's recent actions are signs of his madness for Clive. Vernon's reconciliatory calling and therefore inviting himself to Amsterdam, according to Clive, indicate his tacit acceptance of his inevitable fate. These perceptions are, however, Clive's strongly personal and intramental justifications, evaluation and mental dispositions. The symptoms of the disease that Clive enumerates to his contact, or what he calls »the good doctor,« are strongly aspectual as well. Clive claims that Vernon is »unpredictable, bizarre, and extremely antisocial behaviour, a complete loss of reason. Destructive tendencies, delusions of omnipotence. A disintegrated personality« (*AM* 156). What he calls Vernon's »antisocial behaviour« or his »delusions of omniscience« are in fact the same intramental perceptions based on which Vernon's mind works. Vernon himself eagerly pursues what he considers to be his commitment to their contract. Nevertheless, following their embedded narratives, the reader already knows that they both regretted soon after they had mentioned their proposals.

When Clive hears his music in the distance before entering into the rehearsal hall, we are told that »He was walking toward a representation of himself« (*AM* 156). This TR indicates Clive's equal perception of his music and himself. Their coincidental disintegration at the end of the narrative does also represent their inseparability. The time Clive finds out that in his symphony »dissonance was spreading like a contagion« (*AM* 157), a nostalgic feeling overcomes him. He could have done the last variations or modifications to his music before being forced to take part in the identification process. His music, furthermore, signifies the tantalizing nature of his thoughts too. Clive's inner conflicts concerning his own music and »greatness« suggest the degree he is resisting the facts as well as his stubborn character. When Clive turns into a listener, he defines his own music as »ruined goods.« Therefore, it is possible to claim that the moment Clive comes out of his own mind as a creator or originator and is exposed to his creation, he is able to find out its chief problem:

> For now, it was the music, the wondrous transformation of thought into sound. [. . .] Sometimes Clive worked so hard on a piece that he could lose sight of his ultimate purpose, to create this pleasure at once so sensual and abstract, to translate into vibrating air this nonlanguage whose meanings were forever just beyond reach, suspended tantalisingly at a point where emotion and intellect fused. Certain sequences of notes reminded him of nothing more than the recent effort to write them. [. . .] the music conjured for Clive the disorder of his studio in the dawn light and the suspicions he had had about himself and hardly dared frame. Greatness. Was he an idiot to have thought this way? Surely there had to be one first single moment of self-recognition, and surely it would always seem absurd. [. . .] Clive put his face into his hands. He was right to have worried. It was ruined goods. (*AM* 158–159)

The more Clive is exposed to his own music, the more he takes Vernon as its spoiler. As a result, he persuades himself to take revenge on Vernon—his own old friend who informed the police about Clive's information on the Lakeland »anonymous rambler« (*AM* 157) and that prevented Clive from applying the »exquisite change« to the symphony notes. This provokes in him an act of retaliation against his only close friend:

> This should have been the symphony's moment of triumphant assertion, the gathering up of ail that was joyously human before the destruction to come. But presented like this, as a simple fortissimo repetition, it was literal-minded bombast, it was bathos; less than that, it was a void: one that only revenge could fill. [. . .] The theme was disintegrating into the tidal wave of dissonance and was gathering in volume, but it sounded quite absurd, like twenty orchestras tuning to an A. It was not dissonant at all. Practically every instrument was playing the same note- It was a drone. It was a giant bagpipe in need of repair. (*AM* 158–159)

Nevertheless, Clive reconstructs his own reasoning for his would-be action against Vernon. The more he identifies the distorting problem in his symphony, the more he reframes his own justifications concerning his arrangement for poisoning Vernon. He justifies his action on the grounds that Vernon has already poisoned him through spoiling his music or his true self:

> He had just experienced an auditory hallucination, an illusion, or a disillusion. The absence of the variation had wrecked his masterpiece, and he was clearer than ever now, if such a thing were possible, about the plans he had made. It was no longer fury that drove him, or hatred or disgust, or the necessity of honouring his word. What he was about to do was contractually right, it had the amoral inevitability of pure geometry, and he didn't feel a thing. (*AM* 161)

Not being able to produce something complete and creative, Clive pursues a vengeful action against his old friend who is now turned into an enemy. His egotistic perceptions, therefore, justify his extremely self-centred goals. Since he ascribes failure to Vernon, Clive expects the director of the symphony to praise his work although he is aware of its »flawed« nature: »Despite his awareness of its imperfections, Clive wanted the great conductor to bless his symphony with a lofty compliment« (*AM* 161). He feels that his thoughts and deeds should be respected even if they contain imperfections. However, he is reluctant to confess them too. The critic Paul Lanark also points out the flawed nature of Clive's symphony by addressing him: »They say you've ripped off Beethoven something rotten« (*AM* 164). Clive indignantly repudiates him. Likewise, the two old friends continue on their pretentions even after they give each other the poisoned champagne:

> [Vernon:] »Cheers. And look, I meant what I said. I really am sorry about sending the police round to you. It was appalling behaviour. Unconditional, groveling apologies.«
> [Clive:] »Don't mention it again. I'm terribly sorry about your job and all that business. You really were the best.«
> [Vernon:] »Let's shake on it, then. Friends.«
> [Clive:] »Friends.« (*AM* 165)

After their mutual poisoning, when Clive goes into his room, he enters into his »drugged unconsciousness« or hallucinations before his »fatal injection« (Malcolm 194) prior to death. He is reported as »writhing in pleasurable anticipation« (*AM* 167) while dreaming himself falling in love with Susie, his girlfriend, at it occurs to her: »if he could stop thinking about work for a week, he could bring himself to fall in love with Susie« (*AM* 167). The problem, however, is that his wish is grounded on something impossible, because he is not represented as separable from his own work and he has just entered into post-mortem state. Still, he takes Vernon's agents, the Dutch doctor and the nurse, for Molly and Paul. The narrator's TR, »he experienced an ecstasy of exhausted surrender« (*AM* 166), indicates Clive's last moment perceptions while finding all his intramental intentions unfulfilled in his real life:

> At the thought, he was overcome by a sudden deep affection for himself as just the sort of person one should stick by, and he felt a tear run down his cheekbone and tickle his ear. He couldn't quite be troubled to wipe it away. And no need, for walking across the room toward him now was Molly, Molly Lane! And some fellow in tow. (*AM* 167)

Furthermore, he finds himself in an (imaginary) conversation with Molly reminding him of Paul Lanark and the Lake District event. This conversation becomes significantly revealing when Molly addresses Clive claiming: »You always put your work first, and perhaps that's right.« Clive's reaction is dualistic: »Yes, No« (*AM* 168). Clive's hallucinations come to their end when Molly informs him that Lanark will let him know what she really thinks about his music by entering a huge needle into his arm. Although the injection hurts Clive most, he is satisfied with the critic's »praise.« Accordingly, Clive dies with »dreams of greatness« (Malcolm 194).

Clive's life and thought are also represented between the two certain states. He neither belongs totally to himself being able to control his internal perceptions, feelings and desires nor is he able to maintain a balance between his intramental inclinations and his intermental obligations. Instead, he is represented as being extremely absorbed in his music being enchanted by it without taking into consideration or acknowledging any possibility of problem in it.[78] Likewise, since he believes his aspects, beliefs, judgments, perceptions etc. are the right ones, he cannot stop thinking about those of the others. He is, therefore, unable to make a balance between his own values and those of Vernon's. His intramentally fuelled actions, nevertheless, get more confident as the narrative progresses.

3.4 The Egocentricism and Intermentality: Representation of the Impact of (Intentional) Intramentality on Vernon Haliday's Thoughts and Actions

In a similar manner to Clive, Vernon is represented as disregarding the impact of his actions on the other's life. From the very beginning his propensity to instigate the enmity with Garmony, regardless of Clive's, Molly's or even Garmony's thoughts, suggests his intentional intramental drives. However, he attempts to hide such perceptions behind what he refers to as public interests. Moreover, he is unaware of the impact of his own actions on the other(s) while he accuses Clive for being unaware of his moral duty. Their mutual problem is that they are both primarily unaware of the nature of their own actions and thoughts while at the same time they are criticizing each other for ignoring their moral duties.

The dominant mode of Vernon's mental functioning is also intramental one. He attempts to achieve his ambition of becoming a famous editor for

[78] Florence Ponting in *CB* is also a musician. They both find a separate self in their music, which is superior to their social selves.

the sake of public interests. After Molly's death, he opportunistically gets in touch with her husband, George, in order to defame Garmony. In the earlier part of narrative, he is revealed as concerning with some ontological, existential or self-questionings. For example, as we are told, it occurred to him that »he might not exist« (*AM* 29). Even at his office in *The Judge* his

> exercise of authority did not sharpen his sense of self, as it usually did. Instead it seemed to Vernon that he was infinitely diluted; he was simply the sum of all the people who had listened to him, and when he was alone, he was nothing at all. When he reached, in solitude, for a thought, there was no one there to think it. His chair was empty; he was finely dissolved throughout the building, [. . .] he was [. . .] globally disseminated like dust. [. . .] This sense of absence had been growing since Molly's funeral. It was wearing into him. (*AM* 29–30)

The narrator in this passage is recounting the character's subjectivity through free indirect discourse. This discourse shows the impact of momentary situations on his mental workings. In this way, Vernon's experience of helplessness is shown in more natural way. Therefore, as Clive experiences a dilemma about his music theories and practices, Vernon vacillates between his private self and the public persona, »He was widely known as a man without edges, without faults or virtues, as a man who did not fully exist. Within his profession Vernon was revered as a nonentity« (*AM* 30). Nevertheless, his work ascribes a self to him: »Now that he was in company again, back on the job, his interior absence was no longer an affliction« (*AM* 34). Furthermore, such a fluctuating characteristic helped Vernon in becoming the fifth editor of *The Judge* since he »had shown an instinctive talent for making neither friends nor allies« (*AM* 30). Vernon's present »state of dissociation« (*AM* 30) is also affected by a pain in the right side of his head. It gives him a perception of nonexistence and the feeling that »he was already dead« (*AM* 31). The pain is in the part of brain which is often »associated with emotional intelligence« (Wells, *Ian McEwan* 90). It is »not objectifiable« since, according to Catrinescu:

> He spots the pain and tries to give it a name, [. . .] but fails because his symptoms are not objectifyable; they belong to his subjectivity, to his subconscious. It is an overwhelming sensation that seizes his entire body and mind, that reclaims all his attention, but it is nothing concrete although he is trying to define its organic limits.

Nevertheless, these thoughts disappear or go to the background of his mind when Vernon returns to work.

As we see its primary symptoms in the crematorium scene, Vernon's problem with Garmony is more highlighted when he notices »Garmony's Washington triumph« written by Frank Dibben, the foreign editor. The impact of this title on his consciousness and its recounting in FIT mode display his inner states configured by the past and future implications of the words »Garmony« and »triumph.« Vernon does not intend to let Garmony have any feeling of triumph simply because he loathes him, he is his enemy and he was his rival in the past. The narrator's account of Vernon's consciousness reveals his experiencing mind at that moment: »That would need to be a skeptical piece, or a hostile one. And if it really was a triumph, it could stay off the front page« (*AM* 32). Such presuppositions instigate Vernon's reaction against George's proposal for publishing Garmony's three transvestite photographs. He hopes to disgrace him even though he is banned from doing so before even receiving the photos. Moreover, it is over Garmony's case that Frank's relationship with Vernon becomes suspiciously tenacious. Its teleological contribution to the later replacement of Vernon by Frank shows the scene's importance:

> Vernon heard him [Frank] out, and then: »He's [Garmony] in Washington when he should be in Brussels. He's cutting a deal with the Americans behind the Germans' backs. Short-term gain, long-term disaster. He was a terrible home secretary, he's even worse at the Foreign Office, and he'll be the ruin of us if he's ever prime minister—which is looking more and more likely.«
> »Well, yes,« Frank agreed, his softness of tone concealing his fury about the Ankara put-down. »You said all that in your leader, Vernon. Surely the point is not whether we agree with the deal, but whether it's significant.«
> Vernon was wondering whether he might just bring himself to let Frank go. What was he doing wearing an earring?
> »Quite right, Frank,« Vernon said cordially. »We're in Europe. The Americans want us in Europe. The special relationship is history. The deal has no significance. The coverage stays on the inside pages. Meanwhile, we'll continue to give Garmony a hard time. (*AM* 36)

Presentation of double competing perspectives in this passage signifies their different evaluation of the shared issues. Frank pretends to be concerned only with the professional ethics: »Surely the point is not whether we agree with the deal, but whether it's significant.« Garmony, however, poses as a person who is only concerned with the social or public interests when he says, »The deal has no significance.« Unlike Vernon, Frank is a good mind reader. He digs through Vernon's expressions and sets his future cunning plans based on them while Vernon continues his confidence about the photographs to him. Furthermore, Vernon's worries about his position and his lingering doubts about Frank are shown when Frank follows him to the washroom, »Cassius is hungry, Vernon thought. He'll head his department, then he'll want my job« (*AM* 39). This scene is, however, the beginning of Frank's advancement towards Vernon. Their close relationship continues until Vernon, although very late, finds out Frank's role in the Garmony's case.

The declaration of injunction creates an atmosphere of mistrust towards Vernon in *The Judge*. For example, Vernon perceives that the newspaper's lawyer, Tony, »was looking distrustful.« This TR, focalized through Vernon's perspective, shows *The Judge* community's general opinion of Vernon emphasised by all their »suspicious questions« (*AM* 43). It also implies their lack of trust in him. In other words, an intermental unit is being shaped against Vernon concurrent with his intermental breakdown with his single close friend Clive, over his policy to give »Garmony a hard time« (*AM* 36). To put the same point in other words, Vernon's intramental pursuing of his goals leads him to experience the deadly imbalance in his intermental relationships either with his close friend or with his colleagues in *the Judge*. Nevertheless, before entering into Clive's house, as we are told, »Vernon still took pleasure in his visits.« However, this »pleasure« disappears after their mutually stubborn insistence on intramental perspectives while discussing Garmony's case. Moreover, the bleak outcome of their meeting is indicated in Vernon's feelings as he re-experiences »only vestigially« their shared past rejoices: »he experienced again, though only vestigially, a sensation he never had these days, of genuine anticipation, the feeling that anything might happen« (*AM* 47). This »genuine anticipation« is a symptom of a defining event in their meeting. Its teleological importance increases the more their relationship changes throughout the narrative.

Vernon's distaste is not limited to Garmony or to the grammarians in *The Judge*. It includes George too.[79] When he goes to George's home in order to take a look at Garmony's photographs before buying them, his introductory perception of George is suggesting: »The man was simply preposterous« (*AM* 51). Besides looking at the photographs, Vernon there, at Molly's department in George's house, is reminded of Molly's memories. This evokes his innermost feelings as revealed through [1] to [5] in the following passage. For the first time, he experiences what is it like to imagine Molly as dead. In addition, he experiences the sense of loss as he understands that he has lost a friend. The »homesick« feeling, nevertheless, terminates in this scene,

> [1] Now, as George pushed the door open, Vernon tensed. He felt unprepared. [. . .] [2] Vernon experienced for the first time the proper impact of Molly's death—the plain fact of her absence. [. . .] and until now he had never really missed her in his heart, or felt the insult of knowing he would never see or hear her again. [3] She was his friend, perhaps the best he had ever had, and she had gone. He could easily have made a fool of himself in front of George, whose outline was blurring even now. [4] This particular kind of desolation, a painful constriction right behind his face, above the roof of his mouth, he hadn't known since childhood, since prep school. [5] Homesick for Molly. He concealed a gasp of self-pity behind a loud adult cough. (*AM* 53–54)

This is one of the rare scenes in which the impact of Molly's absence on Vernon's consciousness is represented. As it is stated, Vernon »had never really missed her in his heart« beforehand. As a result, when he finds himself in this »tense« situation he feels »unprepared.« This intermnetal sympathy, however, is a transient moment because Vernon is increasingly concerned with intramental long-term goals. The more he reconsiders his and his friends' agreement concerning Molly's stay in George's, or her husband's, apartment, the more he regrets his contribution to that communal decision: »Vernon and all her other friends advised her to stay in Holland Park, believing familiarity would serve her better. How wrong they had been. She would have been freer, even under the strictest institutional re-

[79] Later in the narrative, it will also include his closest friend, Clive, too.

gime, than she turned out to be in George's care« (*AM* 55). This internal turmoil, however, terminates, as if it had never existed, when Vernon is called back to his profession by the photographs George is showing him:

> Then he studied the second and third again, seeing them fully now and feeling waves of distinct responses: astonishment first, followed by a wild inward hilarity. Suppressing it gave him a sense of levitating from his chair. Next he experienced ponderous responsibility—or was it power? A man's life, or at least his career, was in his hands. And who could tell, perhaps Vernon was in a position to change the country's future for the better. And his paper's circulation. (*AM* 56)

While looking at the photographs, Vernon's inward reactions and teleological calculations are reported first in TR mode and then in free indirect thought or perception mode. The moment he is thinking of the prosperous chances the photographs would bring him, Vernon's »astonishments« give place to »hilarity« and »sense of levitation.« Following that, the narrator takes reader into Vernon's mind and closely displays the manner he pretends to be primarily concerned about »the country's future« and his own »ponderous responsibility.« Using his own continuing consciousness frame and based on Vernon's embedded narratives scattered throughout the narrative, the reader, nevertheless, knows that Vernon abstains acknowledging his real reasons in this case. More than from his »responsibility« feeling for the country's future, Vernon's venomous thoughts and actions about Garmony derive from both his own jealousy and his own ambition. Since he is aware of the fact that Garmony had had an intimate relationship with Molly, he can use the photographs as a peculiar chance to save his paper and hence strengthen his own editorial position in *The Judge*. Besides representing his opportunistic character, this passage, therefore, presents the qualia or what it's like aspect of such a situation on Vernon.

Vernon's mental functioning continues in the same mood the reader has left him in the first scene after his confrontation with his close friend Clive. He is disseminated in the social actions without which he does not feel to exist. If Clive struggles to lessen the interference of the outward with the inward spheres, restricting all his concerns and concentration to his intrametally oriented inner life and feelings, Vernon has no inner life apart from the outward events. Nevertheless, similarly, they are to some extent »non-entities, men taken up by their careers and material success and in a sense absorbed by that« (Malcolm, 2002: 192). Vernon's mind is characterised as being a social mind in action concerned with the issues related to the »furious grammarians,« the sceptical board of directors in *The Judge*, its production staff, its lawyers,« »his own people,« »George Lane's people« and the issues related to the publication of Garmony's photographs (*AM* 98). Based on Vernon's embedded narratives in chapter IV part II (pp. 98–120), the reader finds out that his confrontation with Clive has not dissuaded him from publishing the photographs. Although indirectly, he follows his egoistic intention as he »made his public-interest case for publishing the photographs much as he had made it to Clive, but sleekly, at greater length and speed, with more urgency and definition and proliferating examples, with pie charts, block graphs, spreadsheets, and soothing precedents« (*AM* 98). Vernon, therefore, pretends to defend and adhere to »public-interest,« while his actions turn out to be more self-centred. Likewise, encountering with Molly-Garmony's case, his intramentality shows itself. The more he gets involved with their photographs, the more he gets »away« from her because she was once his intimate friend. Unlike Clive, he is rarely haunted by or reminded of her memories except in his illusions:

> he was back there again, lifting his briefcase high as he waded through water, or blood, or tears coursing over a red carpet that brought him to an amphitheatre where he mounted a podium to make his case while all around him was a silence that towered like redwoods, and in the gloom, dozens of averted eyes, and someone walking away from him across the circus sawdust who looked like Molly but would not answer when he called. (*AM* 99).

Vernon's unconscious perception of his situation is represented as wading through »water, blood, or tear« towards his goal. Moreover, the darkness of the place, its silence, the »averted ayes« gazed at him and above all Molly's carelessness to his calling all show Vernon's perception of his own difficult situation. The narrator's comment on Vernon's dreams given in TR mode, however, emphasises the main reasons behind his actions. Vernon's unconscious mind unceasingly attempts to suppress his real intentions. Therefore,

Clive is hardly able to understand the real reasons of his close friend's behaviour. Nevertheless, the narrator and the reader, but not the character, know that,

> His dreams were simply a kaleidoscopic fracturing of his week, fair comment on its pace and emotional demands but omitting-with the unthinking partisan bias of the unconscious-the game plan, the rationale whose evolving logic had in fact kept him sane. Publication day was tomorrow, Friday. (*AM* 99)

Vernon, therefore, is represented as being mainly concerned with Garmony and Clive in his embedded narratives. He seemingly becomes successful at last in achieving a »broad consensus« about Garmony as a »despicable person« who »was financially, morally and sexually corrupt« (*AM* 100). Vernon's mental states, moreover, are linked with his actions. For example, when he finds himself successful in persuading *The Judge* officials to agree to publish the Molly-Garmony photographs, his self-perceptions transform positively:

> [1] In the accumulating momentum of the week, practically every hour had revealed to Vernon new aspects of his powers and potential, and as his gifts for persuasion and planning began to produce results, [2] he felt large and benign, a little ruthless, perhaps, but ultimately good, capable of standing alone against the current, seeing over the heads of his contemporaries, knowing that he was about to shape the destiny of his country and that he could bear the responsibility. (*AM* 101)

Revealed through TR mode, Vernon's perceptions also show his evaluation of his actions. Having found himself able to persuade the people in *The Judge* to publish the photographs, Vernon conceives the results of his campaign satisfactory. He ascribes new »aspects« to his mind [1]. Furthermore, based on his new perception of his own mental states, Vernon sets new goals with sheer determination. Although he knows that his actions may be »ruthless,« he thinks that they are good for the »destiny of his country.« Finally, Vernon promises himself to »bear the responsibility« [2]. His internal states, therefore, depend largely on his social affiliations. Even his physical state depends on his mental states. For example, when he finds the prospect good, it seems to him that:

> not so long ago he had been afflicted by a numbness of the scalp and a sense of not existing that had provoked in him fears of madness and death. Molly's funeral had given him the jitters. Now his purpose and being filled him to his fingertips. The story was alive, and so was he. (*AM* 101–102)

Thus, Vernon's inner feelings depend mostly on his successes in social plans. Nevertheless his existence is disseminated. Without the others, he does not exist, or »his identity loses coherence« (Wells, *Ian McEwan* 90). It does not mean that his intermental bonds are larger or broader than that of Clive's because he has almost no other intermental or joint thought with anybody other than with Clive, although before their confrontation.

Clive's doubly embedded narratives reciprocally resonate in Vernon's mind. In both cases, there is a traceable course from intermentality to disrupting intramentality. As the thoughts related with Vernon were breaking Clive's concentration in the rocks, the after-effects of their confrontation resonate in Vernon's mind violating his benign feelings:

> [1] But one small matter denied him complete happiness: Clive. He had addressed him in his mind so often, sharpening the arguments, adding all the things he should have said that night, that he could almost convince himself that he was winning his old friend round, just as he was triumphing over the dinosaurs on the board of directors. [2] But they hadn't spoken since their row, and Vernon was worrying more as publication day approached. [3] Was Clive brooding, or furious, or was he locked in his studio, lost in work and oblivious to public affairs? [4] Several times during the week Vernon had thought of snatching a minute alone to phone him. But he worried that a fresh attack from Clive would unsteady him in the meetings ahead. [5: a] Now Vernon eyed the bedside phone beyond the heaped and buckled pillows, and then he made a lunge. [5: b] Best not to let forethought make a coward of him again. He had to save this friendship. Best to do it while he was calm. (*AM* 102)

Vernon's re-evaluations of the confrontation scene and his justifications, represented in TR mode, signify the degree of strong aspectuality in his discourse. Furthermore, Vernon considers his stance on the publishing issue to be the correct one. In his idle imaginations, he conceives overcoming the »dinosaurs of the board of directors« in the same way he did overcome his friend, Clive [2]. Vernon is, nevertheless, reluctant to call Clive because he »worries« more about the photographs than about his friend. Vernon, moreover, makes inferences about Clive's mental states. The FIT mode [3] shows

Vernon's mind in action making assumptions about another mind. Seemingly, he can accurately imagine his friend's mental states after their separation. He is, however, unable to consider or imagine the assessment of the concerned issues from Clive's perspective. His intramental approach grants him the right to disregard the other possibilities. The TR mode in part [4], furthermore, presents the real reasons behind his disinclination to call Clive. Nevertheless, in part [5: a] Vernon is represented as making a decision and putting it into action immediately by making a »lunge.« Overlapping each other for one moment, his decision combines with his action. He finally overcomes his own indeterminacy in terms of the primacy of their friendship to the issues related with their confrontation. Accordingly the war between his professional dreams and his interpersonal relationship subsides for a while within him as the FIT mode [5: b] reveals Vernon in an attempt to overcome his doubts and reconsider his friendship. The last sentence »Best to do it while he was calm,« however, shows the degree of vulnerability concerning their friendship as well as Vernon's worries regarding his ability to control his temper in the future. The passage, therefore, indicates the high degrees of aspectuality. Vernon in both cases—publication and confrontation—considers his stance and views rightful. They will finally persuade both the board of the directors in *The Judge* and Clive.

When Vernon finally calls Clive in order to make reconciliations, they both pretend to be more concerned about their friendship than anything else. For example, when the publication subject arises in their statements are pretentious. Clive maintains that »We'll just have to agree to differ« (*AM* 103). His statement, »agree to differ,« turns out to be a fake statement because Clive will never agree with Vernon's decision concerning Molly-Garmony photographs. Reciprocally, Vernon will easily persuade him to go to the police in order to report the row scene in the rocks. Such disagreements, however, cause the breach and imbalance in their friendship to grow which finally brings about their death. Likewise, Vernon's later actions in the narrative turn out to be unlike his claims, »I wouldn't want it to come between us« (*AM* 103). The reader already knows that their opposing interpretations of the same issues gradually destroy the conventional intermental bond between them. Vernon's phone call to Clive is not because of his worries for him or due to his concern to maintain their friendship. He uses it as a chance to concentrate more on Garmony's case in *The Judge*. When he finds out »Clive wasn't angry with him, so that was fine, and now he needed to get going« (*AM* 104), he does not even listen to Clive's recounting of the row scene. The teleological contribution of this scene to their relationship, however, will appear when Vernon will accuse Clive of his lack of moral duty based on his passivity towards a criminal scene.

As Vernon's mental functioning is revealed through his struggles in *The Judge* building, the perceptions of *The Judge* clerks about Vernon are also revealed through both their intermental thoughts among themselves and their individual actions. They evaluate Vernon's decision to publish the photographs in spite of their strong but mostly tacit oppositions against it. Frank is the only person in *The Judge* that his actions cajole Vernon into an intermental relationship for a while. Their intimacy is, however, not genuine as Vernon is »outmaneuvered« (Malcolm 191) by him the day after the publication of the photographs. Frank's character is disclosed both by the intermental thought in *The Judge* about him and Vernon's perception of him. He was

> [1] rumoured to be restless. They called him Cassius for his lean and hungry look, [2] but this was unfair: his eyes were dark, his face long and pale, his stubble heavy, giving him the appearance of a police cell interrogator, but his manner was courteous, though a little withdrawn, and he had an attractive, wry intelligence. [3]Vernon had always detested him in an absentminded way but had come round to Frank in the early days of the Garmony turmoil. (*AM* 105)

The narrator in this passage, applying TR mode, puts forward three different aspects towards Dibben. One is the intermental thought in *The Judge*. He is compared to Cassius [1].[80] The narrator, nevertheless, does not agree with

---

[80] Gaius Cassius Longinus (85 BC- 42 BC) was an austere Roman republican and an instigator in the plot against Julius Caesar's assassination. Julius Caesar in William Shakespeare' (2012) eponymous play describes Cassius in the following words:
Let me have men about me that are fat,
Sleek-headed men, and such as sleep o' nights:
Yond Cassius has a lean and hungry look;
He thinks too much: such men are dangerous. (ACT I, SCENE II)

the general assumption since Dibben is more like »a police cell interrogator« [2]. This implies something mysterious about Dibben as does his »lean and hungry look« to *The Judge* inhabitants. Vernon's, however, simply detests him without knowing its reason(s) as he »detested him in absentminded way« [3]. The TR mode in the above passage, accordingly, shows the way Dibben is perceived by the unnamed fictional minds in *The Judge*, by the narrator as well as by Vernon. Nevertheless, Dibben's strange and suspicious behaviour towards Vernon becomes more meaningful after his promotion to *The Judge* editorship. Despite that, his words and actions[81] raise the narrator's and narrative readers', but not the character's, doubts from the beginning. He, for example, knows when and how to draw near to Vernon. In other words, he is a good mind reader. Following that, when Vernon is emotionally stuck, Dibben, getting closer to him, coaxes trust out of him:

> The evening after the chapel passed its no-confidence vote in the editor, the evening after Vernon's compact with Clive, the young man stalked Vernon's hunched figure down the street at dusk and finally approached, touched his shoulder, and suggested a drink. There was something persuasive in Dibben's tone. (*AM* 105)

Frank knows how to seem »persuasive« while Vernon does not even think about the strange possibility of making an intermental relationship with him. To put the same point in other words, before being persuaded by Frank's tone, Vernon is persuaded by his own situation. Franks' cleverness refers to his ability to recognise the right place and time. Moreover, his sly Albeguiles Vernon to go »to the bar for another time« and, in his emotional fantasies, underestimate him (Frank). Frank shows himself to be a supporter of »stitching up Garmony« (*AM* 106). At the same time, he ensures Vernon that, to be more effective, he should keep away from him in the public scenes of *The Judge*: »He wanted to be of use, which was why it wouldn't be right for him to be openly identified as the editor's ally« (*AM* 106). Nevertheless, the pretentious nature of Frank's friendship is suggested by his inclination

---

In the same way, McEwan's narrator ascribes the same characteristics to Dibben from the communal perspective within the storyworld of *AM*.

81 His thoughts are not presented through internal focalisation or FIT modes but mostly through his direct speech and also through his actions.

to »look uninvolved, neutral.« That, nevertheless, does not raise Vernon's doubts. Instead, he confides to him everything related to Garmony's photographs wrongly perceiving that »the two passed an agreeable half-hour exploring a shared contempt« (*AM* 107) in that case.

Although the fictional minds in *AM* pursue a »shared« mind or thought, there is not any sustaining one within the storyworld. The central characters, particularly Clive and Vernon, are too much aspectual as at any chance they prefer their intramental persuasions to their »shared« thoughts. Following that, Vernon thinks he and Frank share the same »contempt« towards Garmony. Therefore, based on such a wrong perception, he shows the photographs to Frank and his convincing, although pretentious, comments guile him more:

> Frank gazed at each one at length, without comment, simply shaking his head. Then he put them back in the envelope and said quietly, »Incredible. The hypocrisy of the man.« They sat in thoughtful silence a moment, then he added, »You have to do it. You mustn't let them stop you. It'll wreck his chances for PM. It'll finish him completely. Vernon, I really want to help.« The support among the younger staff was never quite as identifiable as Frank had claimed. (*AM* 107)

His ability to deliver provocative comments, which match with Vernon's expectations, and his pretending postures, for example his »thoughtful silence,« cause Vernon to fantasize an intermental bond with him. Unlike Frank's expressions, he does not see any sign of »the younger staff« support in *The Judge*. Despite that, he continues counselling him in their serial rendezvous. The narrator's free indirect report, moreover, discloses Vernon's mental dispositions related to his dramatic, fantastic, and fanciful intermental relationship with Frank which, according to Vernon, is going to be of service to his »historical mission.« His subjectivity, furthermore, prefers Frank at this moment because, compared to the others, he can assist him to attain his goals. We are told that: »Most of all, Vernon had someone to talk to, someone who shared his sense of historical mission and excitement and instinctively understood the momentous nature of the affair, and who offered encouragement when everyone else was so critical« (*AM* 108). Vernon, however, suspects Frank's loyalty when it is too late. When they are in the lift before joining the last quick conference prior to the Friday edition, we are told that Vernon feels »obliged to conceal his terror and appear nonchalant« (*AM* 110). However, this sense of obligation, which mainly derives from his self-centeredness, persuades Vernon to grab any possible chance in order to realise his strongly intramental goals. For example, when Frank says that »If it's all right with you, I think I should hang back, not show my hand at this stage,« we are told in TR:

> Vernon felt a faint, brief inner disturbance, like the tightening of some neglected reflexive muscle. He was touched by curiosity as much as distrust, but it was too late to do anything now, so he said, ›Sure. I need you in place. The next few days could be crucial‹. (*AM* 110)

Vernon, nevertheless, unlike Clive, does not seem to be at war with himself. When he notices Frank's peeling away, he is no longer haunted with the implications of Frank's behaviour towards himself. Instead, he concentrates on his purpose and on the prospects of his present actions, as Clive does in similar situations:

> Now, as he paced toward room six, Vernon was himself again, large, benign, ruthless, and good. Where others would have felt a weight upon their shoulders, he felt an enabling lightness, or indeed a light, a glow, of competence and well-being, for his sure hands were about to cut away a cancer from the organs of the body politic; this was the image he intended to use in the leader that would follow Garmony's resignation. Hypocrisy would be exposed, the country would stay in Europe, capital punishment and compulsory conscription would remain a crank's dream, social welfare would survive in some form or other, the global environment would get a decent chance, and Vernon was on the point of breaking into song. He didn't, but the next two hours had all the brio of a light opera in which every aria was his, and in which a shifting chorus of mixed voices both praised him and harmoniously echoed his thoughts. (*AM* 111)

Although he pretends his actions to be for the sake of »country,« Vernon's subjectivity is primarily concerned with the relentless pursuing of his professional goals. As Vernon's deputy, Grant McDonald, points out, »Vernon's [opinions] made his case with a passion and a deadly journalistic instinct« (*AM* 114). His »passion« together with his »deadly journalistic instinct,« however, shows Vernon as a character lacking human sympathy. His entire embedded narratives, furthermore, show us that his approach, whether in his relationships or in his profession as a journalist, is more Darwinian rather than anthropomorphic. As focalized from his perspective, »in some respects journalism resembled science; the best ideas were the ones that survived and were strengthened by intelligent opposition.« This »fragile conceit« (*AM* 115), as the narrator calls it, points out the atrocity of Vernon's approach. For example, after seeing the famous front page of *The Judge* covered with Garmony's photograph in its Friday edition, the general view is that »this was work of the highest professional standards« (*AM* 116). Despite that, the action itself, regardless of its falsity or truth, is considered extremely harsh because it primarily followed to destroy Garmony's character not just as a politician but as a person. In this case, the narrator informs us about the adverse consequences of Vernon's harsh action as perceived by the social thought of the people in *The Judge*: »As one young journalist would remark to another later in the canteen, it was like seeing someone you know stripped in public and flogged. Unmasked and punished« (*AM* 116).

Clive's story of the row scene in the Lakeland pops up in Vernon's consciousness after his home editor, Jeremy Ball, informs him that »the Lakeland rapist had struck for a second time in a week and a man had been arrested last night« (*AM* 113). Vernon, however, does not pay attention to Jeremy's report about the news item in the same way his absentmindedness held him back from listening to Clive's Lakeland story. Nevertheless, Vernon, whose »instinct was unerring,« in his proper time is called back to the »Lakeland rapist« (*AM* 116, 113) by the help of what he calls his journalistic instinct. His struggles to remember some lost thought by putting the diffused pieces next to each other is given in the TR mode as following:

> The thought scrolled round and round in his mind, it went well, it went well. But there was something, something important, some new information he had been about to respond to, then he had been Cliverted, and then he had forgotten, it had flashed away from him in a swarm of other, similar items. It was a remark, a snippet that had surprised him at the time. He should have spoken up right then. (*AM* 116–117)

He is happy to be on the threshold of publishing Garmony's photographs. He, nevertheless, worries that some »Cliverted« thought is violating his already achieved happiness. Therefore, Vernon's mind is reported as transcending his skull through thinking about something mostly related to his profession. If he is reported as thinking about Clive and Molly every now and then, that is in fact because of their contribution to his goals or their standing for something Vernon takes to be useful for intramental intentions.

The strong aspectuality of the narrative is more obvious from the comments given by Julian Garmony's Wife, Rose Garmony, on the eve of the publication of Molly-Garmony photographs in *The Judge*. Garmony's party managers decide to use Mrs Garmony, an eminent surgeon, in order to prevent or at least discharge the socio-political effects of Vernon's would-be famous front page through arranging a live TV show. Following that, and while holding »Vernon's front page« up, Mrs Garmony pretends to know everything about her husband and Molly Lane who, according to her, »was simply a family friend« (*AM* 124). The reader knows that she tells lies since, regarding her husband, elsewhere she says, »he had pulled out all Molly Lane's letters, the ones that stupidly indulged his grotesque cravings. Thank God that episode was over, thank God the woman was dead« (*AM* 92). This TR also reveals Molly's power over Garmony as her letters are thought to be liberating for him. This reading is, moreover, closer to Clive's understanding of Molly-Garmony relationship. Clive thinks that Molly gave him what he could not find elsewhere. Furthermore, at the end of her collaboration in the party game, Mrs Garmony, addressing Vernon, says: »Mr Halliday, you have the mentality of a blackmailer, and the moral stature of the flea« (*AM* 125). As mentioned in Mrs Garmony's statement, Vernon is believed to be a »blackmailer« and a »flea« by his critics like Mrs Garmony and Paul Lanark. They imply the self-centred, egotistic and therefore intramental nature of his thoughts and actions. However, the main source of this divulging action, or as Vernon croaks while watching the show on TV, »spoiler« (*AM* 124)[82], is Frank to whom Vernon wrongly thought he could trust.

The communal views after Mrs Garmony's TV show and Vernon's famous front page indicate the central role of »self-advancement« in Vernon's actions. Further, Vernon's heavily aspectual judgment in the name of »public-interest« (*AM* 98) becomes more apparent as, after Mrs Garmony's show, a plethora of »remembered [. . .] misgivings« fills *The Judge* people. Nevertheless, regardless of the right perspective, it is Vernon who is punished by being sacked. A more comprehensive description of Vernon's intramental thought is given in one broadsheet by a leader:

> It seems to have escaped the attention of the editor of *The Judge* that the decade we live in now is not like the one before. Then, self-advancement was the watchword, while greed and hypocrisy were the rank realities. Now we live in a more reasonable, compassionate, and tolerant age in which the private and harmless preferences of individuals, however public they may be, remain their own business. Where there is no discernible issue of public interest, the old-fashioned arts of the blackmailer and self-righteous whistleblower have no place, and while this paper does not wish to impugn the moral sensitivities of the common flea. (*AM* 126)

Furthermore, Vernon's intramental re-examinations of the events leading to his forced resignation show the degree of his egotistic dependence on his own perspectives. After he is forced to resign and on the first morning of his »unemployment« (*AM* 145), he is reported as brooding on »all the indignities and ironies that had accumulated about his dismissal yesterday.« He broods about his colleagues in *The Judge* and its directors recollecting the way they asked him to resign and receive »remuneration« instead of being sacked (*AM* 145). He, furthermore, recollects that no one in his office »was popping in to express their outraged sympathy« (*AM* 146) while he was

82 Dominic Head establishes a relation between the idea of »spoiler« and »McEwan's satirical anatomy of the kind of self-contained professionalism that kills off the ethical sense.« He, moreover, argues that each of the two friends »encounters an ethical dilemma that reveals how morality has been displaced by self-interest in the world of the contemporary professional« (»*On Chesil Beach*« 117).

leaving the office. Nonetheless, Clive's short letter recounted in the narrator's TR, »his mental odometer tallied the insults and humiliations« is more excruciating than his friend's »insults«:

> [1] Not enough that Frank Dibben was treacherous, that all his colleagues deserted him, that every newspaper was cheering his dismissal; [2] not enough that the whole country celebrated the crushing of the flea and that Garmony was still at large. [3] Lying on the bed beside him was a venomous little card gloating over his downfall, written by his oldest friend, written by a man so morally eminent he would rather see a woman raped in front of him than have his work disrupted. [4] Perfectly hateful, and mad. Vindictive. So it was war. Right, then. Here we go, don't hesitate. (*AM* 147)

Reported in FIT mode [1, 2 and 4], Vernon broods on Frank's treacherous action and his own trust in him [1]. For the first time, he gets to know that he was the person who betrayed Vernon's plans about the front page bringing him finally to his resignation. Likewise, he also re-experiences the manner *The Judge* officials and colleagues insulted and humiliated him. Vernon, moreover, is angry that while he is sacked for publishing Garmony's photographs, which he pretends to be only for the sake of public interest, Garmony himself is »at large« [2]. It is discomforting for Vernon to find himself unable to fulfil his dreams. Nevertheless, neither the colleagues' as well as the officials' actions in *The Judge* nor Garmony's situation after the publication of his transvestite photographs with Molly does annoy Vernon as does his oldest friend's letter [3]. The writer of the letter makes him more angry than the content of the letter that Vernon takes to be »gloating over his downfall.« Vernon's ironical judgment considering his friend as a »morally eminent« person refers to Clive's decision in the rocks about not entering into the row scene. Following that, his thought attributions to Clive, cued by the previous events between them, take Vernon to his deadly decision about his friend. Accordingly, he finds Clive »hateful,« [4] a mad person who does not understand what he is doing. In the same way, Clive, after his too long brooding, finds Vernon »loathsome« (*AM* 137, 141). He attributes madness to him when he finds him voraciously pursuing Garmony's case. Furthermore, Vernon views Clive's letter to him as a sign of his friend's indictment. Vernon's attribution is, however, based on his wrong perception that Clive's letter to him refers to their last confrontation when he asked him either he should go to the police and inform them about his Lakeland experience or he himself would inform them about it asking them to go to Clive. Vernon, therefore, interprets Clive's letter to him as his »revenge« against his previous threat. Accordingly, these mental calculations bring Vernon to an understanding that he is in a »war« with his friend. This revelation is a turning point in their friendship although here from Vernon's perspective, as it was the same for Clive after Vernon's last call. Even though Vernon, after his investigations, comes to understanding that Clive did not break the law by his non-involvement in the Lake District row, we are told that he »was still back with his thoughts, still not satisfied. It turned out that Clive had not broken the law. He would be inconvenienced into doing his duty, nothing more than that. But there had to be more. There had to be consequences« (*AM* 147). What makes him sure about the necessary »consequences« of his friend's action is fundamentally his intramental interpretations of the event. Nothing other than the deadly consequences, about which is concerned with, can console him.

Therefore, reviewing the Friday issue of *The Judge*, Vernon once more comes across with the news related to the »medical scandal in Holland[83]« (*AM* 149) which coveys the legal way people can get rid of their old relatives by paying some money. Vernon had promised Clive, after his morbid thoughts triggered by the pain in his left hand, to help him die soon in case of any disease like Molly's. His only condition was that Clive should also do the same for him if necessary because »he had been afflicted by a numbness of the scalp and a sense of not existing that had provoked in him fears of madness and death. Molly's funeral had given him the jitters« (*AM* 101). Likewise, Clive ponders over his own contract with Vernon while reading

83 According to Dana Catrinescu, »the references to the new medical practices accepted in Holland are to be seen as a *mise en abyme*, an anticipation of what is going to happen in the capital of the newly legalized euthanasia, Amsterdam.« Moreover, according to Ingersoll, »Clive's effort to finish the »millennial symphony« provides something of a *mise en abyme* effect for this novel, as his musical composition stands in for the narrative working toward its ending« (»City of Endings« 128).

the same Holland story in Friday's *Judge*. The mutual contract, however, after their last conversation and Clive's ensuing letter to Vernon, becomes merely a pretext for both sides in order to advance their mutually invisible plots. Vernon, nevertheless, attributes all reasons of his present »disgrace« to Clive:

> his thoughts kept returning to that hateful postcard, the twisting knife, the salt in his lacerations, and as the day passed it came to stand for all the major and minor insults of the past twenty-four hours. That little message to him from Clive embodied and condensed all the poison of this affair, the blindness of his accusers, their hypocrisy, their vengefulness, and above all the element that Vernon considered to be the worst of human vices, personal betrayal. (*AM* 148)

Vernon is too much absorbed in Clive's letter, as shown in the above passage in TR mode, to think rationally or at least impartially taking into consideration the other possibilities as well. The more Vernon thinks, the more Clive stands for all the »insults« and humiliations he has had after his forced resignation. He equates his old friend with his enemies accusing him of being hypocrital, vengeful and above all, of betraying him.

His desire for revenge motivates Vernon to devise a plan. He pretends to be only following the promise he gave to Clive while accepting his request in order to help him die soon and easy in case of being afflicted by an immedicable disease. Accordingly, Vernon thinks it is both possible to remain loyal to his commitments in the contract and, at the same time, take his revenge by clinging to the Dutch story. His overwhelming sense of vengefulness swamps his ability to make moral judgements. He invites himself to Amsterdam, which he thinks is the only way for him to reach his goals. The narrator's TR of Vernon's disillusionment is revealing in this case: »contemplating the wreck of his prospects, and wondering whether he should ring Clive and pretend to make peace, in order to invite himself to Amsterdam« (*AM* 149). In his »post-mortem« (*AM* 171) state after their mutual poisoning, Vernon is haunted by his experiences in *The Judge*. He still adores himself: »As he settled, he had an image of himself as a massive statue dominating the lobby of Judge House, a great reclining figure hewn from granite: Vernon Halliday, man of action, editor« (*AM* 170). In his hallucinatory state, he dreams about the morning meeting in *The Judge*. He sees both Frank and Molly Lane there:

> They were all here. Frank Dibben, and standing next to him pleasant surprise-Molly Lane. It was a matter of principle with Vernon not to confuse his personal and professional lives, so he gave her no more than a business-like nod. Beautiful woman, though. Smart idea of hers, to go blond. And smart idea of his to take her on. (*AM* 171)

Nevertheless, unlike his perceptions, Vernon's thoughts and actions are represented in the narrative as all belonging to his professional life. He imagines Frank in a relationship with Molly. She is using her personal influence on Vernon in order to help her lover's, Frank's, promotion:

> It was a matter of some disappointment to Vernon that Molly should approach now to plead Dibben's case. But of course! Molly and Frank. He should have guessed. She was plucking at Vernon's shirtsleeve, she was using her personal connection with the editor to promote the interests of her current lover. [. . .] She truly was a beautiful woman, and he had never been able to resist her, not since she had taught him how to roast porcini. (*AM* 172)

Despite that, Vernon, unlike Clive, at last knows the real story that he has been poisoned: »he had just begun to grasp, though feebly, where he really was and what must have been in his champagne and who these visitors were. But he did interrupt his speech and fall silent for a while, and then at last murmured reverentially, ›It's a spoiler!‹« (*AM* 173). The two friends, however, do not hallucinate, let alone think, about each other in their premortem states. Therefore, their doubly embedded narratives do not continue after their separation for the last time before going into their rooms with the exception that there is a slight reference to Clive in Vernon's last murmuring, »It's a spoiler.«

The frame narrative conclusion as whole »comes to a satisfying conclusion, the two compromised friends punished for their hubris and greed« (Malcolm, 2002: 191). Nevertheless, the narrative, according to Malcolm, does not clarify that »the good are rewarded in *Amsterdam*, because there are no good. [. . .] The world of the great and the good is a foul place in

Amsterdam« (195). Moreover, their deaths at the end of the narrative, according to Ingersoll, are the »logical outcomes of the death having taken place before this novel begins« (»City of Endings« 125).

Finally, according to Stolorow and Atwood, »There is no such thing as a person but only a person in relation to other persons« (qtd. in Segalla 147). Therefore, as it is in the field of intersubjectivity, the characters' embedded narratives within *AM* storyworld are interpenetrated. Because of that, even Clive's absorption in his music and Vernon's immersion in his editorship cannot make them free from the others. In other words, it is possible to say that since they cannot be self-sufficient, they are unable to achieve a balance, in terms of their mental functioning, in the absence of the others too. Their existence, therefore, is a relational subjectivity that depends heavily on the other selves within the storyworld. Thus, the Other becomes the central focus of the narrative. That is why when we are, for example, presented Vernon's narrative, at the same time we are presented Clive's narrative too. In other words, presentation of Vernon's thoughts and actions or his mental functioning are basically concerned with Clive's recollections, reflections, evaluations, assessments, plans, judgments etc. Likewise, Clive's narratives, if emptied from the parts related to Vernon, would be an illogical mass of some event sequences or thoughts and perceptions. His actions and thoughts become meaningful in relation to Vernon although this mutual need does not mean that they necessarily think and act like each other. Their intermentality is not as much as their intersubjectivity. Instead, their narratives are strongly doubly embedded ones while in terms of the manner or function of their thoughts they are intramental fictional minds pursuing fundamentally their aspectual interpretation of the narrative events and situations. It is, accordingly, such alternative approaches to some strongly humane concepts such as morality or moral duty, public or social interest vs. personal one and revenge that gradually widen the imbalance, firstly begun with a slight confrontation between the two old friends, into a fatal one. Therefore, the cognitive activities of the focal fictional minds together with the representation of the way they experience some particular moments within the storyworlds are the fundamental aspects of *AM* narrative. It primarily represents Clive's and Vernon's minds in action throughout the narrative. This is in congruent with Palmer's and Herman's argument according to which the presentation of the function of fictional minds as well as the way they undergo experiences within the storyworlds should be considered as the primary function of narrative.

Palmer argues that presentation of fictional minds should be considered as the primary function of narrative and according to Herman representation of what it's like or qualia aspect of narrative is the most contributing basic element to the narrativity of a narrative. Regarding their discussion, *AM* is a good example in the presentation of the fictional minds' cognitive activities and also what it's like for them to undergo some experiences. That is so because, representing the breakdown process of an intimate friendship between the two close friends, the entire narrative portrays their intramental experiences. The narrative reader also, using his/her natural cognitive frames, shares those experiences. Accordingly, the chapter attempted to examine Clive' and Vernon's incipient intermental mind, their ensuing intramental dissents and their private mental functioning. According to the above discussion, it is possible to say that *AM* narrative represents the outcome of acting merely based on intramental perceptions regardless of the perspectives of the other(s). Clive and Vernon are fundamentally absorbed in their own professions in a way that from their perspectives nothing other than their own purpose deserves attention. Molly's death foregrounds such latent intramental propensities and desires. Being unaware of the impact of their actions on the lives of the others, Clive and Vernon consider their individual aspectuality as their only moral duty. Nevertheless, their mutual egocentric thoughts, that incite their actions, bring about the deadly imbalance to their both private and public selves. Internally and externally, they give themselves totally to the intramental thoughts, which give rise both to their own destruction and to the breakdown of their friendship. In other words, due to the disruption in the usually balanced relation between intermental thoughts and intramental ones, Clive and Vernon not only lose their friendship but also they lose their own lives too. Moreover, *AM* represents the moment by moment mental functioning of the two experiencing minds in terms of the significant events that occur both between them and to them individually. For example, Clive's inability to complete the millennium symphony notes, his indeterminacy to save the woman in danger in the rocks, Vernon's decisiveness to stain Garmony permanently and their determination to seek revenge on each other are represented minutely in order to delineate the processes through which their deadly imtramental dissents pass. Accordingly, *AM* not only presents the cognitive activities of the fictional minds as its core but also it displays what it's like for Clive and Vernon to break their intermental minds and change into enemies.

4. *Atonement*

4.1 An Intramental Thought against Intermental Minds: *AT*

> [McEwan in *Atonement*] wields a prose so clear and straightforward it seems almost invisible, but it's always alive with the thoughts of the characters, as if it were a transparent medium into other minds. He makes such writing look simple but nobody else can do it so well. (David Sexton, qtd. in Albers and Caeners 707)

AT is a narrative primarily about atonement itself. It represents the terrible impact of a total misreading on some fictional minds. Briony Tallis, the protagonist in the first part, commits a dire mistake when she misunderstands the relationship between her sister Cecilia and Robbie Turner. Made up of four parts, the whole narrative is focalised through the perspective of a first person narrator who is the writer of the narrative as well. Through writing, she intends to reconstruct her unavoidable experiences of a fatal misreading in the past so that she might find atonement for her drastic crime then. She thinks that her life-long experience in writing has enabled her to overcome her own egocentrism and gain a strong power of sympathy. As a result, as she perceives, her mental capacity for intermentality enables her to imagine or understand the disruptive impact of her thoughts and actions on the intermental bond between Cecilia and Robbie. Briony-the-author's fictional rearrangement of the real events in the storyworld, in other words, shows her own cognitive development. This derives from the fact that through her fictional or imaginary confession and through narrating the events from different perspectives, she is at least able to evaluate the terrible consequences of her past thoughts and actions.

The narrative situation in *AT* is more similar to *CB* rather than *AM*. In both narratives, the intramentality finally grows into intermentality through time and experience. Writing, or the ability to imagine some (although fictional) people's thoughts, perceptions, perspectives, (re)actions, and even the impact of some external events and situations on the manner of their thinking, enables the character-narrator-author Briony to restore (yet fictionally) some historical situations and, through (re)arranging them, (re)build the already disrupted intermental bond. In other words, construction of a permanent intermental thought between Cecilia and Robbie is represented as the central yearning in *AT* and the narrative is quite successful at doing so. The conflict between intermental thought and intramental one, furthermore, is similarly the main narrative concern both in *AM* and *CB*. Similar to the case in *AT*, in both narratives intramental thought is destructively dominant. While in *AM* Clive's and Vernon's egocentrism not only destroys their old friendship but also it finally brings about their mutual murder, in *CB* intramentality breaks up the newly constructed intermental bond between Edward and Florence. The only difference is the fact that in *CB*, through time and experience, Edward's re-evaluations of the events leading to their break up on their wedding night finally inflames her mind and thoughts with a feeling of regret which can be read as n increasing tendency on his side towards intermentality. Therefore, it is arguable that intramentality in *AT* is portrayed as belonged to the adolescence period when a growing desire to (re)arrange the world based on one's own order appears.

The significance of Briony's misreading and its destructive impact on the lives of Cecilia and Briony have been the subject of some critical analyses. According to Martin Jacobi, misreading acts in two different levels in *AT*: »the author not only dramatizes misreading and implicitly warns readers against misreading, but also induces his readers into misreading« (55). In other words, while the narrative primarily represents the effects of Briony's misreading on the intermental bond between Robbie and Cecilia, its structure imposes another kind of misreading on the reader. Through the last part, the author shows how, unlike her interpretation of the narrative events and situations in the previous parts, the reader herself has experienced a similar kind of misreading. In other words, »the misreading that causes readers to desire the lovers' deaths is generically the same as the misreading of the novel's narrator, Briony Tallis, which led her to act so as to bring about the lovers' suffering« (56). Furthermore, Peter Mathews sees a connection between Briony's misreading and the implications of the secrets she perceives around. When she finds herself unable to understand them, she finds them signs of hidden »guilt,« »But Briony's—and later, the reader's—faulty interpretation of the situation is based on a misreading of the rhetorical surface of things, the falsely symmetrical assumption that concealment equates with guilt and transparency with integrity« (»The Impression« 151).

The first and the last parts of *AT* shows the two opposing aspects of Briony's character. While in the first part the omniscient narrator, through focalising the narrative from the young Briony's perspective, represents the manner a thirteen-year-old young adolescent's mind fictionalises the real events and situations by relying on her intramental perceptions only, the first person narrator in the last part of the narrative illustrates how, through time and experience, she has learned to sympathise with the other people and hence build, although fictionally, an intermental bond with them. The whole narrative, therefore, can be read as a representation of an arduous process through which the narrator replaces the dominance of intramental thinking mode with that of the intermental one. This is, however, only a fictional account, or narrativisation, of a totally different story once happened in the storyworld. The whole narrative structure and content, thus, imply the absolute dominance of the intramental aspect of mind. This chapter, therefore, analyses the first part of *AT* narrative in order to examine closely the manner of Briony's, Cecilia's, Robbie's and Emily's minds before the misreading moment. The chapter mainly tries to show how the conflict between the two opposing modes of mental functioning finally ends with the ever-increasing dominance of the intramental aspect of thought. In other words, the chapter primarily analyses the conflict between the thirteen-year-old adolescent character's, Briony's, mode of mental functioning and that of the newly constructed intermental bond between Cecilia and Robbie. Besides that, the chapter also analyses the function of Lola's impact on Briony as well as the content of Emily's consciousness indicating how her mind is embodied as the only social mind which brings together all the other separate minds within the narrative. Similar to the situation in *AM* and *CB*, McEwan in *AT* displays how the intramental mode of thinking is potential to bring about an irrecoverable situation.

The first part of *AT* is a pure consciousness narrative. Condensation is the dominant characteristic of the narrative plot in this part. *AT* should also be considered as a narrative with a high level of narrativity, because it combines both Palmer's and Herman's concerns together. It demonstrates the way narrative plot is boosted by the conflict between intramental (Briony's mind) and intermental (Cecilia's and Robbie's minds) thoughts. Besides that, it closely presents what Herman describes as the »pressure of events« on the central »consciousnesses affected by the occurrences at issue« (*Basic* 137). It is written in the style of literary modernists as, in its form and structure, it is closer to Virginia Woolf's definition of novel. Criticising the so-called materialists, Woolf in her famous essay, »Modern Fiction« (1919), argues that the consciousness representation should be the main concern of the (modern) narrative where »The mind receives a myriad impressions — trivial, fantastic, evanescent, or engraved with the sharpness of steel. From all sides they come, an incessant shower of innumerable atoms. [. . .] life is a luminous halo, a semi-transparent envelope surrounding us from the beginning of consciousness to the end« (160). Likewise, through enlarging the eventful moments of about a single day, McEwan in the first part of *AT* registers the impact of »impressions« on the mental functioning of the central characters, particularly on the transforming mind of Briony. Doing so, he portrays the way their thinking modes (re)act against the external events and situations.

The first part of *AT* is made up of fourteen short chapters where FIT is the dominant narrating mode. The omniscient narrator focalises most of the fourteen chapters intermittently from the perspectives of Briony (Chapters One, Three, Seven, Ten and Thirteen), Cecilia (Chapters Two and Nine), Robbie (Chapter Eight) and Emily (Chapters Six and Twelve). In the remaining chapters, it is the manipulative function of the narrator that mostly combines the various perspectives revealing the ongoing conflict between the diverging thoughts (Briony's) and the converging ones (Cecilia's and Robbie's). In other words, the omniscient narrator presents a detailed report of the central characters' flow of consciounesses revealing both how they are diverging from each other (intramentality), and how the manner of their mental functioning is affected by the thoughts and actions of each other. The central concern of the narrative plot, thus, is a representation of the two opposing modes of thoughts. While Briony tries to rearrange the world around herself based on her own imaginary understanding of order, Cecilia, relying on the external realities, applies herself to understanding the real order. Their opposing evaluations mostly derive from two different modes of thinking. The narrative, however, puts forward how intramentality or subjective-first side of mind finally overthrows the intermentality or intersubjective first side of that. It does so through representing the impact of external events and situations on the mental functioning of the characters. As a result, the three remaining parts of the narrative and the focal character's/author's whole writing project is an attempt to find atonement. Through (re)writing what once happened, and how it affected her sister's and Robbie's lives, Briony-the-author endeavours to restore the disrupted intermental bond between them. One level beyond the fictional world, it is the (implied) author himself who manipulates all this process possibly to suggest that without a strong feeling of sympathy (intermentality) and an intentional effort to evaluate the impact of one's thoughts and actions on the lives of the others, any person's intramental thoughts and perceptions have potential to bring about the disruptive consequences. Besides that, as it is implied in the whole narrative structure, intermentality is a learnable character trait which can be acquired through time and experience. In addition, compared to the destructive aspect of intramentality, intermental thought is constructive as it is in harmony with the related context.

The dominance of interamental mode of mental functioning in the first part is obvious from Emily Tallis's mental functioning which reveals the centrifugal nature of fictional minds. In other words, Briony's pronounced tendency towards intramental thought and the undercurrent clash between the two modes of mental functioning is primarily revealed through Emily's social mind. It is through her mind that we are shown the true state of the other fictional minds in the Tallis house. Her contemplations not only reveal the grave concerns of a mother about her children and her husband, but also they shed light on the state of both her sister's children and Robbie. She even evaluates Cecilia's marriage to Paul. Although she cannot do anything for them, she is the only fictional mind that understands the other characters' states. This capacity enables her to sympathise with her husband and children. Her mind, therefore, is characterised as functioning mainly based on the other characters' actions. Her migraine pain allows her to focus more closely on both the on-going issues at the house and the past and future issues as well. It also provides us with her »memories, judgments, vague resolutions, questions—uncoiled quietly before her« (*AT* 143). Affected by the pain, she »lay in the dark and knew everything. The less she was able to do, the more she was aware« (*AT* 63). In other words, she »beamed her raw attention into every recess of the house« (*AT* 66). Her mind is the only social mind in the narrative because, as we are told, her:

> Habitual fretting about her children, her husband, her sister, the help, had rubbed her senses raw; migraine, mother love and, over the years, many hours of lying still on her bed, had distilled from this sensitivity a sixth sense, a tentacular awareness that reached out from the dimness and moved through the house, unseen and all-knowing. Only the truth came back to her, for what she knew, she knew. (*AT* 63)

Despite her worries about her children and despite her awareness about the nature of her relationship with her husband, her mind mainly functions based on a realistic evaluative system. For example, she does not expand her worries into future, »She could send her tendrils into every room of the house, but she could not send them into the future. She also knew that, ultimately, it was her own peace of mind she strove for; self-interest and kindness were best not separated« (*AT* 67).

Her reflection on her daughters shows the degree she is aware of the increasingly diverging thoughts of Cecilia and Briony, »Cecilia was not inclined to help [. . .] Briony expecting too much, and no one, especially the cousins, able to measure up to her frenetic vision« (*AT* 20). She is in fact worried about her daughters. She knows that the situation is also caused by her failure in doing her responsibilities as »Illness had stopped her giving her children all a mother should « and »Sensing this, they had always called her by her first name« (*AT* 62–63). In other words, she partly finds herself responsible for the nature of her daughters' relationship, »Cecilia should lend a hand, but she was too wrapped up in herself, too much the intellectual to bother with children« (*AT* 63). Understanding her, she worries about Briony's situation despite the fact that she knows she cannot do anything about it. Accordingly, she is able to read Briony's mind from her moody and mysterious behaviour:

> She had vanished into an intact inner world of which the writing was no more than the visible surface, the protective crust which even, or especially, a loving mother could not penetrate. Her daughter was always off and away in her mind, grappling with some unspoken, self-imposed problem, as though the weary, self-evident world could be reinvented by a child. (*AT* 65)

Upon following Briony's changing behaviour, Emily could notice her »improper« behaviour with Robbie at the table, »Briony had been thoroughly improper at dinner to speak that way to Robbie. If she had resentments of her own, Emily sympathized. It was to be expected. But to express them was undignified« (*AT* 142). Unlike the reader, she does not know anything about Briony's reasons—reading the content of Robbie's letter to Cecilia, observing from the window what happened between him and Cecilia near the fountain and finding them naked in each other's arms in the library. Still she is aware of the impact of Briony's failure in the performance of her play, »the collapse of the play was a terrible blow and the child would need all the comfort a mother could give« (*AT* 6). Her worry in this case is driven by her own experience with her sister Hermione. She is basically concerned about the impact of Lola on her »Poor darling Briony, the softest little thing« who cares too much about her cousins but »how to protect her against failure, against that Lola, the incarnation of Emily's youngest sister who had been just as precocious and scheming at that age, and who had recently plotted her way out of a marriage, into what she wanted everyone to call a nervous breakdown« (*AT* 62). Despite the fact that Emily's egotistic »feeling of resentment« towards Lola and her negative impact on Briony are nourished by »an old antagonism,« she tries to control such feeling or at least avoid imposing its impact on her evaluation of Lola, »The more she felt it, the more she fussed over Lola to hide it« (*AT* 137). Such a sympathetic evaluation is the general tendency of her mental functioning.

Similar to her sympathetic evaluation of Briony and Lola, Emily also sympathises with her husband Jack. Her evaluation of the reasons of his long absence from the house and the secret life he pursues in London shows the degree she can sympathise with other perspectives. Having perceived the true nature of the issues, she feels that »She did not wish to know why Jack spent so many consecutive nights in London. Or rather, she did not wish to be told« (*AT* 140). This is the main difference of her mental functioning from that of Briony:

> [1] she knew he [her husband] did not sleep at his club, and he knew that she knew this. But there was nothing to say. Or rather, there was too much. They resembled each other in their dread of conflict, and the regularity of his evening calls, however much she disbelieved them, was a comfort to them both. [2] If this sham was conventional hypocrisy, she had to concede that it had its uses. [. . .] Even being lied to constantly, though hardly like love, was sustained attention; he must care about her to fabricate so elaborately and over such a long stretch of time. His deceit was a form of tribute to the importance of their marriage. (*AT* 139).

Emily is able to imagine the way she appears in her husband's mind and hence she finds the shared points between themselves [1]. Such a constructive manner of mental functioning helps her to interpret her husband's »deceit« as a »tribute« to their marriage [2]. Furthermore, she remembers a time when a science professor told her that the reason insects are drawn towards light is »the visual impression of an even deeper darkness beyond the light. Even though they might be eaten, they had to obey the instinct that made them seek out the darkest place, on the far side of the light—and in this case it was an illusion.« Still professor's explanation seems to her »like sophistry, or an explanation for its own sake. How could anyone presume to know the world through the eyes of an insect? Not everything had a cause, and pretending otherwise was an interference in the workings of the world that was futile, and could even lead to grief. Some things were simply so« (*AT* 140). It is based on such a philosophy that her mind basically functions with. Unlike Briony, she does not want to change the existing order of the things through imposing her intramental perceptions on them.

Emily's social mind also evaluates Robbie. Her thoughts about him reveals both the reasons her husband likes to support Robbie and the reasons she does not agree with him although she likes him as well. Such a disagreement, however, does not end in a negative emotion about Robbie. This is mainly because of the fact that she is able to go over the issue from her husband's perspective. In other words, she can imagine what it is like (called quails) to Jack to support Robbie:

> She thought of Robbie at dinner when there had been something manic and glazed in his look. [. . .] But really, he was a hobby of Jack's, living proof of some leveling principle he had pursued through the years. When he spoke about Robbie, which wasn't often, it was with a touch of self-righteous vindication. (*AT* 142)

She even critically evaluates her own disposition towards her husband's material support for Robbie, »Something had been established which Emily took to be a criticism of herself. She had opposed Jack when he proposed paying for the boy's education, which smacked of meddling to her, and unfair on Leon and the girls« (*AT* 142).

Having rightly identified Cecilia's introvert behaviour, Emily also evaluates the possibility of Cecilia's and Paul Marshall's marriage, »Thinking of the dinner again—how artfully Mr. Marshall had put everyone at ease. Was he suitable? It was a pity about his looks, with one half of his face looking like an overfurnished« (*AT* 142). This possibility provides her with an excuse to critically evaluate Cecilia's perspective about marriage. She thinks that her education has affected her character negatively in a way that she cannot identify what is good for her future. Unlike her, she regards Paul as an appropriate husband for Cecilia because his chocolate business heralds a life of »comfort« and »untroubled years« to come:

> If he really were to supply the whole of the British Army with Amo bars he could become immensely rich. But Cecilia, having learned modern forms of snobbery at Cambridge, considered a man with a degree in chemistry incomplete as a human being. Her very words. She had lolled about for three years at Girton with the kind of books she could equally have read at home—Jane Austen, Dickens, Conrad, all in the library downstairs, in complete sets. How had that pursuit, reading the novels that others took as their leisure, let her think she was superior to anyone else? Even a chemist had his uses. (*AT* 143)

Emily's mental functioning, therefore, provides the reader with a vital piece of information about the deep layer of the Tallis House. It is through her migraine-affected mind that, more realistically, we learn about her isolated husband Jack, Briony's delicate situation and Lola's negative impact on her,

Cecilia's change, Robbie's situation and her dreams about Paul Marshall. Emily's mind displays the fact that all characters in Tallis house are disconnected from each other and, therefore, the whole narrative plot can be read as the representation of intermental breakdown.

4.2 Briony Tallis's Intramental Mind and the Order of the Real World

Representation of the flow of Briony's consciousness and the dominant manner of her mental functioning lie at the central concern of the narrative plot in the first part of *AT*. Most of the narrative events and situations in this part is mostly done from her perspective which is afflicted with »vile excitement« (*AT* 162). Of fifteen chapters, five chapters are completely focalised through her mind. Besides that, her perceptions and actions influence the narrative events in the remaining chapters. From the immediate flow of her consciousness, we are able to trace the process through which her mind is experiencing growing out of the childhood fancies into an assertive adolescent self. The former is represented as functioning based on a metaphysical order and power while in the latter a desire for the proclamation of an emerging independent self is dominant. Both thinking modes, however, are in a contradiction with the realities of the storyworld. In both cases, it is Briony's continuously active mind that desires to (re)create the imagined or intended reality. In other words, her mind basically functions with an intramental perception of order. Or as Peter Mathews says, »All of Briony's passions—her storytelling, her love of secrets, her penchant for miniaturisation—stem from an obsession with order« (»The Impression« 148). The fabricated reality, however, is the main source of narrative conflict and purpose. It is also a sign of intramentality itself, since it acts as the source of disequilibrium in the narrative. Therefore, it is arguable that through placing such destructive thoughts, which are disconnected from the outside realities, in the childhood period or in the period when there is not enough experience gained by self-consciousness, McEwan's narrative implies that intermentality belongs to the domain of the adults. In other words, learned by experience, it is just a matter of trial and error. Briony-the-author finally obtains it after nearly five decades of mental (re)constructions of the destructive event she caused to happen when she was thirteen.

Briony is symbolised as a reflective character from the very beginning or, as Jacobi says, »the implied author wants us to think of Briony as callow, self-absorbed, and so forth« (58). Her reflections, however, are mostly dependant on her own personal evaluations of the outside realities. She is a promising writer with an overactive mind which functions not based on what exists but mostly based on what should exist. When she gives the final draft of her first drama, *The Trials of Arabella*, to her mother to read and evaluate, we are presented the way she reads her mother's reaction to the play: »Briony studied her mother's face for every trace of shifting emotion« (*AT* 4). Likewise, the more we go on towards her close examination of Cecilia-Robbie case, the more we see how, in her evaluations of the other people's emotions, thoughts, intentions and actions, she tends to colour the reality by her »yearning fantasies« (*AT* 4). Doing so, she desires to impose her own »order« on her surroundings. Writing helps her to rearrange what seems to her unpleasant in the real world. It is the only realm that satisfies her:

> She sensed now how this might be achieved, through desire alone; the world she ran through loved her and would give her what she wanted and would let it happen. And then, when it did, she would describe it. Wasn't writing a kind of soaring, an achievable form of flight, of fancy, of the imagination? (*AT* 147)

Accordingly, through rearranging the actual world, she introduces a world of her own. We are told that unlike her sister, »She was one of those children possessed by a desire to have the world just so« (*AT* 4). Such a desire derives from her »orderly spirit« as well as her »passion for secrets« (*AT* 5). Writing helps her to satisfy such desires since it involves both secrecy and the pleasures of miniaturization. Her everyday life, however, does not provide her with secrets: »she had no secrets. Her wish for a harmonious, organized world denied her the reckless possibilities of wrongdoing. Mayhem and destruction were too chaotic for her tastes, and she did not have it in her to be cruel« (*AT* 5).

Involvement with fiction, appropriately, acts as a »transition« (*AT* 7) to Briony as it does so to the reader at the beginning of reading experience. It helps Briony to fulfil her psychological needs. In other words, Brinoy-the-writer is aware of the fact that »the imagination itself was a source of secrets:

once she had begun a story, no one could be told. Pretending in words was too tentative, too vulnerable, too embarrassing to let anyone know« (*AT* 6). In the first pages of the narrative, she is presented as showing a passionate yearning for the power writing gives her through enabling her to communicate her own intentions in the form of fiction: »she felt foolish, appearing to know about the emotions of an imaginary being. Self-exposure was inevitable the moment she described a character's weakness; the reader was bound to speculate that she was describing herself. What other authority could she have?« (*AT* 6) Her tendency to the fictional constructions, moreover, is self-contained. In other words, not relying on the positive appreciation of the others, it derives from an inner motivation. While reading her works to her family, although she »unapologetically demand[ed] her family's total attention as she cast her narrative spell,« we are told that »Even without their attention and praise and obvious pleasure, Briony could not have been held back from her writing« (*AT* 6–7). Her last work, *The Trials of Arabella*, takes her one step more into the fictional world since it changes her understanding of the storytelling since, through FID mode, it enables her to report the characters' emotions directly to the reader.

Likewise, it is mainly because of satisfying her literary mind that Briony welcomes her cousins Lola, Jackson and Pierrot. When she welcomes them, we are told that, she had a »highly focused artistic ambition« (*AT* 9). Her piles of »ambitions« are, however, repudiated by the external world. It is such a disappointment that gradually drives her into a contradiction with the adult world order. From the very beginning, it is implied that there is an ever increasing rift between her perceptions and those of the adults represented by her parents, sister, brother and Robbie. When she prepares her cousins for the performance of her play, her mother and sister laugh at her planned thought: »Immediately, her mother and sister were there to interpose a blander timetable« (*AT* 9). Briony's involvement in the fictional world, however, enables her to fictionalize their minds. As a result, she tends to impose her own intentions on the others' minds as she advances her desire based on the external facts.

In their rehearsal, Briony unavoidably tries to converge the order of her fictional world fully with that of the actual one. Like a director, she is evaluating the overlapping aspects between the characters of her play and the role actors. Her evaluation manifests itself as tending towards fictionalising or storying the actual world:

> On the face of it, Arabella, whose hair was as dark as Briony's, was unlikely to be descended from freckled parents, or elope with a foreign freckled count, rent a garret room from a freckled innkeeper, lose her heart to a freckled prince and be married by a freckled vicar before a freckled congregation. But all this was to be so. Her cousins' coloring was too vivid—virtually fluorescent!—to be concealed. The best that could be said was that Arabella's *lack* of freckles was the sign—the hieroglyph, Briony might have written—of her distinction. Her purity of spirit would never be in doubt, though she moved through a blemished world. There was a further problem with the twins, who could not be told apart by a stranger. Was it right that the wicked count should so completely resemble the handsome prince, or that both should resemble Arabella's father *and* the vicar? What if Lola were cast as the prince? (*AT* 10)

Such a mental functioning, therefore, derives from both her early adolescent mind which mainly enjoys fantasy and her authorship. When Pierrot expresses his unwillingness to act in the play by saying »It's just showing off,« Brinoy finds his statement as »self-evident truth.« Her internal evaluation of the statement, rendered to us through FIT mode, shows the degree she enjoys fictional world, »This was precisely why she loved plays, or hers at least; everyone would adore her. [. . .] she knew they could never understand her ambition« (*AT* 11). The external world's unwillingness to succumb to her ambition, however, adds o her »unprovable suspicions« (*AT* 32). As a reaction, she tries to fill in the distance between what she thinks should be and what really exists in the real world.

Briony is experiencing some cognitive transformation. Her ontological concerns reveal her obsessive desire to express her emerging self (pp. 33–35). She wants to »find the secret of herself, that part of her that was really in charge« (*AT* 33). Beyond that, she wonders whether the other people, including her sister and father, do have thoughts and feelings as well. This part of her reflection reveals the low state of her theory of mind or her ability to imagine the other people's mental states:

> If the answer was yes, then the world, the social world, was unbearably complicated, with two billion voices, and everyone's thoughts striving in equal importance and everyone's claim on life as intense, and everyone thinking they were unique, when no one was. One could drown in irrelevance. But if the answer was no, then Briony was surrounded by machines, intelligent and pleasant enough on the outside, but lacking the bright and private *inside* feeling she had. This was sinister and lonely, as well as unlikely. For, though it offended her sense of order, she knew it was overwhelmingly probable that everyone else had thoughts like hers. She knew this, but only in a rather arid way; she didn't really feel it. (*AT* 34)

Concurrent with her physical development, Briony's perceptions change as well as the new stage of her authorship influences the manner of her mental functioning. The potentiality of her play in representation and the way her cousins disappoint her about acting it, help her to begin writing in a new genre, fiction or novel. It helps her to explore the relationship between the fictional world and the real one. For the first time, the play experience awakens her from her already established world of fantasy and imagination as its rehearsal experience brings her closer to the real world through affecting »her sense of order. The self-contained world she had drawn with clear and perfect lines had been defaced with the scribble of other minds, other needs; and time itself, so easily sectioned on paper into acts and scenes, was even now dribbling uncontrollably away« (*AT* 34). Her realist approach to writing, however, does not attenuate her tendency to fictionalise the world. Instead, she interprets the new situation as a threat both to her inner self and to her wring. This is the main reason of her destructive intramentality as well. Unable to accept such a change, we are told that, she »squirmed in her oppression« (*AT* 35).

The new genre emboldens her to simulate or virtualise the other character's minds. Having decided not to continue the rehearsal of her play, she chooses to write a story, give it to his brother Leon and »watch as he read it« (*AT* 35). Such a big change in her attitude towards authorship again derives from her intentions. She thinks that in this way she can communicate, by now we can be sure that she means to impose, her thoughts more directly upon the reader. Her reflection on this subject reveals the degree her mind is entangled with functionality: »A story was direct and simple, allowing nothing to come between herself and her reader [. . .]—no intermediaries with their private ambitions or incompetence, no pressures of time, no limits on resources. Reading a sentence and understanding it were the same thing« (*AT* 35). Furthermore, having observed the fountain scene, she thinks that, as her new genre allows her to do so, she should rewrite what happened there, »But how to do justice to the changes that had made her into a real writer at last, and to her chaotic swarm of impressions, and to the disgust and fascination she felt? Order must be imposed« (*AT* 108). Accordingly, she ponders that she is morally allowed to reorder the existing world based on the principles of the new genre:

> There must be some lofty, godlike place from which all people could be judged alike, not pitted against each other, as in some lifelong hockey match, but seen noisily jostling together in all their glorious imperfection. [. . .] Trapped between the urge to write a simple diary account of her day's experiences and the ambition to make something greater of them that would be polished, self-contained and obscure, she sat for many minutes frowning at her sheet of paper. (*AT* 108–109)

She finds the act of writing a responsibility that demands mental activity, »She wondered whether having final responsibility for someone, even a creature like a horse or a dog, was fundamentally opposed to the wild and inward journey of writing. Protective worrying, engaging with another's mind as one entered it, taking the dominant role as one guided another's fate, was hardly mental freedom« (*AT* 149). As a result of such reasoning, she determines to change her writing style from fairy tales to fiction and the other characters are aware of the possible dangers of her changing mood, »she appeared to the world like a girl in the grip of a terrible mood« (*AT* 69).

Parallel with her artistic experience, Briony in concerned about finding her true self. She peels off the layers of her older self away so as to find the genuine one. However, the more she carves out, the more she becomes certain to find what can be taken as her intramental part. She looks backwards to her life thinking:

> it was childhood she set about now, having no further need for it. [. . .] she disposed of her old self year by year in thirteen strokes. She severed the sickly dependency of infancy and early childhood, and the schoolgirl eager to show off and be praised, and the eleven-year-old's silly pride in her first stories and her reliance on her mother's

> good opinion. They flew over her left shoulder and lay at her feet. [. . .] Enough! Take that! (*AT* 70)

Galvanized by such a new feeling, she encounters with her brother Leon. Inwardly, she expects anybody to identify her new self. In other words, she expects them to subdue to the necessities of her new identity. This new manner of mental functioning leads to more powerful intramental perceptions. As she thinks, her brother »must learn that she was independent now of other people's opinion, even his. She was a grand master, lost to the intricacies of her art. Besides, he was bound to stop the trap and come running down the bank, and she would have to suffer the interruption with good grace« (*AT* 71). Despite her expectations, the adult world makes her disappointed as she experiences difficulty in her »realignment« with the actual world:

> The cost of oblivious daydreaming was always this moment of return, the realignment with [. . .] the hard mass of the actual. It was difficult to come back. [. . .] Briony had lost her godly power of creation, but it was only at this moment of return that the loss became evident; part of a daydream's enticement was the illusion that she was helpless before its logic: [. . .] she felt herself shrinking under the early evening sky. She was weary of being outdoors, but she was not ready to go in. Was that really all there was in life, indoors or out? Wasn't there somewhere else for people to go? [. . .] This was the challenge she was putting to existence [. . .] She would simply wait on the bridge, calm and obstinate, until events, real events, not her own fantasies, rose to her challenge, and dispelled her insignificance. (*AT* 72)

Swaying between the two poles, childhood and adulthood, Briony prefers to evaluate the outside world from her childhood perspective although she desires to grow out of it. In her privacy she thinks that she has entered into »an arena of adult emotion« (*AT* 106), her following actions and thoughts do reveal the fact that she is still following her own order. It this based on such an inflexible mentality that Briony evaluates the other characters. She tries to impose her own sense of order upon their lives. In Cecilia-Robbie's case, for example, her reaction mainly derives from her inability to align her own horizon, which acts based on fantasy, closely with that of the adult world, which functions based on some totally different codes. Briony's intramental manner of thought just fails to identify the differences between the two poles as it makes her unable to look at the world from the adults' perspectives which seem to her full of »mysteries« or an »unspeakable world« (*AT* 150). She finds it unavoidable to »discover« it through her stories, »All she had to do now was discover the stories, not just the subjects, but a way of unfolding them, that would do justice to her new knowledge.« The omniscient narrator, however, immediately clarifies the fact that her desire for storying the world would only show to herself her own »ignorance« through time, »Or did she mean, her wiser grasp of her own ignorance?« (*AT* 150). Of all the other characters, Briony's perception about the adult world mostly comes from her cousin Lola. She imagines her as her maid. Her introvert character and meaningful silences at some significant narrative situations motivate Briony's desire enabling her imagine her own stories of the events.

The arrival of Briony's cousins affects her life deeply. It is through their performance of her play that for the first time in her life she becomes aware of the wide distance between imagination and reality. Additionally, by more than any other character in the storyworld, the young Briony is affected by her eldest cousin Lola. She presents her the fake copy of the adult world codes. Imitating and following her finally brings Briony to commit her crime. Lola's presence in the narrative, therefore, is essential for the portrayal of the roots of Briony's potentiality for misreading. Lola causes her misperceptions about the adult social codes. When she and her two brothers arrive, Briony tries to persuade them to act in her play. The more she deals with them in this process, the more Lola affects her reactions. She raises her negative emotions. At the early moments, Lola evokes her jealousy emotion as Briony increasingly finds herself in a kind of competition with her:

> Their sister, who sat between them, with left leg balanced on right knee, was, by contrast, perfectly composed, having liberally applied perfume and changed into a green gingham frock to offset her coloring. Her sandals revealed an ankle bracelet and toenails painted vermilion. The sight of these nails gave Briony a constricting sensation around her sternum, and she knew at once that she could not ask Lola to play the prince. (*AT* 11)

Although they do not exchange many words, Briony closely observes Lola's appearance and behaviour. Lola's silence triggers her flawed evaluations.

When she finds the twins unwilling to act in her play, she ascribes the reason of their behaviour to Lola thinking that »Perhaps Lola was relying on the twins to wreck the play innocently, and needed only to stand back and observe« (*AT* 32). As a result, she continuously adds to her intention to be like Lola—more affective and more adult, »She should have changed her dress this morning. She thought how she should take more care of her appearance, like Lola. It was childish not to« (*AT* 33). She pretends to imitate her behaviour but, like what she pretends to be doing in her realistic style of writing, she does it imperfectly as she only follows her own intended behaviour.

Briony's literary mind enables her to imagine the impact of her own words and actions on the others' thoughts, feelings and actions. Therefore, the problem in her case is the fact that the more she is immersed in her fantasy world of writing, the more she disrupts the balance between the storyworld realities and those perceived and pursued by her mind. For example, although she is aware of her cousins' unwillingness to act in her play, she finally follows her own desire:

> The vulnerable Quinceys were being coerced. And yet, Briony struggled to grasp the difficult thought, wasn't there manipulation here, wasn't Lola using the twins to express something on her behalf, something hostile or destructive? Briony felt the disadvantage of being two years younger than the other girl, of having a full two years' refinement weigh against her, and now her play seemed a miserable, embarrassing thing. (*AT* 12)

Lola, therefore, acts as a good excuse for Briony to get disappointed about her fairy tale or romance style (her childhood period as well) and, instead, begin writing (and acting) in a new genre, novel. It is through Lola that her desire to grow mostly shows itself. This growth does happen both in her art and in her character. As a result of having been affected by what she experiences in her surroundings, Briony ignores her play, *The Trial of Arabella,* and plans to represent the realities of her society in her new genre. Despite that, Briony continues to misinterpret what she sees since her newly emerging self is strange to the adult world codes and conventions as it tends to replace the real reality with the fake one pursued by her literary mind.

Briony shows a good deal of theory of mind as she reveals a capacity to look at herself from Lola's perspective. This, however, does not bring about an intermental thought between her and the other characters. The more she truly assumes how her thoughts and actions are read by Lola, the more she becomes determined to pursue her own retaliatory thoughts: »how could she refuse a cousin so far from home whose family life was in ruins? Lola was reading her mind because she now played her final card, the unrefusable ace« (*AT* 13–14). Briony here thinks that Lola is able to perceive what she is thinking about. In other words, she thinks that Lola reads her mind although it is her artistic mind that enables her to perceive not what exists, but what possibly might exist. Besides that, one should consider the role her intense feeling of adolescent jealousy plays in her evaluations. When such an emotion combines with her writerly imagination, the result becomes a fictional kind of rhetoric because literature is natural part of her mind or, as put by Jacobi »Briony has immersed herself in literature her entire young life and seems to see the world through the lens of romantic melodrama« (59). For instance, when she finds herself unavoidably giving the main role of her play, Arabella's role, to Lola, to cope with its pathetic impact, Briony turns to fiction, »Briony knew her only reasonable choice then would be to run away, to live under hedges, eat berries and speak to no one, and be found by a bearded woodsman one winter's dawn, curled up at the base of a giant oak, beautiful and dead, and barefoot, or perhaps wearing the ballet pumps with the pink ribbon straps« (*AT* 14). Lola's presence, nevertheless, strengthens her sense of self. When she perceives that Lola wants the central role in the play and »The advance of Lola's dominion was merciless and made self-pity irrelevant,« she becomes more determined to »resist« (*AT* 15). In this way she makes a »shift in the balance of power« (*AT* 15) and continues keeping Lola under her close observation. Lola's performance seems to her inappropriate: »she spoke her lines correctly but casually, and sometimes smiled inappropriately at some private thought, determined to demonstrate that her nearly adult mind was elsewhere« (*AT* 16). Besides that, it is under her affective appraisal of Lola and the reception of her mimetic play—she thinks that cousins were »steadily wrecking Briony's creation« (*AT* 16)—that Briony finally decides to »abandon the rehearsals« without anybody's knowledge (*AT* 52).

Lola, however, continues to influence Briony as she continuously reflects on the manner Lola treated her twin brothers: »That a girl so brittle and domineering should be brought this low by a couple of nine-year-old boys seemed wondrous to Briony, and it gave her a sense of her own power« (*AT* 110). As a result of her recollection while walking in the meadow, Briony finally gathers all her mental ability in order to make herself free from the spell of both Lola·and acting or playwriting. Taking a bundle of nettles as incarnation of Lola, she satisfactorily kills her many times for:

> her various sins—pride, gluttony, avarice, uncooperativeness—and for each she paid with a life. [. . .] When Lola had died enough, three pairs of young nettles were sacrificed for the incompetence of the twins—retribution was indifferent and granted no special favors to children. Then playwriting itself became a nettle, became several in fact; the shallowness, the wasted time, the messiness of other minds, the hopelessness of pretending—in the garden of the arts, it was a weed and had to die. (*AT* 70)

Briony's horrific violence in this scene is directed against her past life. After this moment, she is certain that she can only rely on her own way of evaluating people as well as their thoughts and actions. Killing Lola signifies going beyond her. Briony does no longer wish the adult sphere represented to her by Lola; instead, she pretends to act as an adult. It is with this fake mentality that she approaches the ever increasing romantic relationship between Cecilia and Robbie. Not knowing the adult codes or orders enough and relying on her self-contained mind only, she interprets what happens between them.

4.3 In Search of Love: Constructin of an Interminal Mind between Cecilia and Robbie

Of all the fictional minds within the Tallis house, Cecilia's and Robbie's minds are the only centripetal ones. Increasingly, they move towards each other through a strong bond of love. Their growing romantic feeling about each other provides them with a shared space which makes their ultimate sympathy possible. The mode of their mental functioning is in opposition to the domineering course of Briony's intramental mind. Although they suddenly realise their mutual love at the narrative beginning, it has its roots in their friendship from childhood. In other words, the construction process of their intermental unit is as old as their life.

Unlike Briony's desire to impose her own order on her surroundings, Cecilia's busy mind is represented as looking for a shared order. Furthermore, her mental functioning indicates a mind yearning for a unity with another, Robbie's, mind. Unlike her young sister Briony who imposes her own fictional perceptions on the real world, Cecilia's mind functions based on the realities of the external world. She does not desire to reconfigure the world based on her own imaginary order; her order does only exist outside the Tallis house. From the moment of her introduction in the first part of the second chapter, her mind is portrayed as desiring an intermental relationship. Her contemplations reveal »an austere, joyless woman moreover« (*AT* 90).The source of Cecilia's restlessness is her intense awareness about the realities of her environment. She gets disappointed by her family as she feels she is ignored, »She had returned from Cambridge with a vague notion that her family was owed an uninterrupted stretch of her company. But her father remained in town, and her mother, when she wasn't nurturing her migraines, seemed distant, even unfriendly« (*AT* 19). As a result of her home situation, she is experiencing an inner conflict about whether to leave the house or to stay. Having returned from her university, she feels »uncomfortable« at home: »In fact, being at odds with her father about anything at all, even an insignificant domestic detail, made her uncomfortable« (*AT* 44). From this perspective, her situation resembles that of both Edward's and Flurence's in *CB*:

> No one was holding Cecilia back, no one would care particularly if she left. [. . .] She simply liked to feel that she was prevented from leaving, that she was needed. From time to time she persuaded herself she remained for Briony's sake, or to help her mother, or because this really was her last sustained period at home and she would see it through. In fact, the thought of packing a suitcase and taking the morning train did not excite her. Leaving for leaving's sake. Lingering here, bored and comfortable, was a form of self-punishment tinged with pleasure, or the expectation of it; if she went away something bad might happen or, worse, something good, something she could not afford to miss. (*AT* 20–21)

The need Cecilia feels for the other people shows the degree her existence depends on them. Her mind is not self-contained as it desires connection with the other minds. She simply is unable to disconnect herself form the other people. But the more she reflects on the main reason(s) of her restlessness, the more she gets closer to the thought of Robbie. She knows it is primarily for his sake she cannot leave. Such a self-awareness inaugurates the construction process of an intermental unit or mind between them:

> And there was Robbie, who exasperated her with his affectation of distance, and his grand plans which he would only discuss with her father. They had known each other since they were seven, she and Robbie, and it bothered her that they were awkward when they talked. Even though she felt it was largely his fault—could his first have gone to his head?—she knew this was something she must clear up before she thought of leaving. (*AT* 20–21)

Having confessed her emotional attachment to Robbie, Cecilia's mental mode changes. The romantic perception brings about defamiliarisation in her perspective as »the familiar was transformed into a delicious strangeness« (*AT* 19). She re-evaluates her relationship with Robbie as she yearns for an intermental unit with him, »All day long, she realized, she had been feeling strange, and seeing strangely, as though everything was already long in the past, made more vivid by posthumous ironies she could not quite grasp« (*AT* 45). Such a realisation colours her perspective in evaluating her life and relationships. For example, it affects her evaluation of her brother's friend Paul Marshall. When she sees him for the first time, she evaluates him in terms of whether he can be an appropriate husband for her, »Cecilia wondered, as she sometimes did when she met a man for the first time, if this was the one she was going to marry, and whether it was this particular moment she would remember for the rest of her life—with gratitude, or profound and particular regret« (*AT* 44). But the more she examines Paul, the more she gets disappointed, »Watching him during the first several minutes of his delivery, Cecilia felt a pleasant sinking sensation in her stomach as she contemplated how deliciously self-destructive it would be, almost erotic, to be married to a man so nearly handsome, so hugely rich, so unfathomably stupid« (*AT* 47).

Cecilia does also examine Briony's situation carefully. When compared, her thoughts about Briony shows the degree she is aware of her sister's situation. When she is told that Briony has not returned from the outside, different possibilities flood to her mind. Unlike Briony, however, she is able to control the flow of her thoughts through sticking to the actual facts or to the real world possibilities:

> Someone else to worry about [. . .] she was obliged to return to Briony's room for another pair. This time she paused to peer out of the window at the dusk and wonder where her sister was. Drowned in the lake, ravished by gypsies, struck by a passing motorcar, she thought ritually, a sound principle being that nothing was ever as one imagined it, and this was an efficient means of excluding the worst. (*AT* 95)

Cecilia's anxiety also derives from the fact that she feels their house is decentred as her father and brother are escaping or ignoring their duties, her mother is mentally incapable of controlling these issues and Briony is lost in her dreams (*AT* 96–97). She feels that »No one in her family, however, noticed the transformation in her, and she was not able to resist the power of their habitual expectations« (*AT* 97). She is experiencing a new feeling of self-realisation which brings about a new self to her which is, however, a self construction based on the realities of her situation or verisimilitude. The reason she feels she should leave her family life is the fact that she does not see any intermental relationship with any of her family members:

> Two years ago her father disappeared into the preparation of mysterious consultation documents for the Home Office. Her mother had always lived in an invalid's shadow land, Briony had always required mothering from her older sister, and Leon had always floated free, and she had always loved him for it. (*AT* 96)

Such a realistic analysis helps her to notice that she has gone »into the old roles.« Her transformed self, which has grown since her time in Cambridge, however, persuades her to go away from her family although »No one in her family, however, noticed the transformation in her, and she was not able to resist the power of their habitual expectations« (*AT* 97). Her situation is more painful and pathetic, because she is aware of the real nature of her own state. She does not fantasize about the reality as she is aware that »her parents were absent in their different ways, Briony was lost to her fantasies and Leon was in town. Now it was time for her to move on« (*AT* 97). Following her awareness, she rightly feels excited that she should accept her aunt's invitation and go to Paris. Her excitement, however, does not last long. When Leon informs her about inviting Robbie to dinner, she criticises him for doing so. At the same time, she spends some good time on her dressing for the party. She feels excited about seeing Robbie although she disguises her desire, »She was skeptical [. . .] her mind was—in every sense—where she was to spend the evening, and she had to be at ease with herself. [. . .] Relaxed was how she wanted to feel, and, at the same time, self-contained. Above all, she wanted to look as though she had not given the matter a moment's thought, and that would take time« (*AT* 91). When she is walking with her brother in the yard, they reach the fountain and there her intense emotion to Robbie returns back to her:

> [1] They reached the fountain and turned to face the house, and remained in silence for a while, leaning against the parapet, at the site of her disgrace. Reckless, ridiculous, and above all shaming. Only time, a prudish veil of hours, prevented her brother from seeing her as she had been. [2] But she had no such protection from Robbie. He had seen her, he would always be able to see her, even as time smoothed out the memory to a barroom tale. [3] She was still irritated with her brother about the invitation, but she needed him, she wanted a share in his freedom. Solicitously, she prompted him to give her his news. (*AT* 101)

Cecilia is capable of imagining herself as looking at her own action from her brother's perspective. She thinks that he would find her behaviour as »disgrace. Reckless, ridiculous, and above all shaming« [1]. Despite that, when she looks at what she did from Robbie's perspective, she finds it an appropriate reaction. That is so because, unlike Leon, Robbie is able to sympathise with her as he understands her or is »able to see her« [2]. Cecilia, however, thinks that she should »share« his brother's »freedom« and this makes their conversation possible. She honestly shares with her brother what she feels about their other family members. She talks about her »boredom and solitude« complaining that »she had come to be with the family, and make amends for being away, and had found her parents and sister absent in their different ways« (*AT* 103). The omniscient narrator's account of the unconscious level of her mind reveals her desperate situation, »There was desperation in all she said, an emptiness at its core, or something excluded or unnamed that made her talk faster, and exaggerate with less conviction« (*AT* 103). The »unnamed« subject is her attachment to Robbie. She is under the spell of his love. She cannot talk about her recent life to her brother frankly as she knows that, unlike her brother, she cannot maintain a dual life, »The agreeable nullity of Leon's life was a polished artifact, its ease deceptive, its limitations achieved by invisible hard work and the accidents of character, none of which she could hope to rival« (*AT* 103). Her difference from the intramentally operating mind of Briony is the fact that she knows her limitation. Her mind acts as a realist mind which is looking for a shared meaning. When she finally says that she feels the need to go away from the house, the real obstacle reappears, »›I'd love to come up to town.‹ Even as she said the words she imagined herself being dragged back, incapable of packing her bag or of making the train. Perhaps she didn't want to go at all, but she repeated herself a little more emphatically« (*AT* 104). The more she reflects on her situation, the more she gets closer to Robbie's thought. Such a converging manner of thought clashes with the diverging one pursued by Briony's mind.

Cecilia's awareness about her romantic feeling towards Robbie proceeds his proclamation. When she sees him in the yard for the first time, she finds him »looking at her with amused suspicion. There was something between them, and even she had to acknowledge that a tame remark about the weather sounded perverse« (*AT* 24). When Robbie asks her »›How's *Clarissa*?‹« and she abruptly says »›I'd rather read Fielding any day,‹« showing regret about such an answer, Cecilia carefully evaluates Robbie's possible interpretation of her statement. Furthermore, she acknowledges her love:

> She felt she had said something stupid. [. . .] He might be thinking she was talking to him in code, suggestively conveying her taste for the full-blooded and sensual. That was a mistake, of course, and she was discomfited and had no idea how to put him right. She liked his eyes, she thought, the unblended mix of orange and green, made even more granular in sunlight. And she liked the fact that he was so tall. It was an interesting combination in a man, intelligence and sheer bulk. (*AT* 24)

Her private discourse of affection for Robbie influences her behaviour. When she tells him that her brother Leon is coming home with one of his friends, Paul Marshall, his reaction, »›The chocolate millionaire. Oh no! And you're giving him flowers!‹« provokes an evaluative analysis in Cecilia's mind, »She smiled. Was he pretending to be jealous to conceal the fact that he was? She no longer understood him. They had fallen out of touch at Cambridge. It had been too difficult to do anything else« (*AT* 25). Cecilia, nevertheless, tries to find out the exact reason(s) of Robbie's behaviour. Unlike her sister, she does not want to impose her own intention, »She was the one who was overinterpreting, and jittery in his presence, and she was annoyed with herself« (*AT* 25). The more her thoughts about Robbie are presented, the more we get to know the deep level of her emotional engagement with him:

> he was one of the most confident people she had ever met. She was being mocked, she knew. Rebuffed, [. . .] She was being mocked, or she was being punished—she did not know which was worse. Punished for being in a different circle at Cambridge, for not having a charlady for a mother; mocked for her poor degree—not that they actually awarded degrees to women anyway. (*AT* 26)

In this way, Cecilia carefully evaluates Robbie's behaviour towards her. Her primary purpose is to be sure about his feeling and perceptions. She observes his actions critically. At the same time she tries not to include her own perception about his actions in her evaluation of them, »she could tell from his expression—a forced, stretched smile that did not part his lips—that he regretted what he had said« (*AT* 26). Besides that, she is aware of the main reasons of the recent problems or misunderstanding between them:

> There was no ease, no stability in the course of their conversations, no chance to relax. Instead, it was spikes, traps, and awkward turns that caused her to dislike herself almost as much as she disliked him, though she did not doubt that he was mostly to blame. She hadn't changed, but there was no question that he had. He was putting distance between himself and the family that had been completely open to him and given him everything. (*AT* 26–27)

His apparent indifference towards her, nevertheless, makes Cecilia angry. The more she thinks about the possible reasons of the distance between herself and Robbie, the more her evaluative discourse becomes harsh. She interprets his behaviour as a sign of »masculine authority« (*AT* 27).

Cecilia's and Robbie's confrontation at the fountain is a turning point in their relationship. It sparks the flame of their profound love. The exchanged assumptions between them show the deep level of their emotional engagement. Furthermore, it is through their later reflections on what happens at this moment that they mutually come to the same conclusion—they are in love with each other. Being in love enables them to perceive the mental states of each other. The real process of such a realisation inaugurates with the moment Cecilia, feeling angry about the flower vase, shouts at Robbie »You idiot! Look what you've done.« Although through his looking and gesture Robbie meant to accept »full responsibility,« we are told that »she hated him for the inadequacy of the response.« As a result, when she sees him intending to get into the basin, she finds it »intolerable.« She does so under the effect of a previous misunderstanding, »He had come to the house and removed his shoes and socks—well, she would show him then« (*AT* 28). She decides to get into the cold water mainly as an act of revenge, »Denying his help, any possibility of making amends, was his punishment. The unexpectedly freezing water that caused her to gasp was his punishment. [. . .] Drowning herself would be his punishment« (*AT* 28–29). Having come out of the basin and being aware of the »savage« manner of her movements, she continues her revenge, »she would not meet his eye. He did not exist, he was banished, and this was also the punishment« (*AT* 29). Cecilia, therefore, is aware of the impact of her actions on Robbie. Although, she does not express her love to him, she tries to show him how she feels about him and his actions. In privacy, she praises him for his »liberation«:

> Some said that it was innocence, or ignorance of the world, that protected Robbie from being harmed by it, that he was a kind of holy fool who could step across the drawing room equivalent of hot coals without harm. The truth, as Cecilia knew, was simpler. He had spent his childhood moving freely between the bungalow and the main house. Jack Tallis was his patron, Leon and Cecilia were his best friends, at least until grammar school. At university, where Robbie discovered that he was cleverer

> than many of the people he met, his liberation was complete. Even his arrogance need not be on display. (*AT* 81)

She even becomes more aware of her romantic feeling towards him after reading Robbie's letter for the first time. When Briony gives her the letter, Cecilia re-considers the strange nature of her own behaviour at about that time as she finds the same bizarre traces there. In other words, the letter brings her some clarity. It acts as her guide to his feelings about her:

> Initially, a simple phrase chased round and round in Cecilia's thoughts: *Of course, of course.* How had she not seen it? Everything was explained. The whole day, the weeks before, her childhood. A lifetime. It was clear to her now. Why else take so long to choose a dress, or fight over a vase, or find everything so different, or be unable to leave? What had made her so blind, so obtuse? (*AT* 105)

The content of the letter, furthermore, establishes and moulds her reaction to Robbie. When she opens the door and he begins to make excuses about his (wrong) letter, sympathising with him, she only guides him to the library where they willingly make love and establish their intermental unit.

Likewise, Robbie's reflection on the fountain scene later in the bathroom helps him to decode the intended meanings of Cecilia's behaviour. In this way, they decrease the unequal level of their intentions and expectations. Being deeply influenced by the basin event, Robbie is doubtable whether to take in the dinner party, Leon has invited him to, at the Tallis house. Before meeting her at the dinner, he finally decides to write an excuse letter to Cecilia. He reviews his fountain experience in the bathroom. His reflection reveals the dominance of sexual feeling in his affection at the beginning, »his blood and, so it seemed, his thoughts warmed the water« (*AT* 73). It is, however, through the defamialarising effect of (physical) love that he, like Cecilia, is able to achieve an intermental bond with her finally. In the bathroom, Robbie reviews what happened at the fountain:

> A drop of water on her upper arm. Wet. An embroidered flower, a simple daisy, sewn between the cups of her bra. Her breasts wide apart and small. On her back, a mole half covered by a strap. When she climbed out of the pond, a glimpse of the triangular darkness her knickers were supposed to conceal. Wet. He saw it, he made himself see it again. The way her pelvic bones stretched the material clear of her skin, the deep curve of her waist, her startling whiteness. When she reached for her skirt,

> a carelessly raised foot revealed a patch of soil on each pad of her sweetly diminishing toes. Another mole the size of a farthing on her thigh and something purplish on her calf—a strawberry mark, a scar. Not blemishes. Adornments. (*AT* 74)

This is a totally new feeling to him because for many years »She was like a sister, almost invisible« (*AT* 74). He acknowledges his own mistake, »Was that why she was angry now, because he had ignored her for years?« (*AT* 77). Even while experiencing such a moment, his interpretation of Cecilia's mind and intentions is closer to the reality. He feels the need to talk to her »He would have to speak to her soon.« His memory helps him to go beyond his overwhelming desire for Cecilia's body and instead want her whole self. His recollection of the fountain scene and the way Cecilia's body appeared to him while she was going down into the pool help him to find in her something beyond sexual attraction. He decodes the reasons of her behaviour there. It is through his reflections that he comes to a new understanding about Cecilia's attempt to give an indirect message to him. In other words, Robbie's love begins with physical affection as sex plays the basic role in his deep emotional involvement in her:

> The sweetness of her, the delicacy, his childhood friend, and now in danger of becoming unreachable. To strip off like that—yes, her endearing attempt to seem eccentric, her stab at being bold had an exaggerated, homemade quality. Now she would be in agonies of regret, and could not know what she had done to him. And all of this would be very well, it would be rescuable, if she was not so angry with him over a broken vase that had come apart in his hands. But he loved her fury too. (*AT* 75)

The more he reflects on the fountain scene, the more he finds himself able to decode Cecilia's message. Being caught between fantasy and real, he tries to interpret the real state of the event. In other words, he avoids ascribing his own intention and intramental perceptions to Cecilia's behaviour:

> [his] eyes fixed and unseeing, and indulged a cinema fantasy: she pounded against his lapels before yielding with a little sob to the safe enclosure of his arms and letting herself be kissed; she didn't forgive him, she simply gave up. He watched this several times before he returned to what was real: she was angry with him, and she would be angrier still when she knew he was to be one of the dinner guests. Out there, in the fierce light, he hadn't thought quickly enough to refuse Leon's invitation. Automatically, he had bleated out his yes, and now he would face her irritation. He

> groaned again, and didn‹t care if he were heard downstairs, at the memory of how she had taken off her clothes in front of him—so indifferently, as though he were an infant. Of course. He saw it clearly now. The idea was to humiliate him. There it stood, the undeniable fact. Humiliation. She wanted it for him. She was not mere sweetness, and he could not afford to condescend to her, for she was a force, she could drive him out of his depth and push him under. (*AT* 75)

Like a psychologist, he carries on reading Cecilia's intentions based on her behaviour. As a result of his psychological analysis, he finds her right to be angry with him. However, he is unable to find the main reason of Cecilia's »show of temper.« His effort to understand the main implications of Cecilia's behaviour shows the deep level of his engagement with her. At the same time, it suggests his inclination towards sympathy which is the basic condition for intermentality:

But perhaps—he had rolled onto his back—he should not believe in her outrage. Wasn't it too theatrical? Surely she must have meant something better, even in her anger. Even in her anger, she had wanted to show him just how beautiful she was and bind him to her. How could he trust such a self-serving idea derived from hope and desire? He had to. [. . .] What might Freud say? How about: she hid the unconscious desire to expose herself to him behind a show of temper. Pathetic hope! It was an emasculation, a sentence, and this—what he was feeling now—this torture was his punishment for breaking her ridiculous vase. (*AT* 76)

His final decision to go to the dinner party does in fact explain his active and constructive part in the emerging intermental bond with Cecilia. Unlike Edward in *CB* who did not go after Florence and that brought their promising indumenta unit into end, Robbie goes after Cecilia and she accepts her regretful return. The construction of an intermental bond requires such a mutual voluntary involvement. When he considers the possibility that »He should never see her again,« he immediately revolts against his own thought, »He had to see her tonight. He had no choice anyway—he was going.« The prospect of seeing her vitalises him even if he does not know what will happen, how Cecilia will receive him:

> He'd be in a room with her tonight, and the body he had seen, the moles, the pallor, the strawberry mark, would be concealed inside her clothes. He alone would know,

> and Emily of course. But only he would be thinking of them. And Cecilia would not speak to him or look at him. Even that would be better than lying here groaning. No, it wouldn't. It would be worse, but he still wanted it. He had to have it. He wanted it to be worse. (*AT* 76)

The prospect of seeing Cecilia makes him feel elated, »The anticipation and dread he felt at seeing her was also a kind of sensual pleasure, and surrounding it, like an embrace, was a general elation—it might hurt, it was horribly inconvenient, no good might come of it, but he had found out for himself what it was to be in love, and it thrilled him« (*AT* 85). As a result of his strong will to see Cecilia, he finds himself writing an excuse letter to her. After many times of (re)writing, he finally decides to send this to her, »›You'd be forgiven for thinking me mad—wandering into your house barefoot, or snapping your antique vase. The truth is, I feel rather lightheaded and foolish in your presence, Cee, and I don't think I can blame the heat! Will you forgive me? Robbie.‹« However, he finds himself typing another letter, which expresses his sexual desire towards her, »›In my dreams I kiss your cunt, your sweet wet cunt. In my thoughts I make love to you all day long‹« (*AT* 80). By mistake, he puts the letter into an envelope and on his way to the Tallis house, he asks Briony to take it to Cecilia. The word cunt, we are told, »contained everything he felt, and explained why he was to dwell on this moment later. Freedom. In his life as in his limbs« (*AT* 85). He himself did not know »How had it crept up on him, this advanced stage of fetishizing the love object?« (*AT* 79). Therefore, it is his deep emotional attachment to Cecilia that persuades him to choose going towards Cecilia. When he finds out that he has sent her the wrong letter, the one that includes the embarrassing word »cunt,« he becomes more decisive to go to Tallis house and explain to her everything:

> It came down to this: go in now and face her anger and disgust, give an explanation which would not be accepted, and most likely be turned away—unbearable humiliation; or go home now without a word, leaving the impression that the letter was what he intended, be tortured all night and for days to come by brooding, knowing nothing of her reaction—even more unbearable. And spineless. He went over it again and it looked the same. There was no way out, he would have to speak to her. (*AT* 123)

When she opens the door for him, he finds her »even more beautiful than his fantasies of her« (*AT* 123). Distressed by the content of the letter he has already sent her by mistake, he tries to explain everything to her. He excuses her and acknowledges that »It was a stupid thing. You were never meant to read it. No one was« (*AT* 124). While Cecilia pretends to be listening to him, she gradually guides her into the library, »So he walked toward her slowly as she slipped back, until she was in the corner where she stopped and watched him approach« (*AT* 125). The dark place of the library acts as a confession box. In response to his letter, Cecilia pours out her repressed desire for him. Their mutual confession illustrates their shared interest in establishing a joint unit. For the first time, Cecilia begins revealing the history of her love to him:

> »It's been there for weeks [. . .] Perhaps it's months. I don't know. But today . . . all day it's been strange. I mean, I've been seeing strangely, as if for the first time. Everything has looked different—too sharp, too real. Even my own hands looked different. At other times I seem to be watching events as if they happened long ago. And all day I've been furious with you—and with myself. I thought that I'd be perfectly happy never seeing you or speaking to you again. I thought you'd go off to medical school and I'd be happy. I was so angry with you. I suppose it's been a way of not thinking about it. Rather convenient really . . .« (*AT* 125)

Robbie, nonetheless, is not quite sure what Cecilia is talking about as he does not know what »it« might refer to. This inquiry provokes or explanation from Cecilia. She reminds him of what he pretends not to know, »You knew before me. Something has happened, hasn't it? And you knew before me. It's like being close up to something so large you don't even see it. Even now, I'm not sure I can. But I know it's there« (*AT* 125). Finally, she acknowledges how she found out her new feeling. Furthermore, she admits the reason of her rebellious behaviour at the fountain. She expects him to recognise her affection and to respond to that as well. In other words, she expects his sympathy without which her affection would be meaningless:

> »I know it's there because it made me behave ridiculously. And you, of course ... But this morning, I've never done anything like that before. Afterward I was so angry about it. Even as it was happening. I told myself I'd given you a weapon to use

> against me. Then, this evening, when I began to understand—well, how could I have been so ignorant about myself? And so stupid?« (*AT* 126)

Despite her description of the way she feels, she does not name it, since she is uncertain about his feeling, »She was afraid that there was nothing shared at all, that all her assumptions were wrong and that with her words she had isolated herself further, and he would think she was a fool« (*AT* 126). She does not clearly utter the fact that she loves him or she is in love with him. Instead, she indirectly examines his reaction to her confessing words. She assumes that he should be able to infer what she is talking about if he is experiencing the same kind of emotion. When she asks him »›You do know what I'm talking about. Tell me you do,‹« he says »›I do. I know it exactly. But why are you crying? Is there something else?‹« (*AT* 126). The omniscient narrator's comment shows how they both were aware of the main »obstacle« on their way to express their love to each other as they both »felt watched by their bemused childhood selves« (*AT* 127). Such a co-understanding lies at the basic level of their intermentality. Unlike, Edwards in *CB*, Robbie not only identifies Cecilia's mental state, but also his reaction is in congruence with her emotional need. Furthermore, they both avoid enforcing the egoistic intentions:

> He thought she was about to broach an impossible obstacle and he meant, of course, *someone*, but she didn't understand. She didn't know how to answer and she looked at him, quite flummoxed. Why was she crying? How could she begin to tell him when so much emotion, so many emotions, simply engulfed her? He in turn felt that his question was unfair, inappropriate, and he struggled to think of a way of putting it right. They stared at each other in confusion, unable to speak, sensing that something delicately established might slip from them. (*AT* 126)

> Out of their mutual love, a new shared self is born which belongs to both of them and at the same time does not belong to any one of them separately. In other words, as it is implied, an intermental unit demands construction of a new self. Cecilia and Robbie are aware that to achieve to that level, they should transcend their previous selves. This knowledge is the key reason for the immortality of their intermental unit:

> That they were old friends who had shared a childhood was now a barrier—they were embarrassed before their former selves. Their friendship had become vague and even constrained in recent years, but it was still an old habit, and to break it now in order to become strangers on intimate terms required a clarity of purpose which

> had temporarily deserted them. For the moment, there seemed no way out with words. (*AT* 126)

Through going beyond language and time, they help other to overcome the dominance of their old selves, »What had been self-conscious was now impersonal, almost abstract« (*AT* 127). They both recreate each other and themselves as they begin from the zero point, »At last they were strangers, their pasts were forgotten. They were also strangers to themselves who had forgotten who or where they were« (*AT* 127). As a result, we are told that they were »too selfless now to be embarrassed« (*AT* 128). Furthermore, they go beyond the limiting presence of time, »They were beyond the present, outside time, with no memories and no future. There was nothing but obliterating sensation, thrilling and swelling, [. . .] Despite these limitations, it did not surprise them how clearly they knew their own needs« (*AT* 128). Accordingly, they embrace each other and willingly make love. Consolidating it, their love-making acts as a final seal on their intermentality in the same was, as the narrator says, their »I love you« murmuring were as »signatures on an unseen contract«:

> The closeness of a familiar face was not ludicrous, it was wondrous. Robbie stared at the woman, the girl he had always known, thinking the change was entirely in himself, and was as fundamental, as fundamentally biological, as birth. Nothing as singular or as important had happened since the day of his birth. She returned his gaze, struck by the sense of her own transformation, and overwhelmed by the beauty in a face which a lifetime's habit had taught her to ignore. She whispered his name with the deliberation of a child trying out the distinct sounds. When he replied with her name, it sounded like a new word—the syllables remained the same, the meaning was different. Finally he spoke the three simple words that no amount of bad art or bad faith can ever quite cheapen. She repeated them, with exactly the same slight emphasis on the second word, as though she had been the one to say them first. He had no religious belief, but it was impossible not to think of an invisible presence or witness in the room, and that these words spoken aloud were like signatures on an unseen contract. (*AT* 129)

Their new shared self is a daring self. Interrupted by Briony's unexpected presence at the library, they both feel renewed without any embarrassing feeling at the dinner table. Feeling »afraid of nothing« and willingly waiting for their shared moments ahead, Robbie thinks about the prospect of their changed life, »the dinner would not last forever, and he would find a way to be with Cecilia again that night, and together they would confront the extraordinary new fact in their lives—their changed lives—and resume. At the thought, his stomach plunged« (*AT* 121). The more he looks at Cecilia at the table, the more he becomes bewitched by her beauty. At the same time, she appears to him as a strange person who is, at the same time, familiar an unfamiliar, »His excitement was close to pain and sharpened by the pressure of contradictions: she was familiar like a sister, she was exotic like a lover; he had always known her, he knew nothing about her; she was plain, she was beautiful; she was capable [. . .]« (*AT* 122). He is happy that he sent the wrong letter to her since, in his re-evaluation of its impact on her, he finds out that »his stupid letter repelled her but it unlocked her. He regretted it, and he exulted in his mistake« (*AT* 122). The reason he feels so is the fact that his letter did act like a key to unlock her invisible emotions and he feels enchanted that, under its influence, »They would be alone together soon, with more contradictions—hilarity and sensuousness, desire and fear at their recklessness, awe and impatience to begin. [. . .] And this was no fantasy, this was real, this was his near future, both desirable and unavoidable« (*AT* 122). In this way, Robbie's refreshed self is a shared self which includes Cecilia as a constitutive part.

4.4 The Destructive Impact of Briony's Intramental Thoughts on the Emerging Intermental Bond between Cecilia and Robbie

Briony evaluates the relationship between Cecilia and Robbie in two opposing ways. The young adolescent Briony is a strange person to the adult codes of the romantic relationship between Cecilia and Robbie. On the contrary, disapproving her own behaviour in the childhood period, the experienced adult Briony attempts to immortalise the intermental bond between her sister and Robbie through her fiction so that she might atone herself for her deadly crime in the past. In the following part, focusing on the manner of her mental functioning at different steps, the process through which Briony finally dares to publicise her complete misreading is analysed.

Although her (mis)reading of the emerging intermental bond between Cecilia and Robbie is configured by what she sees, it is the habitual manner of her mental functioning that increasingly ascribes nonfactual states to their minds. As a result, her misreading at the end of that day is the result of a sequence of events she observes from a totally individualistic perspective without having the cognitive capacity to understand them. Briony publically accuses Robbie of adultery based on her false perceptions about the content of the fake letter Robbie gives her to take to Cecilia; the fountain scene she observes from the window with Cecilia and Robbie at the centre; the way she finds them in the library; and finally the way she finds Lola in the heart of darkness while looking for the twins. Her mental functioning both before and after the accusation moment reveals a mind, functioning solely based on its intramental perceptions, obsessed with pursuing its own goals. She finds herself under an obligation to save her sister from the menace of the »maniac« Robbie. Her evaluation of Cecilia's situation and Robbie's monstrous character mainly is the impact of the mental state she has achieved recently. For example, »she arrives at her accusation,« as Jacobi emphasises, »through the employment of a literary logic developed from her reading« (59).

Having been affected by the experience she gains through her contemplation about the relationship between fiction and reality, Briony, not knowing what is the matter, is observing Cecilia and Robbie by the fountain from the »wide-open windows« (*AT* 32). This scene is the first narrative evidence which sets out how she is following a subjective realism. Having been provoked by the external events and situations, she is in fact writing her own story of what might be happening between Cecelia and Robbie. Her mind is unable to differentiate between the real world and the fictional one:

> [1] There was something rather formal about the way he stood, feet apart, head held back. A proposal of marriage. [2] Briony would not have been surprised. She herself had written a tale in which a humble woodcutter saved a princess from drowning and ended by marrying her. What was presented here fitted well. [3] Robbie Turner, only son of a humble cleaning lady and of no known father, Robbie who had been subsidized by Briony's father through school and university, had wanted to be a landscape gardener, and now wanted to take up medicine, had the boldness of ambition to ask for Cecilia's hand. [4] It made perfect sense. Such leaps across boundaries were the stuff of daily romance. (*AT* 36)

Briony ascribes intentions to Cecilia's and Robbie's behaviour based on her own experience in writing fiction [1 and 2]. Following that she focuses her attention on Robbie and his »boldness of ambition.« She find them unequal [3]. Her fictional mind submerged in romance, however, does provide her with the similar examples of the »leaps across boundaries.« As a result, she thinks that she understands the reason of Robbie's action (of proposal). Briony does in fact reinvent what happens between her sister and Robbie. The window provides her the situation without its real content. As a result, she reconstructs the scene following her own perceptions. She increasingly associates her sister's situation with mistreatment while she ascribes all atrocious things to Robbie's side:

> What was less comprehensible, however, was how Robbie imperiously raised his hand now, as though issuing a command which Cecilia dared not disobey. It was extraordinary that she was unable to resist him. At his insistence she was removing her clothes, [. . .] What strange power did he have over her? Blackmail? Threats? [. . .] She should shut her eyes, she thought, and spare herself the sight of her sister's shame. But that was impossible, because there were further surprises. Cecilia, mercifully still in her underwear, was climbing into the pond, was standing waist deep in the water, was pinching her nose—and then she was gone. There was only Robbie, and the clothes on the gravel, and beyond, the silent park and the distant, blue hills. (*AT* 36)

The more Briony observes them, the more she thinks that she understands their intentions. Such a wrong perception acts as the basis for her succeeding evaluations of their, particularly Robbie's, behaviour. The reverberation of this scene in her (un)conscious mind keeps it alive for her until the last scene of the narrative when Briony, the famous author, returns back to their Tallis House. It is only through time that she is able to find out the degree she misunderstood the scene. Therefore, her writing is her attempt to atone herself for her guilty action. It is through the mature perspective of adult Briony that we are told »The sequence was illogical—the drowning scene, followed by a rescue, should have preceded the marriage proposal. Such was Briony's last thought before she accepted that she did not understand, and that she must simply watch« (*AT* 36–37). Despite such a »weak intimation,« Briony later on is quite sure that that she understood what was going on between the two. In other words, although she is confused about what she sees since it is against the habitual order of her mental functioning, she imposes her own reading or voice on the silent and »empty« scene. When Cecilia leaves the scene without exchanging any words with Robbie, Briony changes her focus of attention back to him thinking, »He was [. . .] no doubt satisfied.« She ascribes such a mental state to him and her later interpretation of Robbie's actions are all only based on such a flawed perception because when Cecilia leaves, we are told that »Suddenly the scene was empty; the wet patch on the ground where Cecilia had got out of the pond was the only evidence that anything had happened at all« (*AT* 37). Following that, the omniscient narrator, manipulated by Briony's narrating I, delineates the flawed nature of her perception:

> Unseen, from two stories up, with the benefit of unambiguous sunlight, she had privileged access across the years to adult behavior, to rites and conventions she knew nothing about, as yet. [. . .] Briony had her first, weak intimation that for her now it could no longer be fairy-tale castles and princesses, but the strangeness of the here and now, of what passed between people, the ordinary people that she knew, and what power one could have over the other, and how easy it was to get everything wrong, completely wrong. (*AT* 37)

Briony's later reflections on the fountain scene is a sign of her growing tendency to fictionalise the fact. She rewrites the scene many times and the whole *AT* narrative is based on that. Her mental functioning at this moment uncovers an intentional resistance against realism. She stubbornly refuses any possibility which is against her own thought and perceptions [1]. Her adult perspective, however, does reveal the flawed nature of such perception [2]:

> [1] It was a temptation for her to be magical and dramatic, and to regard what she had witnessed as a tableau mounted for her alone, a special moral for her wrapped in a mystery. [. . .] Briony resisted because she wanted to chase in solitude the faint thrill of possibility she had felt before, the elusive excitement at a prospect she was coming close to defining, at least emotionally. [2] The definition would refine itself over the years. She was to concede that [. . .] she may have attributed more deliberation than was feasible to her thirteen-year-old self. (*AT* 37–38)

She gets infatuated by her own interpretation of the scene she observed and this encourages her to begin a story based on what she saw. She justifies her own version of the scene. The extradiegetic narrator's discourse in this part is coloured with the central character's discourse. As an emerging writer, Briony believes that she can reinvent the other minds since understanding their true content is difficult. Even for a short time, she wants to disclose her »revelation« to her sister Cecilia (*AT* 41). Her adult self calls this technique an »impartial psychological realism«:

> she sensed she could write a scene like the one by the fountain and she could include a hidden observer like herself. [. . .] There did not have to be a moral. She need only show separate minds, as alive as her own, struggling with the idea that other minds were equally alive. It wasn't only wickedness and scheming that made people unhappy, it was confusion and misunderstanding; above all, it was the failure to grasp the simple truth that other people are as real as you. And only in a story could you enter these different minds and show how they had an equal value. That was the only moral a story need have. (*AT* 38)

The intervening omniscient narrator once more reveals the discrepancy between the real events and Briony's intramental interpretation of them. Therefore, she thought that as a result of »some kind of revelation,« she could invent »the truth« and was able to represent it from different perspectives, »the scene could be recast, through Cecilia's eyes, and then Robbie's« (*AT* 39).

The fountain experience acts as a background against which Briony's later evaluation of Robbie's behaviour depends. As a result of her recent revelation, she ponders she has the moral right to read Robbie's letter, »A savage and thoughtless curiosity prompted her to rip the letter from its envelope—she read it in the hall after Polly had let her in—and though the shock of the message vindicated her completely, this did not prevent her from feeling guilty. It was wrong to open people's letters, but it was right, it was essential, for her to know everything. (*AT* 106). Having read the letter he had given her to take to Cecilia, when Briony finally gives it to her, Cecilia evaluates her state. In her little sister's »unhappiness,« she finds »an element of autonomy« (*AT* 41). This becomes more obvious when she discloses the content of the letter to Lola and, both by her own revenge seeking mind and by the encouragement Lola provides her, she ascribes more negative intentions to Robbie.

Out of her psychological need for a companion, Briony tries to get closer to Lola by telling her about the content of the letter:

> from a mixture of motives—a practical need to change the subject, the desire to share a secret and show the older girl that she too had worldly experiences, but above all because she warmed to Lola and wanted to draw her closer—Briony told her about meeting Robbie on the bridge, and the letter, and how she had opened it, and what was in it. Rather than say the word out loud, which was unthinkable, she spelled it out for her, backward. The effect on Lola was gratifying. [. . .] and so was her hoarse whisper. »Thinking about it *all the time*?« (*AT* 111–112)

Accordingly, when Lola concludes that »›How appalling for you. The man's a maniac,‹« the word »maniac« brings about a re-evaluation process of their past relationship from Briony's perspective. This is in fact the reconstruction moment of all her past knowledge and experience of Robbie:

> A maniac. The word had refinement, and the weight of medical diagnosis. All these years she had known him and that was what he had been. When she was little he used to carry her on his back and pretend to be a beast. She had been alone with him many times at the swimming hole where he taught her one summer how to tread water and do the breaststroke. Now his condition was named she felt a certain consolation, though the mystery of the fountain episode deepened. She had already decided not to tell that story, suspecting that the explanation was simple and that it would be better not to expose her ignorance. (*AT* 112)

Their following discussion on this topic elucidates how Lola acts as a mediator and evoker for Briony to advance her own interpretation of Robbie's character and intentions. In other words, as Jabobi points out, Briony »has the benefit of believing the accused to be a »maniac« because of evidence and a subsequent logic she believes to be compelling, and her self-assurance allows her accusation to sound true to the constables and to her family« (60). Having heard Briony's account of the letter, Lola is encouraged to feed her desire more. When she says that »D'you know, on our first afternoon I thought he was a monster when I heard him shouting at the twins by the swimming pool« (*AT* 112), Briony, as if for competition, remembers the same moment, »Briony tried to recall similar moments when the symptoms of mania might have been observed. She said, »He's always pretended to be rather nice. He's deceived us for years« (*AT* 112). As a result of such mutual (mis)understanding, Lola finally offers her suggestion, »She took Briony's hand. ›I think the police should know about him‹« (*AT* 112). Lola's poisoning words influence her deeply in restructuring his concept in her mind. Her unfamiliarity with the codes and conventions of the symbolic order should also be considered as another reason for her evaluation of the experience, »Naturally, she had never heard the word spoken, or seen it in print, or come across it in asterisks« (*AT* 107). Again, it is the adult Briony's writerly perspective that, through controlling the narrative discourse in this part, highlights the limitation of the young Briony's perspective:

> she needed to be alone to consider Robbie afresh, and to frame the opening paragraph of a story shot through with real life. No more princesses! The scene by the fountain, its air of ugly threat, and at the end, when both had gone their separate ways, the luminous absence shimmering above the wetness on the gravel—all this would have to be reconsidered. With the letter, something elemental, brutal, perhaps even criminal had been introduced, some principle of darkness, and even in her excitement over the possibilities, she did not doubt that her sister was in some way threatened and would need her help. (*AT* 106–107)

The omniscient narrator's comment in this part overlaps with Briony's first person narration in the last part of the narrative. From a general perspective, it signifies the degree Briony pursues her intramental perceptions in her evaluation of Robbie. At the same time, it shows the lasting impact of such intramental perceptions on her character. Having carefully considered Robbie's case in her mind, she comes to the conclusion that »Something irreducibly human, or male, threatened the order of their household, and Briony knew that unless she helped her sister, they would all suffer« (*AT* 107). Being haunted with the thought of such a new revelation, she reimagines what she saw at the fountain as if writing a story based on a real event she observed from the window. Affected by this thought, her behaviour becomes more prudent, »And Cecilia, whom she ought to protect, she dared not go near. Robbie, obviously, she should avoid for safety's sake« (*AT* 111).

Having been emotionally affected by her revisions of the letter and fountain scenes and while passing the library towards the dinner hall, Briony is visited by some memories she had with her father there:

> [1] from behind the library door, a scraping noise followed by a thump and a murmur that could have been a man's or a woman's. [2] In memory—and Briony later gave this matter some thought—she had no particular expectations as she placed her hand on the brass handle and turned it. But she had seen Robbie's letter, she had cast herself as her sister's protector, and she had been instructed by her cousin: what she saw must have been shaped in part by what she already knew, or believed she knew. (*AT* 115)

Quite accidentally, as in her two previous experiences, Briony hears some noise [1]. Her curious mind takes her towards the noise and there she, again, sees Robbie against her sister. Her interpretation and evaluation of this scene is, therefore, both under the influence of her experiences and Lola's affect [2]. As a result, »Though they were immobile, her immediate understanding was that she had interrupted an attack, a hand-to-hand fight.« Her manner of evaluation of the library scene is similar to the two previous scenes. She imposes her intramental flawed perceptions on the silent scene. Since she cannot understand what is happening, she ascribes all the negative concepts to Robbie and the positive ones to Cecilia, »He looked so huge and wild and Cecilia with her bare shoulders and thin arms so frail.« While Cecilia is leaving the library, Briony shockingly finds out that »there was no sign in Cecilia of gratitude or relief. Her face was expressionless, almost composed, [. . .] Briony was left alone with him. He too would not meet her eye« (*AT* 116). Therefore, such scenes look to her as images upon which she writes her own stories.

It is with this mentality that Briony sits around the dinner table »Conscious that she was sharing the night expanse with a maniac [Robbie]« (*AT* 146). When it is found out that the twins have gone away and everybody goes out looking for them, Briony, setting out alone, waters her thought about Robbie more. She feels troubled with her malicious thoughts about him:

> But there was a maniac treading through the night with a dark, unfulfilled heart—she had frustrated him once already—and she needed to be earthbound to describe him too. She must first protect her sister against him, and then find ways of conjuring him safely on paper. Briony slowed to a walking pace, and thought how he must hate her for interrupting him in the library. And though it horrified her, it was another entry, a moment of coming into being, another first: to be hated by an adult. [. . .] she would protect her sister, even if Cecilia failed to acknowledge her debt. And Briony could not be afraid now of Robbie; better by far to let him become the object of her detestation and disgust. [. . .] The pretense, and how she ached to expose it! Real life, her life now beginning, had sent her a villain in the form of an old family friend with strong. (*AT* 147–148)

The more she goes into the darkness, the more her mind pursues Robbie reminding her that »Someone hated her, that had to be remembered, and he was unpredictable and violent« (*AT* 152). It is with such a mental mode that all of a sudden when she »heard the helplessness in Lola's voice« (*AT* 154), the first possibility that came to her mind is Robbie. When Lola says that »›I saw him. I *saw* him,‹« Briony immediately says that »›It was him, wasn't it?‹« and, as she did in the previous occasions, she imposes her own perception on the existing indeterminate situation. »Meekly« saying »Yes,« Lola grabs this chance and lets Briony to speak the truth for her (*AT* 155). Again, it is the narrating perspective of Briony that controls the flow of the narrative discourse in this part. This reveals the process of a crime formation against Robbie:

> She [Lola] [. . .] may have been about to speak, But it did not matter because Briony was about to cut her off and the opportunity would be lost. So many seconds had passed—thirty? forty-five?—and the younger girl could no longer hold herself back. Everything connected. It was her own discovery. It was her story, the one that was writing itself around her. (*AT* 157)

Briony's autonomy and her dominant intramental perception at that moment lead her to the point that she thinks, by such a discovery, she has solved all the mysterious points. Therefore, she says »›It was Robbie, wasn't it?‹« and continues the next part in her own mind, »The maniac. She wanted to say the word« (*AT* 156). The more she insists, the more Lola's inactive reaction encourages her to assert her own intention. Accordingly, as the narrator states, »their respective positions [. . .] were established in these moments by the lake, with Briony's certainty rising whenever her cousin appeared to doubt herself« (*AT* 157). Thus, despite the fact that she herself was not certain about the cause of Lola's situation, still, she proceeds her own interpretation of the scene as she was practising a new form of writing at that time. This brings about her re-evaluation of her past perceptions about Robbie one step more. In other words, rejecting her previous intramental thoughts about him, she devises some new, more radical and false, perceptions about him:

> If only she, Briony, had been less innocent, less stupid. Now she saw, the affair was too consistent, too symmetrical to be anything other than what she said it was. She blamed herself for her childish assumption that Robbie would limit his attentions to Cecilia. What was she thinking of? He was a maniac after all. Anyone would do. And he was bound to go for the most vulnerable—a spindly girl, stumbling about in the dark in an unfamiliar place, bravely searching around the island temple for her brothers. Just as Briony herself had been about to do. That his victim could easily have been her increased Briony's outrage and fervor. If her poor cousin was not able to command the truth, then she would do it for her. *I can. And I will.* (*AT* 158)

Briony's early certainty, however, disappears when she thinks the same scene over and over through time. Through time, she will reconsider her own evaluation pursuing a kind of atonement for the crime she did since, as implied by Briony's narrating perspective, she loses her »initial certainty« from the following hours of her accusation, »As early as the week that followed, the glazed surface of conviction was not without its blemishes and hairline cracks« (*AT* 159). If she persisted that it was Robbie who molested Lola by saying »I saw him. I know it was him,« it was mainly because of the social expectation that demanded a clear answer, »Either she saw, or she did not see,« (*AT* 160) from her. Briony's grown up perspective illustrates the problem the adolescent Briony was caught:

> She trapped herself, she marched into the labyrinth of her own construction, and was too young, too awestruck, too keen to please, to insist on making her own way back. She was not endowed with, or old enough to possess, such independence of spirit. An imposing congregation had massed itself around her first certainties, and now it was waiting and she could not disappoint it at the altar. Her doubts could be neutralized only by plunging in deeper. By clinging tightly to what she believed she

> knew, narrowing her thoughts, reiterating her testimony, she was able to keep from mind the damage she only dimly sensed she was doing. When the matter was closed, when the sentence was passed and the congregation dispersed, a ruthless youthful forgetting, a willful erasing, protected her well into her teens. (*AT* 160)

Moving between certainty and uncertainty, the representation of Briony's mental functioning reveals an ambivalent state of mind. She loses her certainty about Robbie's adultery even before vindicating him publically and his victorious return adds to her doubt. Her young adolescent psyche is caught between the two opposing states, »All that lay between was too clamorous, too fluid to understand, though she sensed she had succeeded, even triumphed« (*AT* 172). As an effect of this situation, Briony (re)evaluates the outcome of her efforts, »In her dizzy state she was not able to say exactly what her success had been.« Furthermore, she feels as if she is a child again, »She wanted her mother, she wanted to put her arms round her mother's neck and pull her lovely face close to hers« (*AT* 172). Despite the »crack« on her certainty about the true identity of the assaulter, when Robbie finally returns home with the twins, all her vengeful feeling restore: »as she looked at Robbie waiting calmly, she experienced a flash of outrage. Did he believe he could conceal his crime behind an apparent kindness, behind this show of being the good shepherd? This was surely a cynical attempt to win forgiveness for what could never be forgiven. She was confirmed again in her view that evil was complicated and misleading« (*AT* 171). The scene, nevertheless, frightens her. When she sees Robbie »handcuffed,« we are told that, »The disgrace of it horrified her. It was further confirmation of his guilt, and the beginning of his punishment. It had the look of eternal damnation »(*AT* 173). Despite all her psychological turmoil, her mind peruses her intramental intentions until the end. When Robbie is taken away, Briony is observing Cecilia's conversation with him. Not knowing anything about the content of the exchanged words between the two, Briony, again like an author, writes a dialogue for the others. Not surprisingly, she ascribes the mal intentions to Robbie:

> [1] If she was delivering the bitter indictment Robbie deserved to hear, it did not show on his face. Though Cecilia was facing away from her, Briony thought she was speaking with very little animation. Her accusations would be all the more powerful

> for being muttered [. . .] It seemed a kindly gesture and Briony was touched by her sister's capacity for forgiveness, if this was what it was. Forgiveness. The word had never meant a thing before, though Briony had heard it exulted at a thousand school and church occasions. And all the time, her sister had understood. [2] There was, of course, much that she did not know about Cecilia. But there would be time, for this tragedy was bound to bring them closer. (*AT* 173)

The narrator's discourse [2], however, delineates the limited nature of Briony's perspective at this time. It is through time and contemplation that Briony would finally be able to perceive her sister's perspective at that time. Besides that, Grace Turner's shouting at the police car, »›Liars! Liars! Liars!‹ Mrs. Turner roared. [. . .] ›Liars! Liars!‹ Grace Turner shouted again« (*AT* 174–175), would be meaningful to Briony through time.

The narrator's comment reveals a teleological impact of this situation on Briony's later development, »if it was to have gained a new maturity, she could hardly feel it now when she was so helpless, so childish even, through lack of sleep, to the point where she thought she could easily make herself cry« (*AT* 172). Through implying the fact that she was »too young« at that time to understand the different aspects of her own action, it is the grown up Briony's perspective that controls the omniscient narrator's discourse after her attestation. It is only through time that Briony understands her testimony was in fact based on nothing real, »Briony was to have no memory of what suddenly prompted her. An idea of great clarity and persuasiveness came from nowhere, and she did not need to announce her intentions, or ask her sister's permission. Clinching evidence, cleanly independent of her own version. Verification. Or even another, separate crime« (*AT* 165). Accordingly, through time Briony cannot forget how her testimony affected the lives of her sister and Robbie at that night as, through time, her intense feeling of guilt »refined the methods of self-torture, threading the beads of detail into an eternal loop, a rosary to be fingered for a lifetime« (*AT* 162). She considered herself as an all-knowing omniscient narrator who can read other people's intentions and thoughts. Therefore, through time, she comes to the understanding that, while committing the crime, »she had not permitted herself to think of the consequences before acting, or how the writer she had only that day become needed to know, to understand everything that came her way« (*AT* 169).

Briony's first person discourse at the last part of her narrative, nonetheless, shows her continuing attempt to represent the lost intermentality between Cecilia and Robbie. The last part of *AT* narrative, »London, 1999,« is Briony the author's narrative of confession. She considers herself an »unreliable witness« (*AT* 338) and acknowledges the fact that truth is something to be discovered: »Like policemen in a search team, we go on hands and knees and crawl our way toward the truth« (*AT* 339). Accordingly, she thinks that her writing ability helped her to restore the distorted truth. Furthermore, she does not think that the actual facts play any role in the fictional world(s). In this way, the analysis of McEwan's narrative reveals the fact that although intermental units between and among character are constructed, they are continuously threatened by the dominant presence of intramental minds. In other words, intramentality is a prevalent mode of mental functioning. The novelist, however, can act against this course. Through imagination, s/he can let the intermental unit last forever. representations, »If I really cared so much about facts, I should have written a different kind of book« (*AT* 340). As she persuasively admits, accepting her role in the crime, she tried to recreate the lost romantic intermental unit between Cecilia and Robbie, »There was a crime. But there were also the lovers. Lovers and their happy ends have been on my mind all night long« (*AT* 349). She thinks that her atonement for the crime only passes through her art which justifies any deviation from the factual course of the events: »I've made a huge digression and doubled back to my starting place. It is only in this last version that my lovers end well, standing side by side on a South London pavement as I walk away« (*AT* 350). Briony the author, however, does not believe in the possibility of the atonement in the traditional sense. Finding any attempt to do so as absurd, she thinks that the primary function of art is not moral teaching:

> The problem these fifty-nine years has been this: how can a novelist achieve atonement when, with her absolute power of deciding outcomes, she is also God? There is no one, no entity or higher form that she can appeal to, or be reconciled with, or that can forgive her. There is nothing outside her. In her imagination she has set the limits

> and the terms. No atonement for God, or novelists, even if they are atheists. It was always an impossible task, and that was precisely the point. The attempt was all. (*AT* 350–351)

Besides that, she emphasises that her »attempt« will continue in the future. In other words, it is an unending activity to look for redemption. She finds it as »a final act of kindness« to let her »lovers live and to unite them at the end.« She, however, only wanted to give »them happiness,« not to be »self-serving as to let them forgive me« (*AT* 351). Accordingly, the narrating Briony, unlike her young egoistic experiencing self, relies on love as the only surviving aspect of human beings. Indirectly, she finally puts intermentality higher than intramentality:

> I no longer possess the courage of my pessimism. When I am dead, and the Marshalls are dead, and the novel is finally published, we will only exist as my inventions. Briony will be as much of a fantasy as the lovers who shared a bed in Balham and enraged their landlady. No one will care what events and which individuals were misrepresented to make a novel. I know there's always a certain kind of reader who will be compelled to ask, But what really happened? The answer is simple: the lovers survive and flourish. As long as there is a single copy, a solitary typescript of my final draft, then my spontaneous, fortuitous sister and her medical prince survive to love. (*AT* 350)

Briony-the-author's first person narration in the last part of *AT* narrative, all in all, shows the lifelong impact of her past crime on her adult mentality. She considers her writing the only way towards the truth as well as atonement. Similar to was she desired to do in *AT*, it is only through literary imagination that the true lovers can be given the chance to live permanently with each other because, as a writer, she is aware of the fact that »her novel cannot change that crushing reality« (Jacobi 64).

5. *On Chesil Beach*

5.1 A Narrative of Unfortunate Misreadings: *CB*

> For me the moral core of the novel is inhabiting other minds. That seems to be what novels do very well and also what morality is about: understanding that people are as real to themselves as you are to yourself, doing unto others as you would have done to yourself. (McEwan, »Missing«)

This chapter explores the two central characters' mental functioning in *CB*. Edward's and Florence's mental functioning such as inferences, assumptions, decisions, and (mis)reading of each other; the representational modes of their consciousness; and the impact of the represented events and situations on their consciousness or what it's like, qualia, nature of the presented experiences are mainly explored. The chapter argues that Edward and Florence's intramental mental functioning is the main cause in bringing about the deadly imbalance in their intimate relationship on their wedding night. In a close exploration of their behaviours, the study shows how Edward's uncontrollable anger, egoistic perceptions and continual misreadings of, or his wrong inferences about, Florence's thoughts contribute to the breakdown of their already established intermental unit. The study also reveals how Florence's uncontrollably horrible feeling about »to be ›entered‹ or ›penetrated‹« (*CB* 9) as well as her obstinately conscious persistence in widening the gap between themselves add to their separation.

»Delineated in painstaking detail« (Mathews, »After« 82), *CB* is the story of a couple's failure in consummating their marriage. It begins with their arrival at a hotel on Chesil beach in 1962 and ends with Edward's retrospective re-evaluation of his treatment with Florence at that night of their separation in the early part of 1960s. The narrative, however, applies a complicated plot. In five parts, it skilfully weaves together the events of their stay at the hotel on the beach, their stories from acquaintance to marriage, their lives before meeting each other at home and at university and their diverging fates after their open confrontation on their wedding night focalized through Edward's perspective. In many parts, the narrator (in)directly points out the important role of historical time and place in their failure. Nevertheless, Edward and Florence (un)consciously and egoistically pursue their own intramental thoughts and plans. Their dissent over them, mostly revealed through their consciousness representation, can be taken as the most important reason for their failure on their wedding night. In other words, they find themselves unable to build any dialogic relationship between their intramental thoughts. Moreover, they are not successful at (re)constructing each other's minds shown in different versions in their own embedded and doubly embedded narratives. In other words, their theories of minds are not sound. As a result, there is a good deal of doubly embedded narratives, but no intermental unit, between Edward and Florence, as it is the case between Clive and Vernon.

CB, similar to *AM* and *AT*, has gained considerable critical attention. According to Wells, Edward and Florence »have no socially acceptable way of communicating with one another,« and »their relationship [. . .] represents the coming together of two very different worlds.« Wells, moreover, believes that both Edward and Florence »are guilty of poor interpretation of the other: Florence cannot perceive how her imagined scenario excludes a very important form of intimacy for him, and he believes he can represent her entire, complex problem with a single word [frigid]« (*Ian McEwan* 85, 92, 96). Wells, nevertheless, does not seemingly take into account the last confrontation scene on the beach when Edward remains passive while Florence, expecting him to do something, is leaving him forever. If he had overcome his egotism and for a moment considered her proposal from her perspective with compassion and sympathy, they would have had different destinies. What he lacked then was in fact the »imaginary identification with other(s) [Florence]« which, according to Nicklas, »becomes such an important ingredient of McEwan's poetics« (*CB* 11). Moreover, the storytime in *AM*, before the annus mirabilis in 1963[84], and its story place, Chesil Beach

84 *CB* clearly returns to Philip Larkin's poem »Annus Mirabilis« which is, according to Childs, »most famous for its observation that sex started in 1963, the year after Chesil Beach is set« (»Contemporary« 30).

where their »open confrontation« (Spitz 201) and separation take place, are considered to be symbolic. According to Head, »one failed wedding night in 1962 can be taken as emblematic of the dividing line between the sexual liberation of the 1960s and the repression that preceded it. Specifically, Chesil Beach [. . .] is made to symbolize this epochal change« (»*On Chesil Beach*« 118). Nevertheless, having pointed out that there is a »critical consensus« regarding Edward and Florence as »victims of a system of puritanical values that dominated England until 1960s.« Peter Mathews suggests that »such an overwhelmingly positive sense is nonetheless deeply problematic« (»After« 82). Instead, he argues:

> McEwan's main concern in *On Chesil Beach* lies less with the looming cultural revolution of the 1960s, which occupies a few scant pages at the book's end, than with the wider effects of the past on the present. He takes care to emphasize their influence on even the smallest aspects of Florence and Edward's lives. [. . .] McEwan thus peppers the novel with numerous examples of how the passing of time affects and shapes the lives of his characters. (»After« 84)

Therefore, Mathews regards »the story of Florence and Edward as a qualified continuation of the Victorian trajectory rather than a break« (»After« 90). Likewise, refuting Head's opinion, Puschmann-Nalenz observes that there should have been more than »sexual liberation« of the 1960s in the novella:

> The crucial event of the narrative is set on the brink of the great change which happened a little later, and it is important to observe that much more than a sexual liberation took place. The novella marks 1962 as a date where a shift of generations was approaching and a fundamental change caused by the independence of British colonies much argues about, where the class system had equally begun to crumble, and educational opportunities and wealth were spreading. (204–205)

In spite of the importance of time on the formation of Edward's and Florence's thoughts and actions, one can also argue that the impact of the »particular moment in history and the history of the moment« (Ingersoll, »The Moment« 131) on the newlyweds' mental functioning also deserve attention. Accordingly, this study analyses *AM* from this perspective in order to examine the manner or mode of their thoughts as well as the impact of their experiences on that. That is so because, according to Ingersoll, »Recently

McEwan has focused on narratives in which the impulse of the moment can chart the course of life« (»The Moment« 132). Furthermore, *CB* is considered as a narrative that engages readers deeply since »One consequence of telling the couple's story on their wedding night in something close to »real time,« to borrow John Lethem's term, is an intensification of the reader's psychological investment in this narrative« (Ingersoll, »The Moment« 137).

The narrative events in *CB,* additionally, are presented alternately through Edward's and Florence' perspectives. As a result, *CB* »is considered a realistic portrayal of the workings of interpersonal relationships by many readers« (Spitz 197). This technique makes the characters' perceptions about the other fictional characters as well as about themselves available for the readers. Despite that, in some passages the narrator's voice either harmonises or differs openly with the characters' discourses. Or, as Puschmann-Nalenz states, »The narrator treats them [Edward and Florence] with equal sympathy and understanding, yet does not spare them criticism of their demeanour either, when the outcome is disastrous, since both their lives have definitely been impaired« (205). Taking into account the duality of narrator/character discourse in *CB,* Head argues that »there is something arch about the novel, governed by a sexually knowing narrator manipulating his innocent creations. Indeed, the gap between their understanding and experience, and the knowledge of the narrator—and also the author, as the governing intelligence—is discomfiting« (»*On Chesil Beach*« 122). Referring to *CB,* McEwan himself points out the principal role of omniscient narrator in the narrative:

> I've lost all interest in first-person narrative. [. . .] I want narrative authority. [. . .] Although the narrator of *On Chesil Beach* is not a character you could describe, or has nay past or future, it is a presence which assumes the aesthetic task of describing the inside of two people's minds. Then the reader can make a judgement. (»Journeys« 133)

Therefore, because of the availability of the inside or content of the two characters' minds, *CB* reader, as well as *AM* reader, »can make his own judgement after the writer had fulfilled the aesthetic task of describing the inside of people's minds« (Puschmann-Nalenz 208). Accordingly, Palmer's and

Herman's terminologies can be helpful in the analysis of the fictional minds' workings, experiences and presentation. Since the couple's central conflicts in *CB* are similar to real life conflicts, the story anchors well to the readers' real world knowledge and experiences. This characteristic adds to the degrees of narrativity in *CB*. For example, according to Spitz, »the authenticity of the dialogue in the final section of Ian McEwan's *On Chesil Beach* is achieved by exploiting the underlying mechanisms of real-life conflict talk« (211).

One of the fundamental questions for the *CB* reader might be whether Edward or Florence should be blamed for the disruption of their intermental unit. Some critics blame each of the couple for having equal role in their disaster. Roberta Gefter Wondrich, for example, states that »their [Edward's and Florence's] great expectations miserably flounder on their honeymoon night in Dorset, by the famous Chesil Beach, when their first attempt at sexual intercourse ends in disaster, due to Edwards's eager inexperience and Florence's deep-rooted sexual anxieties« (119). While some other critics underscore Edward's role in their conflict and the ensuing separation. For example, Puschmann-Nalanez states that »Readers sometimes have polarized opinions about who is more to blame for the ›mess‹, he or she. While Florence immediately expresses a sense of regret and guilt, Edward comes to see his fault only much later, as an elderly man« (206). Accordingly, the narrative mainly »narrows the focus to a man's decision to do nothing, locking himself and his new wife out of a future they might have had« (Ingersoll, »The Moment« 132). Edward's last perceptions are too late to rectify their broken intermentality.

Finally, as Herman argues in his latest book, »storytelling practices are inextricably interlinked with ascriptions of intentions to persons. More expansively, narratives are bound up with ascriptions of reasons for acting that consist of clusters of beliefs, intentions, goals, motivations, emotions, and other related mental states, capacities, and dispositions« (*Storytelling* 23). As it is the case with the frame narratives of Clive and Vernon in *AM* and those of Briony and Cecilia in *AT*, Edward's and Florence's frame narratives in *CB* reveal the »ascriptions of [their] reasons for acting.« Furthermore, Herman believes that »texts like McEwan's [*CB*] may help explain the special fitness of storytelling for folk-psychological purposes« (*Storytelling* 300) in the same way folk psychology can help narrative understanding. Thus, Herman finds *CB* a sample narrative for »building models of action sequences« which »enable storytellers and story-interpreters to assess the motivations, structure, and consequences of actions by varying perspectival and attitudinal stances towards those actions and the situations in which they occur« (*Storytelling* 294). This capacity makes *CB* considerable from the narrativity perspective. That is so because, according to Herman, McEwan in *CB* »uses the powerful action-modelling resources of narrative to configure and reconfigure this situation [Edward's and Florence's situation] from different temporal, spatial and evaluative standpoints« (*Storytelling* 300). Focusing on the narrative order, Herman (*Storytelling* 306–307) argues that in *CB* McEwan frames the newlyweds' present moment in a larger life span including past, present and future:

> On the one hand, McEwan attaches Edward's actions to a longer storyline stretching back through a history of violent outbursts—and forward to a time when Edward will come to regret his own propensity to overreact. [. . .] Combining analeptic shifts back into Edward's past, proleptic glimpses of how his actions during his and Florence's wedding night will affect his future life, and, in the closing pages of the novel, a sped-up chronological recounting of Edward's later years, the temporal structure of the narrative affords recourse for modelling Edward's reasons for acting. [. . .] On the other hand, Florence's attitudes toward and actions during her wedding night are rooted in a more disuse—and difficult-to-built—action structure or storyline.

Therefore, based on their erroneous intramental perceptions during the bedroom scene[85] and the beach scene, the study attempts to show how Edward

---

85 According to Courtney, »the bedroom scene specifically allows for more *narrated thought* [Palmer's FIT] to enter the text [... It] is solely focalized through Florence, and thus it is her perspective and reactions we hear through an ebb and flow between *psycho-narration* [Palmer's TR] and *narrated thought* (and briefly, *quoted thought*). In focalizing the scene in this way, McEwan has shifted the focus from the event-based physical climax (Edward's premature ejaculation) to the psychological climax (Florence's reaction to what she perceives as a horrific event)« (191). Furthermore, McEwan in this scene, as Courtney says, uses »*slowed scene*—a scene in slow motion in which narrative time exceeds story time« (183)—which »allows McEwan to effectively and sharply contrast this moment in time with the next forty years of the characters' lives, which are delivered in compressed narration« (194).

and Florence equally fail to read each other's minds in general and each other's intentions in particular. While Edward seems to be much more responsible for their separation, Florence disregards Edward's mentality. Nevertheless, she is represented as being able to come out of the restrictions of her own perspective and righteously, at least she tries to do so, evaluate their situation form Edward's perspectives too. Immediately after their separation, she dares to admit her defining role in their inevitable failure, whilst Edward does not refine his thoughts about Florence's behaviour on the beach until his mid-sixties. In other words, if Florence is represented as a forerunner of the new order brought by the changes towards the end of 1960s, Edward is represented as being caught in the conventionalised order before that time. The asymmetric relationship between the two orders, however, brings about the bitter intramental dissents in their relationship. Therefore, in the next three sections the imbalance between Edward's and Florence's incipient intermental minds, their embedded and doubly embedded narratives as well as the private and social impact on their consciousness are examined.

5.2 The Imbalance in the Intermental Unit between Edward and Florence

Edward and Florence's inchoate intermental minds change into highly insolvable intramental dissents only during some short moments. Despite that, the omniscient narrator embeds their past stories in the frame narratives. In this way, the reader can trace the historical formation of their latent selves that primarily function through putting intramental perspective higher than the intermental one. The narrator, moreover, displays the echo of their experiences on their present experiencing minds. Edward is represented as being primarily absorbed in his own imagination of possessing Florence, partly regardless of her feelings at that moment. Florence, nonetheless, is represented as experiencing an internal conflict between her own feelings and Edward's expectations that she tries to read or perceive from his behaviours. Although she desperately struggles to maintain their already established delicate intermental minds, she loses the capacity to overcome her internal conflicts when, in their final open confrontation in the beach, she finally finds a chance to speak loudly her intramental thoughts. Edward and Florence, therefore, equally undergo the impact of some embarrassing moments on their mental functioning which lead to their totally intramental, life-changing decisions and actions.

Edward and Florence are intermental at the beginning of *CB* and there is no sign of their imminent separation. They are represented as undergoing some subjective experiences. The newlyweds »seem the closest of friends, trusting and needing one another. Their story is ominous from the onset« (Henry 82). However, this intermental bond is »superficial,« as suggested by the omniscient narrator's TR, »superficially, they [Edward and Florence] were in fine spirits' (*CB* 3). This cues in readers' mind the possibility of a distance between the characters' thoughts and their actions suggesting the »superficial« nature of their behaviours. At the same time, this in-between situation is considerable from the historical perspective too. The narrative's catastrophic event, the couple's separation, takes place in England 1960s. During the decade, the nation was gradually recovering itself from the ruins of the WWII and, at the same time, it was recovering through laying the foundations of economic improvement and a cultural revolution. The particular context of the storyworld, therefore, is a dividing moment in the social history of the country. Furthermore, the generational gap[86] is also a main factor of the gloomy atmosphere in the storyworld. It is mainly elucidated through some interspersed comments by the extradiegetic or non-character narrator, which bring about the focalized characters' past, present and future together. Nevertheless, the focal concern of this study is the analysis of the fictional minds' reactions to the awkward situations on their wedding night. In other words, the study explores how Edward and Florence manage their relationship at their marriage night without relying on the socio-familial as well as historical factors which are usually considered as responsible

86 The gap is more obvious in terms of Florence's contradictions with her parents. For example, we are told that »Florence was beginning to realize that her parents had rather objectionable political opinions« (McEwan, *CB* 52). Although she contradicts her mother's »typical pattern of pro-American propaganda« openly, she is unable to do so with his father, »Florence found it harder to contradict Geoffrey [her father]« (McEwan, *CB* 52, 54).

for the couple's present situation. Accordingly, one can say that the narrative, at the moment of its beginning, is closer to disequilibrium rather than being at a pure equilibrium state. One the one hand, such an indeterminate worldmaking at the inception of the narrative inclines swiftly to disruptions caused by the couple's inexpressible sexual problems. On the other hand, it reveals how Edward's and Florence's self-centred, egotistic and intramental thoughts and actions act as an insurmountable obstacle to their intersubjectivity.

The intermental thought exists between the two fictional minds in their early presentation where Edward is represented as imagining Florence's thoughts. In order not to seem impolite to her, he behaves as he thinks she expects him to do so repressing his intramental intrusive thoughts. For example, when Florence states that the weather is not quite warm enough »to eat outside on the terrace as they had hoped« (*CB* 4), Edward thinks the opposite. However, in order to show his respect to her, in FIT mode, we are told that »Edward thought it was, but, polite to a fault, he would not think of contradicting her on such an evening« (*CB* 4). Such intermental thoughts and actions are, however, prone to the characters' dissenting intramental orientations and their egoistic behaviours. The first narrative sign of such propensities is shown when two servants come to the couple's honeymoon suit in the Georgian inn in order to serve their dinner. Edward's readiness for wrong inferences and perceptions is shown by his cynical observation of the servants' gestures and expressions. His assumptions about the possible consequences of »any sniggering« from their side indicate the degree he is capable of misjudgements in pursuing his intramental perceptions:

> Proud and protective, the young man [Edward] watched closely for any gesture or expression that might have seemed satirical. He could not have tolerated any sniggering. But these lads from a nearby village went about their business [. . .] and their manner was tentative, their hands shook as they set items down on the starched linen tablecloth. They were nervous too. (*CB* 4)

The omniscient narrator's TR in this passage indicates the two different states of mental functioning beside each other. It shows the shared agitated state of Edward and Florence. The teleological impact of Edward's personality traits such as being »proud« and »protective« becomes more clear in the late scenes. Edward's passive and egoist character will stop him asking Florence to stay while she expects him to do so and, above that, he himself is aware of such expectation from her side the moment she pretends to be leaving him forever.

Furthermore, although, Edward and Florence are reported as possessing some similar thoughts, for example, they are »desperate for the waiters to leave« (*CB* 5), nevertheless, their shared thoughts and plans are not certain but »giddy.« In other words, their future seems to be »misty« which suggests the indeterminate nature of their present situation and the non-articulated, anxious mental states concerning their future. This mist of doubts will reappear later in the beach when they will reconstruct their relationship after a long internal struggle in the bedroom. As in the following passage, the omniscient narrator recounts their shared plans:

> And they had so many plans, giddy plans, heaped up before them in the misty future, as richly tangled as the summer flora of the Dorset coast, and as beautiful. Where and how they would live, who their close friends would be, his job with her father's firm, her musical career and what to do with the money her father had given her, and how they would not be like other people, at least, not inwardly. (*CB* 6)

They are, furthermore, represented as being in agreement about their »parental errors,« their childhoods[87] and their marriage which they intermentally believe is going to be the »beginning of a cure« both from the »social encumbrances« and from their embarrassing condition as the young. Therefore, their marriage presents them with a prospect of freedom as they think it is a marriage of minds or a marriage based on shared thoughts. At their wedding night, nevertheless, they are reported as being »Almost strangers, they stood, strangely together, on a new pinnacle of existence, gleeful that their new status promised to promote them out of their endless

---

87 In this context, Ingersoll states that »As the entries to the consciousness of Florence and Edward reveal, childhood was not a valued stage for their generation, and the young were encouraged to abandon the imperfect state of childhood as quickly as possible to become responsible adults. And there was no better way to prove that one was an adult than by getting married« (»The Moment« 133).

youth-Edward and Florence, free at last!« (*CB* 6). They hope their marriage will heal the rift between their thoughts curing them from their time's indictments. Their bright prospects, however, change into mist when they find themselves unable to go beyond their present »strange« states. In this case, the narrator's TRs reveal their fundamental shared concerns in terms of fulfilling their marriage:

> but they could not describe to each other certain contradictory feelings: they separately worried about the moment, some time soon after dinner, when their new maturity would be tested, when they would lie down together on the four-poster bed and reveal themselves fully to one another. (*CB* 6)

Edward's and Florence's intermentality, however, is not so developed to enable them to share their private feelings and perceptions as they are both concerned with their individual problems—the anxiety about wedding night sex. The teleological impact of such shared concerns becomes more significant when they change into the main cause of the imbalance in their relationship.

While Edward and Florence are struggling with their internal worries before the consummation of their marriage, the omniscient narrator's comments on their complicated situation is more revealing. For example, the narrator informs us that »They were adults at last, on holiday, free to do as they chose. [. . .] But for now, the times held them. Even when Edward and Florence were alone, a thousand unacknowledged rules still applied« (*CB* 18). However, as the narrator emphasises, time alone cannot justify their personal shortcomings. The problem is not mostly that they are interrupted by the »unacknowledged rules« or their behaviours are under the control of them. Rather, their greatest problem is their inability to deal with the growing anxiety about their consummation. They cannot manage their own thoughts and actions efficiently at that moment. To put the same point in other words, if Edward was able to perceive the two aspects of his own behaviour, just like Florence, the outcome would totally be different. Although they both live in the same time with the same socio-historical problems, only Florence who is concerned with the two faces of her problem. She is aware of her own anxiety or internal fear of sex while at the same time she is aware of Edward's expectations or her responsibilities towards him too. Edward, nonetheless, is concerned with his own desires and the way she can fulfil them. Therefore, more than Florence, Edward is desperate to jump forward experiencing what he has waited for so long. However, this drive stops him from taking into account Florence's feelings at that particular moment.

They both, moreover, suffer emotionally from their reluctant, but unavoidable, decision to get married. The narrator iteratively reminds us that if they had been living in a different time, they might have known what they wanted because of the advancements in language, psychology and the other scientific fields. Following that, we can claim that *CB* is the analysis of the impact of time on the central characters' consciousness. The narrative represents the reality of living in a time when there are powerful socio-cultural taboos, to be single and lonely, to get married without loving sex, to feel anxious about consummation and to have a traumatic experience in the past. Through the narration of the socio-political events during 1960s England, the narrator also represents how Edward and Florence build an intermental bond through sharing viewpoints. They »shared sense that one day soon the country would be transformed for the better, that youthful energies were pushing to escape, like steam under pressure, merged with the excitement of their own adventure together« (*CB* 25). The omniscient narrator displays the generation gap between the newlyweds and the »other [older] guests« present in the ground floor. For example, they support »wartime habit« and take »a different view« from Edward and Florence in the upstairs. The presentation of different perspectives reveals the richness of the *storyworld* within which the elder generation's old »habits« are in contradiction with the unusual thoughts followed by the new generation. The dialogic aspect of the represented world, or the plurality of the voices within that, however, is not limited to the boundary between the »old« and the »new« or between the war generation and the post-war generation. It also exists within the new order since the consequences of the old habits afflict the inhabitants of the new world. To emphasise the importance of time on one's thoughts and actions, the narrator informs us emphatically that, »Time, gentlemen, please!« (*CB* 25). The inexpressible internal conflicts imposed on them by time, as the narrator iteratively reminds us, accompany them at their diner table in the hotel: »they continued their pretence of eating, trapped in the moment by private anxieties« (*CB* 26). TRs like this enable *CB* reader to experience Edward's and Florence's minds in relation both to each other and the others represented by those sitting in the downstairs. Although unacknowledged by the characters in the early parts of the narrative, the conflicts primarily orient the narrative progression in a way that the narrative seemingly desires a fulfilment for them.

Therefore, the narrator's TRs show a growing disparity between Edward's and Florence's mental functioning. They also portray the impact of the momentary experiences on their consciousness: »He wanted to engage her tongue in some activity of its own, coax it into a hideous mute duet, but she could only shrink and concentrate on not struggling, not gagging, not panicking« (*CB* 29). Their perceptions and desires are dissimilar. For example, Edward draws wrong inferences from Florence's compulsory reactions to his assertive acts:

> [1] When he heard her moan, Edward knew that his happiness was almost complete. He had the impression of delightful weightlessness, of standing several inches clear of the ground, so that he towered pleasingly over her. There was pain-pleasure in the way his heart seemed to rise to thud at the base of his throat. He was thrilled by the light touch of her hands, not so very far from his groin, and by the compliance of her lovely body enfolded in his arms, and the passionate sound of her breathing rapidly through her nostrils. It brought him to a point of unfamiliar ecstasy, [. . .] [2] Perhaps he could persuade her one day soon—perhaps this evening, and she might need no persuading—to take his cock into her soft and beautiful mouth. But that was a thought he needed to scramble away from as fast as he could, for he was in real danger of arriving too soon. He could feel it already beginning, tipping him towards disgrace. (*CB* 30–31)

Edward's inferences from Florence's »moan« and her gestures [1], displayed in TR, indicate his overwhelmed state or his »unfamiliar ecstasy.« This state coaxes him into imagining further intimacy with Florence although, as shown in FIT [2], he thinks it may be necessary to persuade her first. However, he immediately negates his earlier hypothesis, »she might need no persuading.« At the same time, remembrance of his own problem, repressed by Florence's thoughts, prevents him from further broodings which are full of assertiveness. The intramental assertiveness, moreover, makes Edward recollect some socio-political issues in order to forget his own problem, »real danger of arriving too soon.« When the danger is removed, he returns to his mental explorations. He is once again so enmeshed in his sexual desires that he even does not consider for a moment Florence's situation or her existence.

Applying flashback mode in part two (pp. 37–75), the omniscient narrator embeds in the frame narrative the way Edward and Florence got to know each other and then fell in love. Moreover, the narrator provides some background information about their families and the socio-historical events of the storytime in order to unfold for the reader the history of Edward's stubbornness and Florence's »shyness.« Having taken into account the significance of the »idiosyncratic backgrounds of the central characters.« As Dominic Head argues, the represented backgrounds:

> reveal them [Edward and Florence] to be curiously *unrepresentative*. For both protagonists [. . .] there is an element dysfunctionality in their upbringing—dysfunctional by the standards of 1962—and this implies a degree of emotional and psychological disorder for both that could be taken as an explanation of their failure to connect, quite as much as can the social mores of the time. (»*On Chesil Beach*« 118)

Furthermore, the narrator's TRs in part two reveal the impact of the socio-historical events on the manner of the newlyweds' mental functioning at present. Compared to their predecessors, although they totally belong to a different generation having unorthodox beliefs, still their life is controlled by some uncontrollable and mysterious forces which have their roots in the past. Therefore, the haphazard nature of their life and fate is revealed from their mutual perspectives at the beginning of part two when we are told: »What a terrifying possibility, that it might never have happened at all« (*CB* 37).

Although the narrator represents Edward's and Florence's shared characteristics in many ways, the narrative plainly shows how they are two different people. For example, they have totally different music tastes. While rock and roll is Edward's favourite music, classical music has always been Florence's interest and profession. Changing the time of story and in a teleological manner, the narrator reports on the impact of his favourite music on Edward's personality: »for years to come he considered that this was the music that formed his tastes, and even shaped his life« (*CB* 38–39). The defining effects of this »taste« on Edward's thought and action, or his life as a whole, become more considerable when we find out Florence, the would-be musician »revered the ancient types« (*CB* 41), as a practitioner of the classical music and its impact on her calm, introvert and speculative self. Therefore, their friendship, followed by engagement and then marriage, could not eliminate or even soften the already internalised tastes, which were also shaped by their socio-familial contexts. The college years, however, were the time of some permanent changes for both of them. It is reported that Florence suffered for a while from the lack of intimacy with her professor mother, her younger sister and her father. At university, she builds her own quartet with three of her friends in the group where she attempts to conform to the group rules and conventions. Accordingly, her introvert, or what Edward labels as »shy,« character was the result of the imposed social situations. Accordingly, her concept of freedom was dissimilar to the conventionalised or canonical sense of the term since, compared to her life at home, the college years looked like her free years. That was so because she had some people in the group to whom she could confide. The impact of university years on Florence's thoughts are also noticeable here: » Since it did not seem possible to go out with a boy and still keep up with the old friends, Florence preferred to stick with her hostel group. She liked the banter, the intimacy, the kindness, [. . .] Her college years felt like freedom to her« (*CB* 43). This group[88] adaptability and its broadening effects on Florence's intermental disposition, changing her habits, prepare her for the construction of necessary small intermental thought needed for a married life. Nevertheless, despite the fact that they had had some similar experiences, still their different circles at university affected their characters in totally different ways. Likewise, the accidental nature of their meeting, highlighted by the

88 The concept of group used here is closer to Palmer's concept of the term: »I will be exploring a very fluid and flexible notion of a group as any aggregate of characters, including a pair and even including people who may not be particularly close, but who are, for however short a period, thinking intermentally« (*Social* 219).

narrator, »How easily the encounter might not have happened« (*CB* 44), signifies the unpredictable nature of their future too.

After their meeting in the CNL (Campaign for Nuclear Disarmament) hall and their ensuing friendship, Edward and Florence, »enriched by a private mythology« (*CB* 58), are impatiently looking forward to experiencing the biggest change in their life. They hope it will enable them to experience what had been totally strange or unknown for them till then. For example, when they »held each other's gaze,« we are told that »It was still a novel and vertiginous experience for them, to look for a minute on end into the eyes of another adult, without embarrassment or restraint« (*CB* 58). Nevertheless, the omniscient narrator's following TR account reveals the existence of their problem before their meeting:

> Had it taken her this long to discover that she lacked some simple mental trick that everyone else had, a mechanism so ordinary that no one ever mentioned it, an immediate sensual connection to people and events, and to her own needs and desires? All these years she had lived in isolation within herself and, strangely, from herself, never wanting or daring to look back. In the stone-floored echoing hall with the heavy low beams, her problems with Edward were already present in those first few seconds, in their first exchange of looks. (*CB* 61)

Florence's inability to establish »an immediate sensual connection« both to the other people and events and to her own ›needs and desires« is the result of her own long time »isolation.« She does not know her own needs and those of the others. She is completely absorbed in the abstract world of her own music and this has a considerable role in the failure of their marriage.

Florence and Edward had a somewhat similar situation at home. If Florence's unspeakable story with his father and her cold relationship with her mother were her motivations to go way from home, the story of Edward's mother's brain damage, disclosed to him by his father when he was fourteen, was a defining excuse for him to isolate himself from his family household. When he hears from his father that »his mother was brain damaged« (*CB* 69), as put by Head, »a mood of instantaneous withdrawal overtakes him« (»*On Chesil Beach*« 118). Edward's reaction to his father's story discloses his propensity to get into fights easily. He never gets out of this habit:

> his mother was brain-damaged. The term was an insult, a blasphemous invitation to disloyalty. Brain-damaged. Something wrong with her head. If anyone else had said that about his mother, Edward would have been obliged to get in a fight and deliver a thrashing. But even as he listened in hostile silence to this calumny, he felt a burden lifting. Of course it was true, and he could not fight the truth. Straight away, he could begin to persuade himself that he had always known. (*CB* 69)

This revelation causes Edward to grow a new self[89], hidden from the others. It heartens him in order to leave his family as »he continued to help maintain the fiction that she ran the house and that everything she said really was the case, but now he was consciously acting a part, and doing so fortified that newly discovered, tough little core of selfhood« (*CB* 74).

Therefore, through embedding their background stories, the narrator presents, mainly by TRs, the formation processes of their selves at home, college and post-graduation period. The lack of a strong mental bond with their parents brings about their obligatory formation of a hidden self, which is a stubborn self pursuing solely its concealed intramental goals. The after-effects of these historical selves as well as the need to an intermental mind, in order to share their loneliness, bring about a mutual longing in them for an intermental relationship upon which they both act in their first meetings. Nevertheless, their pasts »make them entirely unsuited to establishing a domestic life of their own, with a healthy sexual relationship at its heart. [. . .] Their home lives, from which model experience is absent, have caused both of them to develop in ways that militate against marriage« (Head, »*On Chesil Beach*« 121). Despite his emphasis on the role of Edward's and Florence's pasts on their present behaviour, Head continues his discussion observing that »They are more complex creations than this [his prior argument] implies, with private lives that make the novella's crisis an emotional (rather than a historical) inevitability« (»*On Chesil Beach*« 121). Likewise, the primary focus of this research is also the analysis of the »emotional inevitability« that leads to the total disintegration of the characters' intermentality.

---

89 Both Edward and Florence realise the emergence of a new self and, according to Head, »These realizations—the emergence of a new sense of self, the self-conscious feeling of separation from family—are familiar aspects of adolescent experience« (»*On Chesil Beach*« 119).

All in all, part two, rendered in a flashback, broadens the reader's perception of the couple's personality providing him/her with the chance to evaluate the characters' behaviour towards each other more thoroughly.

Part three (pp. 79–107) is strongly focalized through the couple's competing perspectives. The first section (pp. 79–89) is highly focalized through Florence's perspective restoring the reader into the newlyweds' bedroom in the hotel on Chesil beach. Focusing on the heart-stopping moment, they both try not to think about either the past or the future. Edward, for example, tries not to yield to anger as he did in the past although »The ghost of Harold Mather still troubled him« (*CB* 98). Likewise, Florence endeavours to release herself from the thought of the past and future since they are both disturbing to her. Furthermore, for the second time in part three (pp. 99 to 107), the narrative perspective changes to Florence and the remaining events in the bedroom are recounted totally from her perspective although later, in the last section of part four (pp. 130–135), the events are recounted retrospectively from Edward's perspective too. Presentation of the events from both central characters' and narrator's perspectives displays the impact of the stressful situation on the manner of their argument. They (un)intentionally utter some problematic words and in this way »What had been suppressed (by conventions of politeness and fear of humiliation) now rushes to the surface with a force that overwhelms both characters« (Spitz 201). At the time of their open confrontation on the beach, one can see the distance between what they think (or thought before that time), or their state of minds, and what they say:

> He was preparing to tell her what he had come to say, and he moved a step closer.
> ›Look, this is ridiculous. It was unfair of you to run out like that.‹
> ›Was it?‹
> ›In fact, it was bloody unpleasant.‹
> ›Oh really? Well, it was bloody unpleasant, what you did.‹
> ›Meaning what?‹
> She had her eyes shut as she said it. ›You know exactly what I mean.‹ She would torture herself with the memory of her part in this exchange, but now she added, ›It was absolutely revolting.‹ (*CB* 144)

The word »revolting« incites some retaliatory words from Edward's side. The narratorial comments in these pages increase in order to show the disastrous course of their exchanges. They intentionally say whatever they know is dangerous to their relationship and their mutual »accusations tend to initiate conflict sequences« (Spitz 210). Edward's response to Florence's accusation, »revolting,« is more fatal: »›You don't have the faintest idea how to be with a man. If you did, it would never have happened. You've never let me near you. You don't know a thing about any of it, do you? You carry on as if it's eighteen sixty-two. You don't even know how to kiss‹« (*CB* 144). These accusations are more than she can bear or, as the narrator puts, »How much accusation was she supposed to bear in one small speech?« Florence does not see Edward's face, even if she tries, when they speak. In that pose, they exchange accusations using offending words or phrases such as »bullying,« ridiculous,« »wheedling« etc. (*CB* 145). In this way, their mutual misreadings continue.

Florence is represented as a calculating or shrewd character. She evaluates the available options in their future based on their unsuccessful past. She knows herself well and is aware of Edward's expectations too. Since she does not know how to say it, she skilfully hides her real problem. This makes the rift between them grow further. That is because she tries, on the one hand, to be herself without being forced into a »disgusting« life and, on the other hand, to be in love: »She wanted to be in love and be herself. But to be herself, she had to say no all the time. And then she was no longer herself. She had been cast on the side of sickliness, as an opponent of normal life« (*CB* 146). Still, she cannot speak her mind to Edward. As their conversation continues, they dare to addresses issues that were previously unspoken. In the beach scene, Florence's perspective is given priority because the events and situations are focalized through her perspective. At the final pages of the narrative and in a retrospective manner, Edward's perspective regarding their final decision is also given. It seems that Edward lacks the richness of Florence's internal broodings and her determination. Florence's perceptions in this part are thought to be a communal perception or social consciousness where the narrator's and character's voices are overlapping each other:

> [1] suddenly thought she understood their problem: they were too polite, too constrained, too timorous, they went around each other on tiptoes, murmuring, whispering, deferring, agreeing. They barely knew each other, and never could because of the blanket of companionable near-silence that smothered their differences and blinded them as much as it bound them. They had been frightened of ever disagreeing, [2] and now his anger was setting her free. [3] She wanted to hurt him, punish him in order to make herself distinct from him. It was such an unfamiliar impulse in her, towards the thrill of destruction, that she had no resistance against it. (*CB* 149)

Edward's »anger« [2] acts as an excuse for Florence to reconstruct her already conventionalised perceptions. For the first time, she finds out that their enormous problem is their politeness. This revelation leads to some conflict sequences and »once the conflict frame has gained momentum, the characters orient towards the expectation of dissent« (Spitz 206). Moreover, having perceived that they »barely knew each other.« Florence discovers that their fear to talk about such problems has made them too much similar [1]. Following this reasoning, Florence is so bold as to decide that she should »hurt« him in order to be »distinct« from Edward and this »unfamiliar impulse« exacerbates the destruction of their intermental unit. The desire to be »distinct« could be controlled by Edward if he, getting out of his own perspective, could take into account their problem from her perspective too. He is rarely doing that and even though she is doing it every now and then, still that does not end at a balance in their shaking intermental relationship. Consciously and shrewdly, she tries to read Edward's mind by what he says and how he acts based on his thoughts. As a result, her actions and reactions are mostly the result of her own inferences and ascriptions. For example, when Edward says: »›You were wanting to humiliate me‹« (*CB* 148). The word »humiliate« stirs in her mind a chance to play a card towards her intention. Her answer to Edward, Edward's insult and her asking »get away from me« show the accidental part of their shared life brought to its end by their extremely intramental dissents:

> [Florence:] ›Oh, all right then. If that's what you want. I was trying to humiliate you. It's no less than you deserve when you can't even control yourself.‹
> [Edward:] ›You're a bitch talking like that.‹
> The word was a starburst in the night sky. Now she could say what she liked.

›If that's what you think, then get away from me. Just clear off, will you. Edward, please go away. Don't you understand? I came out here to be alone.‹ (*CB* 148–149)

Although Florence is able to perceive Edward's regret about his own statements, nevertheless, she finds it unacceptable the moment she thinks about their reunion. She finally finds courage to propose her suggestion to him. Having imagined her quartet, she finds herself »heading towards a rehearsal with the quartet, towards an encounter with beauty and difficulty, with problems that could actually be resolved by friends working together« (*CB* 149). Despite that, she cannot find a way out of this stressful situation made up of both »beauty« and difficulty.« Further, since there is no cooperation or »working together,« which can be considered as a sign of intermentality, there is no »resolution«. This analogy, made in an imaginary way, encourages her more to find herself »unfree« with Edward: »How unfree she was, her life entangled with this strange person from a hamlet« (*CB* 150). The reader is also entangled closely with her situation because s/he is closely presented, more in FIT mode, the impact of that situation of Florence's mind. Nevertheless, she does not prefer to speak her mind. Instead, she reacts to Edward's statements. While Edward, in a confessing mode, talks about their relationship using past tense, »›I loved you, but you make it so hard‹.« Florence immediately thinks about the intentional nature of Edward's application of the past tense. Without noticing it, Edward continues his speech: »›We could be so free with each other, we could be in paradise. Instead we're in this mess‹« (*CB* 150). The word »mess,« we are told, »brought back to her the vile scene in the bedroom, the tepid substance on her skin drying to a crust that cracked. She was certain she would never let such a thing happen to her again« (*CB* 151). At the same time, she inwardly acknowledges Edward's statements through looking at herself from his perspective. This ability is her superiority to Edward. She is aware about what it's like to be in a »stalement« as he suggested:

She disliked herself for the way she was calculating the moment when she should turn round, and she saw herself as he might, as awkward and brittle like her mother, hard to know, making difficulties when they could be at ease in paradise. So she should make things simple. It was her duty, her marital duty. (*CB* 151)

Florence finds herself and Edward unpredictable and therefore difficult to read. At the same time, she hardly stops doing so. Such a dichotomy is the driving force for the progression of the frame narrative plot. When she finally stoops to one of them, the intramental one, the denouement appears as a solid fact in front of them. In other words, Florence can be considered as the central controlling force of *CB* plot. In the following passage she is represented as an explorer of her own existence:

> he was clearly before her, the man she loved, her old friend, who said unpredictable, endearing things. But it was uncomfortable laughter, for she was feeling a little mad. She had never known her own feelings, her moods, to dip and swerve so. And now she was about to make a suggestion that from one point of view was entirely sensible, and from another, quite probably—she could not be sure—entirely outrageous. She felt as though she were trying to re-invent existence itself. (*CB* 152)

Florence is, therefore, aware of the divergence of their perspectives. The only thing she cannot imagine is Edward's possible reaction to her proposal because »he remained unreadable,« but, as the narrator says, »she was bound to set it wrong« (*CB* 154 and 152). Her proposal, nevertheless, seems to be multilateral. She is aware of their mutual love; at the same time, she is aware of both sides' needs and desires as she confesses to Edward: »›I'm pretty hopeless, absolutely hopeless at sex [. . .] I have no idea why that is, but I think it isn't going to change. Not immediately. [. . .] it's going to cause you a lot of unhappiness, and me too‹ « (*CB* 153). However, she tries to save herself: »Like a skater on thinning ice, she accelerated to save herself from drowning. She tore through her sentences, as though speed alone would generate sense, as though she could propel him too past contradictions, swing him so fast along the curve of her intention that there could be no objection he could grasp at« (*CB* 154). While Florence growingly emphasises her private or individual self rather than the social or communal one, Edward endeavours to maintain it from the very beginning. She is following a consciously built intermental unit through her proposal. She expects Edward to agree with her in terms of her proposal, to accept that they can remain lovers and at the same time be free.[90] She attempts to clarify to Edward what she means: »We're free now to make our own choices, our own lives. Really, no one can tell us how to live. Free agents! And people live in all kinds of ways now, they can live by their own rules and standards without having to ask anyone else for permission« (*CB* 154). Her proposal, offered under the veil of words, is centrifugal or non-canonical while Edward tends to the centripetal or canonical conventions. In order to persuade Edward, Florence stipulates that since she does not like to have sex and cannot persuade herself into doing it, he can have sexual relationship with whomever he wishes. At the same time, they can still be in love and live together. Such a disruptive proposal brings Florence's long internal conflicts to an end. At the same time, it destroys their apparent intermental unit too. Moreover, it brings the narrative of that storytime to its end. In other words, her proposal not only is against Edward's perspective and worldviews but also it is against the standards or norms of the storytime. Her ideas are, in other words, unorthodox.

Edward's reaction to Florence's proposal, nevertheless, is extremely egoistic and intramental. Its emphasis on dissenting rather than assenting brings about the total breakdown of their already constructed intermentality. The narrative reader, however, experiences the main part of their intermentality since, applying continuing consciousness frame, s/he is able to imagine the characters' states in their absence. Edward considers their situation and her proposal from only his own perspective without being able to come out of himself and look at both the proposal and their tense situation from her perspective too. Instead, yielding to his already established and unavoidable trait, anger, he accuses her of insulting and tricking him. This

---

90 Florence's proposal to Edward is similar to Garmony's proposal to Clive in *AM* when he says, »To air differences and remain friends, the essence of civilized existence, don't you think?« (McEwan, *AM* 21) They both ask for an intermental unit, which includes their mutual thoughts. Nevertheless, no one finds them acceptable at that moment.

does not suppress his bitter anger. Therefore, he calls her a »frigid,« an accusation that legitimises for Florence her mutual accusations. These exchanges finally bring their intermentality to its end:

> Don't you realise how disgusting and ridiculous your idea is? And what an insult it is. An insult to me! I mean, I mean‹—he struggled for the words—›how dare you!‹ [. . .] ›You tricked me. Actually, you're a fraud. And I know exactly what else you are. Do you know what you are? You're frigid, that's what. Completely frigid. But you thought you needed a husband, and I was the first bloody idiot who came along.‹ (*CB* 156)

Edward in this scene »feels overcome by the temptation to be violent again« (Puschmann-Nalenz 206). Florence's proposal and her preceding and proceeding broodings on that signify both the significance and advantages of the two sides. Despite that, Edward's accusation that she is »frigid« triggers a reconstruction in her mind. The (re)construction ability is peculiar to Florence at that time. Edward's only reconstruction takes place with a profound regret after some forty years of Florence's proposal. This time, she comes out of her own perspective and evaluates her own situation and proposal from Edward's perspective. She ironically agrees with his calculations. The following FIT passage reveals Florence's reconstruction of the conventional values, her submission to Edward's centripetal evaluations and her determination to end the relationship:

> She knew she had not set out to deceive him, but everything else, as soon as he said it, seemed entirely true. Frigid, that terrible word—she understood how it applied to her. She was exactly what the word meant. Her proposal was disgusting—how could she not have seen that before?—and clearly an insult. And worst of all, she had broken her promises, made in public, in a church. As soon as he told her, it all fitted perfectly. In her own eyes as well as his, she was worthless. (*CB* 156–157)

After their last exchanges, Florence, aware of the degree she offended him, offers him her excuses: »›I am sorry, Edward. I am most terribly sorry‹,« nevertheless, Edward remains silent and motionless: »She paused a moment, she lingered there, waiting for his reply, then she went on her way« (*CB* 157). As it is obvious, she expects Edward to say or do something in order to dissuade her from going away while Edward, not being able to overcome his own egoist pride, remains passive. Therefore, for the disruption of their intermental, although simulated, unit, more than Florence, Edward should be blamed. That is because not only has his anger forced him to be hasty in rejecting Florence's proposal but also, when she apologised, he could not persuade himself into forgiving her despite the fact that he knew that she was right.

Accordingly, presentation of Edward's and Florence's passage from intermentality to intramentality as well as emphasis on their mutual impact on each other's minds or thoughts and actions are the central concerns in *CB*. After Florence leaves at the beach »Suddenly the narrative appears to have spun out of control, lurching forward with Edward's decline, as though even the rapid motion forward is a repudiation of the intensely slow movement of time in the present of the wedding night« (Ingersoll, »The Moment« 143). Decades later, Edward will bitterly regret remaining passive at the moment of Florence's departure. Although it did not happen in the storyworld, it is implied that he could have asked her to remain and they could overcome their mutual shortcomings after only some time.

5.3 What It's Like to »Love, and Set Each Other Free«: Florence Ponting's Passage from Intermentality to Intramentality

Compared to Edward's non-pragmatic character, Florence is a thinker who tries to solve her problems in a sensible way. From the narrative beginning until the bitter confrontation scene in the beach, she examines the ways she can bring forward her proposal to Edward. Having evaluated her proposal's possible impact on Edward, Florence goes beyond her own perspective and looks at it from his perspective too. She attempts to do so in order to attenuate it according to his mentality. In other words, she is able to make some theories of mind from Edward's perspective. Despite that, her proposal instigates the total breakdown of their intermentality too. From the very beginning and until their open confrontation in the beach, Florence's mind is traversing between intramentality and intermentality. In other words, her mind is nearly always intersubjective. Florence's reactions to Edward's behaviour and her own perceptions are minutely registered in the narrative in order to both represent their impact on her mental functioning and show the significance of their contribution to her final outbreak which comes as a blow to their already preserved intermental bond.

Thus, Florence is reported as being at war within herself from the very beginning. In order to maintain her intermental relationship with Edward, she endeavours more consciously to overcome the deviating thoughts that lead her towards intramental dissents. We are told that her »anxieties were more serious« (*CB* 7) than Edward's. She attempts to avoid any dissuading thoughts pushing them behind her consciousness or simply repressing them. At the same time, she desperately intends to »draw on all her courage to speak her mind« (*CB* 7). Therefore, she is unable to talk about her anxieties in terms of wedding night sex to Edward. Likewise, she attempts to avoid acknowledging those feelings to herself. In other words, she finds her problem »unutterable« in both senses:

> [1] But what troubled her was unutterable, and she could barely frame it for herself. [2] Where he merely suffered conventional first-night nerves, she experienced a visceral dread, a helpless disgust as palpable as seasickness. [3] For much of the time, through all the months of merry wedding preparation, she managed to ignore this stain on her happiness, but whenever her thoughts turned towards a close embrace—she preferred no other term—her stomach tightened dryly, she was nauseous at the back of her throat. (*CB* 7)

Florence cannot, as shown in TR mode, »frame« her problem as it is disseminated in her thought and body [1]. Having compared her problem with Edward's, while the narrator finds his problem more »conventional,« implying its transitory nature, it considers Florence's problem as »a visceral dread« which indicates the more private and personal nature of it [2]. She is aware of her problem and is represented as being caught in a real dilemma. The »nauseous« feeling »at the back of her throat« is like a »stain« on her »happiness« [3]. Throughout the narrative she is represented as struggling inwardly in order to suppress those feelings. As shown in the following FIT report, her anxiety derives mostly from her ontological, dealing with being and existence, and phenomenological, dealing with experience or consciousness, concerns:

> Was she obliged on the night to transform herself for Edward into a kind of portal or drawing room through which he might process? Almost as frequent was a word that suggested to her nothing but pain, flesh parted before a knife: *penetration*.« She simply finds having sex with Edward as »horrifying« and »repulsive.« (*CB* 8)

Nevertheless, she does feel that her dissuading feelings are going to change. To persuade herself in this thought, she firstly devaluates her problem, then overcomes it as we are told: »In optimistic moments she tried to convince herself that she suffered no more than a heightened form of squeamishness, which was bound to pass.« Thus, she does not suffer from her problem, fear of sex, as much as she is hurt by the dilemma it has put her in. She is aware of her problem, as she knows that there is »something profoundly wrong with her« (*CB* 8):

> [1] Her problem, she thought, was greater, deeper, than straightforward physical disgust; her whole being was in revolt against a prospect of entanglement and flesh; her composure and essential happiness were about to be violated. She simply did not want to be ›entered‹ or ›penetrated‹. Sex with Edward could not be the summation of her joy, but was the price she must pay for it. She knew she should have spoken up long ago, as soon as he proposed, long before the [. . .] irreversible arrangements. But what could she have said, what possible terms could she have used when she could not have named the matter to herself? [2] And she loved Edward, not with the hot, moist passion she had read about, but warmly, deeply, sometimes like a daughter, sometimes almost maternally. [. . .] She thought he was original, unlike anyone she had ever met. She adored his curious mind, his mild country accent, the huge strength in his hands, the unpredictable swerves and drifts of his conversation, his kindness to her, and the way his soft brown eyes, resting on her when she spoke, made her feel enveloped in a friendly cloud of love. At the age of twenty-two, she had no doubt that she wanted to spend the rest of her life with Edward Mayhew. [3] How could she have dared risk losing him? (*CB* 9–10)

Florence fairly evaluates her own problem. She knows that having sex with Edward will bring her joy. At the same time, she is aware that, compared to the high price she should pay for it, she will get less pleasure out of it. Besides that, she does not know how to describe her own real feeling, as she herself does not exactly know what kind of feeling it is [1]. Therefore, despite her doubts, both about her own feelings and about her sex with Edward, she thinks that he is the right man she has found. Having reviewed her own reasons, she comes to the conclusion that he is the exact person she wants to marry [2]. When she compares her own contradictory feelings about her sex with Edward and the advantages of Edward's character, she criticises the declining mode of her own thought about him [3]. In this way, the flow of her consciousness projects different aspects of her dilemma.

Florence's intermental bond with Edward is so strong in the early periods of their relationship that she at last persuades herself »to spend the rest of her life« with him in spite of her internal sexual/ontological anxieties. Her specific condition at home[91] and school also indirectly enforces her to go on with Edward in spite of her inward contradictory feelings. We are told that her only sibling, Ruth, was »too young,« her mother »too intellectual, too brittle« and her school friends »terrific.« Therefore, »She was alone with a problem she did not know how to begin to address, and all she had in the way of wisdom was her paperback guide« (*CB* 10–11). Through the narrative progression, however, the more Edward will push her sexually, the more the delicate balance between her internal anxieties and her desire for Edward will break down. The main reason for this disastrous breakdown, however, is Edward. He is unable to read in proper time her mind or intentions, feelings, emotions and the impact of the tense situations on her overall mental functioning. Conversely, Florence is able to read Edward's mind although she cannot quit her intramentality too. She is aware of the effects of her actions and words on his mind. For example, when Edward offers her cherry, we are told:

> Playfully, she sucked it from his fingers and held his gaze as she deliberately chewed, letting him see her tongue, conscious that in flirting with him like this she would be making matters worse for herself. She should not start what she could not sustain, but pleasing him in any way she could was helpful: it made her feel less than entirely useless. If only eating a sticky cherry was all that was required. (*CB* 11)

She is aware of her own weakness in not being able to »sustain« her »flirting with him« and, at the same time, she finds herself justifying her own actions

---

91 Considering his relationship with his mother, Edward's situation at home was similar to Florence's. Because of her »derangement« (McEwan, *CB* 65), he could not make connection with her. However, unlike Florence's, there was an intermental cooperation among his family members.

in terms of her own behaviour towards Edward as »pleasing.« Therefore, Florence endeavours to broaden the intermental thought or bond with Edward although that requires her to struggle with her own unavoidable inclinations.

Unlike Edward, Florence is represented as having two selves—Florence the musician or artist who is very confident and a »leader,« and Florence the ordinary person who is inefficient:

> When the business was music, she was always confident and fluid in her movements [. . .] She was the undisputed leader, and always had the final word in their many musical disagreements. But in the rest of her life she was surprisingly clumsy and unsure, forever stubbing a toe or knocking things over or bumping her head. (*CB* 15)

Florence is represented as struggling against her own inner conflict. She should either control her own distaste of the marriage responsibilities or turn Edward's proposal down which will enable her to get rid of his ensuing voiced and unvoiced requests. As in TR we are told: »She loved him, she wanted to please him, but she had to overcome considerable distaste. It was an honest attempt–she may have been clever, but she was without guile« (*CB* 23). Despite their internal reluctances, they both pretend, to themselves and to each other, not to have any obstacle to their marriage. At the same time, they are enmeshed with emotion rather than intellect and with living the present moment rather than grounding their present actions on their experiences. Moreover, that moment Edward's proposal and Florence's tacit acceptance is their moment of intermentality because they are able to reach at a shared thought although the consequences of that action are not calculated. The would-be disequilibrium in the narrative and the imbalance in their relationship are, nevertheless, the results of their seemingly intermental decisions. We are told that, prior to Edward's proposal:

> she momentarily forgot her little shock. And he was so astonished by his own decisiveness, as well as mentally cramped by unresolved desire, that he could have had little idea of the contradiction she began to live with from that day on, the secret affair between disgust and joy. (*CB* 23)

The narrator's TR combines their states of mind together in this passage. Once Edward proposed and she accepted it immediately, it is revealed that

Florence »momentarily« forgot her earlier sensations and Edward was ruled by his own »unresolved desire.« Moreover, the thought did not even occur to him to imagine the impact of his proposal on her character. Unlikely, through Florence's embedded narratives, the reader is able to follow the way she deals with »the secrete affair between disgust and joy« during their engagement up until their wedding night.

Nevertheless, the narrator's TRs delineate the impact of Edward's sarcastic statement on Florence's consciousness. They, moreover, reveal the contradictory side of her behaviour, mainly verbal one, and her thoughts:

> To demonstrate how wrong he was, she was proposing what she knew he most wanted and she dreaded. She really would have been happier, or less unhappy, to go down to the lounge and pass the time in quiet conversation with the matrons on the floral-patterned sofas while their men leaned seriously into the news, into the gale of history. Anything but this. (*CB* 27)

Florence attempts to postpone what she dreads experiencing. She acts as if she knows what Edward wants or needs. She also knows that what he says about her longing for the news is true. At the same time, since she cannot express her fear, because she does not want to hurt him, she continues her pretension. Likewise, the disparity between subjective and objective or what is meant/intended and what is uttered in their discourses displays the breach in their intermental relationship. The narrator, who is combining the two diverging perspectives, reports the critical condition Florence lives in prior to their intramentally oriented growing dissents. As we are told:

> [1] There was nothing she could do, beyond fainting, and she was hopeless at acting. [2] She stood and took his hand, certain that her own returning smile was rigidly unconvincing. [3] It would not have helped her to know that Edward in his dream-like state had never seen her looking lovelier. (*CB* 27)

Shown in TR mode [1], Florence's conflicts are between her own felt states and her double behaviour. As a result, she is suffering from a kind of dualism. She is at the same time »helpless.« Her own interpretation of her smile, »unconvincing« [2] and narrator's omniscient report [3], which ruffles the narrative chronotop, reveal the angle between their perspectives. This revealing, however, would be impossible without the narrator's narration of the various possibilities. The primary purpose of this technique is to present the couple's problem from at least three angles—the narrator's, Florence's and Edward's.

Moreover, Florence is consciously struggling between Edward's assertiveness and her own unwillingness. Although she steadily cooperates with Edward simply because she does not want to »offend« him, »Her claustrophobia and breathlessness grew even as she became more determined that she could not bear to offend him« (*CB* 29). Despite the perceivable differences between herself and Edward, Florence is represented as considering the other possibilities as well, evaluating their probable consequences as rendered in the following FIT passage:

> [1] If she was sick into his mouth, was one wild thought, their marriage would be instantly over, and she would have to go home and explain herself to her parents. She understood perfectly that this business with tongues, this penetration, was a small scale enactment, a ritual tableau Vivant, of what was still to come, like a prologue before an old play that tells you everything that must happen. [. . .] [2] In deciding to be married, she had agreed to exactly this. She had agreed it was right to do this, and have this done to her. [. . .] And if she didn't like it, she alone was responsible, for all her choices over the past year were always narrowing to this, and it was all her fault, and now she really did think she was going to be sick. (*CB* 29–30)

Florence is represented as looking at her problem more realistically finding herself, her past decision and her personal trait, as the only reason of her present stressful situation. She, moreover, is aware of the following consequences of the »business of tongues« as she takes it a »penetration« although in small scale [1]. The frightening »enactment,« however, is the result of her own action in the past. The event sequences, represented from the first part to the second part, indicates the way Florence attempts to calm herself down. In this way, she makes a connection between her present helplessness and her past carelessness. Finally, she persuades herself to be »responsible« for her own action in the past although it is difficult [2].

While Edward interprets her gestures and mental states only opportunistically in order advance his »entrance« into Florence, she feels »nauseous,« »smothered,« »pinioned« and »suffocating.« Her reaction in this situation is not selfish. She is not ready psychologically to have sex and Edward's instinctive behaviour makes him unable to understand this fact:

> [1] Steadied at last. Edward's thoughts dissolved, and he became once more his tongue, the very tip of it, [2] at the same moment that Florence decided she could take no more. She felt pinioned and smothered, she was suffocating, she was nauseous. [3] And she could hear a sound, rising steadily [. . .] She may even have been making the noise herself. [4] She did not care—she had to get out. (*CB* 32)

Edward's inclination to give himself to his feelings, indicated in the above passage [1], reveals his failure to control his own behaviour. It seems that he uses thinking as a safety valve in order to prevent his »arriving too soon.« The moment he can regulate his emotions, he is able to remember his thoughts before that time. He astonishingly finds out that, compared to other thoughts, Florence is the least thought subject in his mind. In other words, he is unaware of his own action and thought at that moment. Despite that, the strong impact of the same situation on Florence's consciousness is largely different. She is primarily concerned with the causes, process and impact of her own actions. She finds Edward's advancement »suffocating« and intolerable, therefore she decides to bring the smothering situation to an end [2]. Nevertheless, being so much haunted with the nauseous feelings at that moment, she is unaware of or indifferent to the sound of her own moaning [3]. All she wants is to »get out.« That is the result of her decisiveness in order to put an end to his extravagance and her suffocation. Nevertheless, she is not persistent enough to align her actions with her thoughts. Unexpectedly, she does not »get out«; instead, as we are told: »she seized his hand and led him towards the bed« (*CB* 32). Her actions, therefore, are incongruent with her thoughts. She acts the opposite of what she thinks she should act because she feels obliged to act against her true internal feelings. Although she loves Edward, she is worried about the others' or social reaction to her unconventional behaviour. The consequences of her actions are, however, Edward's reactions. In other words, Edward's behaviour in the bedroom is the sequence of her behaviour. In the following scene, she attempts to control her situation:

> [1] It was perverse of her, insane even, when she wanted to run from the room, across the gardens and down the lane, onto the beach to sit alone. [2] Even one minute alone would have helped. [3] But her sense of duty was painfully strong and she could not resist it. She could not bear to let Edward down. [4] And she was convinced she was completely in the wrong. If the entire wedding ensemble of guests and close family had been somehow crammed invisibly into the room to watch, these ghosts would all side with Edward and his urgent, reasonable desires. They would assume there was something wrong with her, and they would be right. (*CB* 32–33)

As indicated in the FIT passage, Florence's evaluation of her own decision to »go out« is strongly under the control of the social minds. Having had such a presupposition in mind, she finds her own action as the result of her »perverse« and »insane« character [1]. In addition, she knows that if she could go out, it would have refreshed her [2]. Again, the word »but« indicates her attempts to nullify her own earlier thoughts and reasoning. This time, she tries to justify her passivity regarding going out. On the one hand, she finds herself unable to ignore her duties toward Edward and, on the other hand, she pretends to Edward that her decision is the result of her love to him [3]. Accordingly, as Ingersoll argues:

> By allowing access to Florence's consciousness, the novel brilliantly reminds readers of how easy and understandable it is for a Florence to sense she is headed for disaster and yet be unable to avert disaster. It is akin to the paradox of Florence's clumsiness in simple acts and her dexterity in playing the violin. (»The Moment« 136)

Whatever the reason may be, Florence not only stays inside but also, looking at herself from the eyes of the »ensemble of guests and close family,« she finds herself alone and inevitably surrendered to Edward's desires. Such a perception makes her feel safe [4].

Furthermore, Florence is desperately aware of the consequences of her pretentious behaviour towards Edward. She knows that her actions house the potential to give Edward the wrong impressions of her psychological state. In other words, she is represented as a character with multifarious perspectives—she can perceive herself from Edward's, the other social minds' and her double selves' perspectives. However, she feels helplessly trapped into accepting the terms of the social contract concerning the customs of marriage its consequent responsibilities. Therefore, in the first part of *CB* narrative (pp. 3 to 33), McEwan highlights the central characters' consciousness operations applying a combination of intermittent triple perspectives—the narrator's, Edward's and Florence's. This technique helps the reader to evaluate the value of the each of them in/dependently from the other. In the last scene, Florence's anxieties during waiting time for the »final act« and the impact of subsequent actions on her mental functioning or the qualia aspect of a private experience are presented:

> [1] She also knew that her behaviour was pitiful. [2] To survive, to escape one hideous moment, she had to raise the stakes and commit herself to the next, and give the unhelpful impression that she longed for it herself. [3] The final act could not be endlessly deferred. The moment was rising to meet her, just as she was foolishly moving towards it. [4] She was trapped in a game whose rules she could not question. She could not escape the logic that had her leading, or towing, Edward across the room towards the open door of the bedroom and the narrow four-poster bed and its smooth white cover. [5] She had no idea what she would do when they were there, but at least that awful sound had ceased, and in the few seconds it would take to arrive, her mouth and tongue were her own, and she could breathe and try to take possession of herself. (*CB* 33)

The FIT passage indicates Florence as a person with disseminated self. Commenting on her own behaviour, she finds it »pitiful« [1]. She also helplessly criticises herself for »raising the stakes« in order to defer the next step since she was aware of the »unhelpful impression that she longed for it herself« [2]. Despite that, the impression of what is going to happen, as she accurately imagines it, puts her under great strain. She knows that she is the only person who, decreasing the distance, is »foolishly moving towards it« [3]. Nevertheless, she perceives her action as the result of a »game« or »logic« whose rules she does not know [4]. When she finds herself helpless at changing the present situation, she tends to forget all about the consequences of going towards the bed. Momentarily, she is happy that she has regained her tongue or self from Edward [5]. This passage is in agreement with Florence's embedded narratives in showing the impact of the tense situation on her consciousness which acts in different layers at the same time. She endeavours to preserve the intermental bond through her internal reasoning. She repeatedly reminds herself of her responsibilities towards him as well as her social duties, her personal weaknesses and her love for Edward. Considering its narrativity, the passage is also rich since it represents the impact of just some seconds on Florence's consciousness. It is able to both remind the reader of the similar experiences and produce »conscious experience« (Ridley viii) for him/her.

Edward's unsatisfactory familial life, loneliness, and suppression of sexual desires are responsible for his intention to get into a conversation, and if possible make friends with, Florence at the moment of their meeting in the hall. By the same token, Florence's life at home in those days was not satisfactory for her. Her mother did not pay attention to her and did not understand or even respect her music. Her father was busy with his own business and Florence had a hesitant feeling toward him loving and hating him at the same time. Further, as we are told, »her younger sister got on her nerves« (*CB* 50). Florence's mother, a university professor, was cold towards her. For example, »She had never kissed or embraced Florence, even when she was small« (*CB* 55). In addition, she »was intolerant of Florence's regular practice.« In TR mode, we are told that Florence interpreted »her mother's disapproval of her career and hostility to music in general« as a hostility to herself (*CB* 49). She could not understand Florence's situation and work because she was too busy and musically »tone-deaf.« The narrator, moreover, makes an indirect comparison between Edward's mother and Florence's mother in order to show the intricate situations they both had at home, although in different ways. In this way, the narrator justifies their initial attraction towards each other at the moment of meeting.[92] We are told that her mother's situation »was no less a disability and misfortune than a clubfoot or a harelip.« Thus, her overall family life, after her London experiences and freedom in the college life, was »minutely oppressive and could not muster her sympathies.« In the same way, we are told that Florence's »father aroused in her conflicting emotions« (*CB* 49). Her memories with him in the

92 Edward and Florence find their family life intolerable as Cecilia in *Atonement* finds it so mainly because they all are unable to build an intermental relationship with anyone in the family.

past provoke her inconsistent feelings towards him as well.[93] Despite the fact that she hates him because of their shared secret in the past while sailing, she is driven to him out of their father-daughter tie:

> There were times when she found him physically repellent and she could hardly bear the sight of him. [. . .] She hated hearing his enthusiastic reports about the boat [. . .] It grated on her, his accounts of a new kind of sail. [. . .] He used to take her out with him, and several times, when she was twelve and thirteen [. . .] They never talked about those trips. He had never asked her again, and she was glad. But sometimes, in a surge of protective feeling and guilty love, she would come up behind him where he sat and entwine her arms around his neck and kiss the top of his head and nuzzle him, liking his clean scent. She would do all this, then loathe herself for it later. (*CB* 49–50)

The above TR text displays the unspeakable experience that Florence had in the past. It acts as a barrier in her way to him as if he stands for her father. Therefore, besides the other reasons, this experience is a strong provocation for Florence to leave home. In spite of her problems at home, Florence »was adept at concealing her feelings from her family« (*CB* 50). Therefore, at her particular familial context, she is being accustomed to »conceal« her true feelings form the others, as she is doing so at the wedding night before finally speaking her mind to Edward. Thus, Florence, like Edward, was in a waiting state just before Edward's appearance: »like Edward fifteen miles away in the wooded hills to the east, she passed her days in a form of anteroom, waiting fretfully for her life to begin« (*CB* 52).

Like Edward, Florence also goes to the CNL meeting without any prethought decisions or plans and quite »absentmindedly« (*CB* 55). They were both CNL members. Her inferences about Edward at the moment of seeing him for the first time resembles Edward's attempt to draw meaningful inferences out of her facial expressions. Her propensity to hide her true inner feelings is shown when she sees a North Oxford man that she had known beforehand. She does not like the man who asks her »help him distribute« the CNL pamphlets about the town; nevertheless, »incapable of rudeness,

---

93 Her father's »guilty« action with her in the past, hinted here, acts as a veil in the continuation of the newlywed's intermentality. Drawing on her experience, Florence finds herself entrapped in the same situation she once had with her father.

[she] settled her face into an attentive grimace« (*CB* 56). Florence's perception of love, as both a »thrill« and »vague dread,« is also revealing in terms of both her need, and her internal fears. The following TR reveals how the dominance of her need to love is fortified by her own intentional accordance:

> A month ago they had told each other they were in love, and that was both a thrill and afterwards, for her, a cause of one night of half waking, of vague dread that she had been impetuous and let go of something important, given something away that was not really hers to give. But it was too interesting, too new, too flattering, too deeply comforting to resist, it was a liberation to be in love and say so, and she could only let herself go deeper. (*CB* 59)

The passage signifies the impact of their blossoming love and Edward's proposal on Florence's consciousness. She is represented as experiencing a tense situation. In their private conversation along the stretch of the river, Florence, while recollecting their first meeting in the CNL hall, tries to remember her primary inferences from Edward's »face« at the moment of his arrival. In the earlier part, the scene was presented from Edward's perspective. This time, the same scene is restricted to Florence's consciousness. She looks at herself from Edward's perspective, »what she had noted was the face—a thoughtful, delicate oval, a high forehead, dark eyebrows widely arched, and the stillness of his gaze as it roamed across the gathering and settled on her, as if he were not in the room at all but imagining it, dreaming her up« (*CB* 60). This perception is, nevertheless, gained in a recollected manner after a while. That is so because, as the narrator's TR shows, Florence's mental states at that time were, like Edward's, busy with her thoughts without being even aware of her own mental states:

> But it was even more abstract than that. At the time it did not even occur to her to satisfy her curiosity. She did not think they were about to meet, or that there was anything she should do to make that possible. It was as if her own curiosity had nothing to do with her—she was really the one who was missing from the room. (*CB* 60)

This TR also shows the degree Florence is prone to her unconscious propensities. She is being de-famialarised by the sensation of being in love. It means that she is aware of her own bizarre behaviour because she finds herself giving »awkward answers« to Edward's questions as she is conscious about how »habitually« she is »sealed off in her everyday thoughts« (*CB* 61). Accordingly, despite the fact that Florence is able to imagine the possible impact of her actions on Edward's perceptions, unavoidably she finds herself leading Edward into the bedroom:

> The bride was not hurried in her movements—this was yet another of those delaying tactics that also committed her further. She was aware of her husband's enchanted gaze, but for the moment she did not feel quite so agitated or pressured. Entering the bedroom, she had plunged into an uncomfortable, dreamlike condition that encumbered her like an old-fashioned diving suit in deep water. Her thoughts did not seem her own—they were piped down to her, thoughts instead of oxygen. (*CB* 79)

The thoughts, however, are the reflections of her auditory memory. Florence finds herself comfortable with her husband's »enchanted gaze« from which she has been struggling to keep away. This becomes possible through delivering herself into music. She consciously tries to lessen or nullify the agitation or pressure of the nervous moment. Nevertheless, as Ingersoll expounds,

> Her invitation arouses his anticipation [Edward's] that she has after all become the willing partner in love-making he had hoped for, but more important it suddenly forces her to recognize that her effort to escape the sense of nausea and suffocation of his tongue penetrating her mouth is going to lead more quickly now to the even more intrusive penetration she has been trying not to even think about. (»The Moment« 139)

Florence tries to overcome the anxiety of this moment through the memories related with her music performance. Relying on them, she thinks that she can control the present situation as she controls the united performance of her music group. Her leadership should also help her here. Therefore, she feels as if she is leading Edward as they walk into the bedroom. At the same time, she draws the conclusion that she ought to utter her well-thought proposal to him. Whenever she becomes determined to do so, she feels overcome by her internal conflicts. Given in FIT mode in the following passage, her inner thought and perceptions display both the impact of the tense situation on her mental functioning and her daring unconventional solution to the problem:

> The Florence who led her quartet, who coolly imposed her will, would never meekly submit to conventional expectations. She was no lamb to be uncomplainingly knifed. Or penetrated. She would demand of herself what it was exactly she wanted and did not want from her marriage, and she would say so out loud to Edward, and expect to discover some form of compromise with him. Surely, what each of them desired should not be at the other's expense. The point was to love, and set each other free. Yes, she needed to speak up, the way she did at rehearsals, and she was going to do it now. (*CB* 81)

Florence's main problem is her unavoidable delay in expressing her proposal. She does love Edward; at the same time, she does not want the burden of the conventional marriage. Therefore, she wants to speak her mind to Edward but she postpones it until it is too late. If Edward is unable to calculate or imagine her situation and if he is primarily concerned with his own desires and intramental wishes, Florence is a woman of brooding, dreaming, calculating and doubt or, as Ingersoll put, her »motivation is more a matter of speculation than Edward's« (»The Moment« 142). As revealed in her long introspections, although her Hamletian dilemma restrains her from uttering her proposal for a long time, she finally dares to verbalise her component proposal at least in her own mind: »to love, and set each other free.« Florence, nevertheless, does not succeed in offering her proposal because the moment she looks back at Edward, we are told: »the liberating idea—as if never quite her own—was gone« (*CB* 81). The priority of saving their intermental bond or maintaining the balance in their relationship is the main reason why she forgets any thought about her proposal when she looks at Edward. She is, moreover, more aware of and eager to keep the established intermental unity between themselves. She is careful not to violate it. For example, when Edward cannot open the zip of her dress, her thoughts indicate her ultimate care for him: »She would have reached over her shoulder to help, but her arms were trapped, and besides, it did not seem right, showing him what to do. Above all, she did not wish to hurt his feelings.« The FIT passage, therefore, shows Florence's ultimate efforts to make Edward comfortable. She even ascribes the faults, concerning undoing her zip, to herself after Edward's voicing: »Oh God, Flo. Just keep still, will you« (*CB* 82).

Edward is so important to Florence that she »automatically« finds herself guilty without taking into account her previous decision to share her proposal with him. In order to help Edward unzip her dress, she thinks about »moving nearer the window for the light.« In addition, finding it »unaffectionate,« she looks at her action from Edward's perspective:

> Obediently, she froze, horrified by the agitation in his voice, automatically certain that it was her fault. It was, after all, her dress, her zip. It might have helped, she thought, to get free and turn her back, and move nearer the window for the light. But that could appear unaffectionate, and the interruption would admit to the scale of the problem. (*CB* 82)

Not only does Florence ascribe the faults to herself but she is also exploring the other possibilities that would have made the situation easier for Edward. However, the more they find themselves closer to the »final act,« the more she finds Edward agitated and frightening: »She was sorry for him, and she was a little frightened of him too. To make even a timid suggestion might enrage him further. So she stood patiently« (*CB* 83). Represented from Florence's perspective, this perception continues to improve until their confrontation scene along the beach. Florence, nevertheless, tries both to control the situation through »delaying tactics« and to lessen Edward's expectations. In order to lower his expectations indirectly, she whispers into his ear, »Actually, I'm a little bit scared« (*CB* 84). Her panic is the result of not only her inability to satisfy him, but also her failure in overcoming her own anxieties. Above all, she does not know how to talk about her problem with Edward because she does not find the appropriate words to describe her feelings.[94]

---

[94] This implies the socio-historical aspects of their problem. At their time (before 1962), talking about sexual issues, the narrative implies, was »never easy« (McEwan, *CB* 3). Therefore, this narrative examines the impact of one historical moment on the characters' consciousness since »again and again, McEwan shows how the decision of a moment can determine the future and in this novel; *On Chesil Beach* he further narrows the focus to a man's decision to do nothing, locking himself and his new wife out of a future they might have shared« (Ingersoll, »The Moment« 132).

Such a feeling of helplessness is indicated in the following FIT passage, which shows the impact of the tense situation on Florence's mental functioning. It is registered in her mind after her own confession, »I'm a little bit sacred,« to Edward:

> [1] This was not strictly accurate but, thoughtful though she was, she could never have described her array of feelings: a dry physical sensation of tight shrinking, general revulsion at what she might be asked to do, shame at the prospect of disappointing him, and of being revealed as a fraud. [2] She disliked herself, and when she whispered to him, she thought her words hissed in her mouth like those of a stage villain. [3] But it was better to talk of being scared than admit to disgust or shame. [4] She had to do everything she could to begin to lower his expectations. [5] He was gazing at her, and nothing registered in his expression to show he had heard her. [6] Even in her difficult state, she marvelled at his soft brown eyes. Such kindly intelligence and forgiveness. Perhaps if she stared into them and saw nothing else, she might just be able to do anything he asked of her. She would trust him utterly. But this was fantasy. (*CB* 84)

Florence finds herself unable to describe her feelings to Edward and is nervous by the »prospect« of being accused of »fraud« [1]. Although just a moment ago, she confided to Edward that she was »scared«; nevertheless, she does not even believe her own word now. Instead, taking the place as a »stage,« she imagines herself as a »villain« on it. This metaphor, »stage villain,« implies that not only does she consider the bedroom ceremony as a play in which she should take a part but also she imagines herself as a character with bad intentions or a »villain« [2]. Nevertheless, as shown by the word »but,« she reconstructs her own reasoning [3]. As a result, she finds her confession, being scared, better than admitting to what she considers as her »disgust or shame« [4]. Furthermore, based on his facial expression, she indulges in speculation on the impact of her words on Edward's consciousness although she finds »nothing registered« there [5]. Then, she tries to deliver herself to some fantasies so that she might be able to forget about her awkward situation. However, focusing on Edward's »soft brown eyes« which would enable her to »trust him utterly,« she finds such a thought merely a »fantasy« and hence counterfactual [6].

Thus, the more Florence finds herself closer to the disgusting moment of penetration, the more she becomes determined to postpone it or at least lessen Edward's expectations about it. While Florence is deeply concerned with keeping the balance between her love of Edward, or their small intermental unit, and her internal anxieties and disgusting feelings, or her intramental dispositions, Edward continues his misreadings mistaking Florence's actions, words, gestures and even postures as signs of her »eagerness.« Such a diverging duality shows how Florence consciously tries to maintain their intermental relationship. She constantly attempts to adjust herself to his expectations. She is even concerned that the involuntary movement of a muscle in her leg might give Edward the impression that his action gives her pain [1]. Nevertheless, the narrator's conjecture about Edward's internal feelings based on his facial expressions emphasises the way he is misreading Florence's intentions:

> [1] She felt it [a muscle in her leg]
> was letting her down, giving the first indication of the extent of her problem. [2] He surely felt the little storm beneath his hand, for his eyes widened minutely, and the tilt of his eyebrows and the soundless parting of his lips suggested that he was impressed, even in awe, as he mistook her turmoil for eagerness. (*CB* 85)

It seems that Edward has removed any possibilities from his mind other than Florence's »eagerness« in what they are about to do. He extends his counterfactual interpretations through intending to »dissuade her from some headlong action,« because he had »storm of his own« (*CB* 85, 86). Her »unruly muscle,« nevertheless, does not cease. The narrator's commentary on the relationship between body and emotion or how it is »shamming« (*CB* 87) that body does not or cannot lie about emotions displays the incongruity between Florence's actual emotions and its manifestation in her body. Therefore, in order to control the »unruly muscle« and lessen her internal »tumult.« Florence reminds herself of Edward's relation to her as well as his rights. Moreover, she tries to justify the existence of his hand on her leg by comparing herself to his college friends. Nevertheless, she finds her own situation unique and herself alone. Through ascribing »aloneness« to herself, Florence gets one more step closer to her egotism:

> his hand was there because he was her husband; she let it stay because she was his wife. Certain of her friends—Greta, Hermione, Lucy especially—would have been

> naked between the sheets hours ago, and would have consummated this marriage—noisily, joyously—long before the wedding. In their affection and generosity, they even had the impression that this was precisely what she had done. She had never lied to them, but neither had she set them straight. Thinking of her friends, she felt the peculiar unshared flavour of her own existence: she was alone. (*CB* 87)

The FIT passage, like most of Florence's embedded narratives, represents the impact of the moment on her consciousness. Once more, Florence looks at her own action from the eyes of the other(s), her friends in this case, feeling »the peculiar unshared flavour of her own existence.« Although she is represented as being aware of her own dispositions, propensities, flavours, abilities and disabilities, she desperately attempts to conform to the communal perspective. Nevertheless, she finds out that »her love for Edward was associated with a definable physical sensation, as irrefutable as vertigo, [. . .] Now here at last were the beginnings of desire, precise and alien, but clearly her own.« She gets excited for a moment because as her revelation »was relief that she was just like everyone else« (*CB* 88).[95] Despite such a »pleasing sensation.« Florence is aware of its transient nature. As the narrator's report of her subjectivity in the following FIT passage reveals, a sense of »apprehension« does not leave Florence in the bedroom:

> there remained her apprehension, a high wall, not so easily demolished. Nor did she want it to be. For all the novelty, she was not in a state of wild abandonment, nor did she want to be hurried towards one. She wanted to linger in this spacious moment, in these fully clothed conditions, with the soft brown-eyed gaze and the tender caress and the spreading thrill. But she knew that this was impossible, and that, as everyone said, one thing would have to lead to another. (*CB* 88–89)

Florence never intends to »demolish« the high wall between themselves since she can imagine what lies beyond that. Although she wants is to »linger in this spacious moment,« she is aware of its impossibility. Therefore,

---

95 Florence is filled with the same kind of happiness when »she had a similar moment of revelation in front of the mirror the evening she first discerned and probed a novel tight swelling around her Nipples [...] It was undeniable: she was not a separate subspecies of the human race. In triumph, she belonged among the generality« (McEwan, *CB* 88). However, referring to this statement, Puschmann-Nalenz states that »her [Florence's] difficulties in socialising are greater than Edward's« (204).

she is looking forward to devising a new »postpone tactic.« However, the narrative perspective changes to Edward from this moment (pp. 89–97). Despite that, the reader, applying continuing consciousness frame[96], is able to imagine Florence's internal »tumult« as well as the impact of the tense situation on her psyche.

Florence's present horrible, painful, and uncomfortable feeling towards the idea of penetration is partly the psychic effects of a vaguely rendered experience with her father about ten years earlier than her wedding night experience. In a telling simile, we are told, »She was trying not to think of the immediate future, or of the past, and she imagined herself clinging to this moment, the precious present, like an unroped climber on a cliff, pressing her face tight against the rock, not daring to move.« In spite of her efforts, the repressed memory returns to her consciousness when Edward, like her father in the past, is undressing. Besides that, she remembers the way she overcame her fears then: »Her only task was to keep her eyes closed and to think of a tune she liked. Or any tune« (*CB* 99). Likewise, she chooses not to move or change her position; instead, she concentrates on the tune hoping, »it would grow and overwhelm her and be an anaesthetic to her fears, and deliver her from disgrace. It appeared unlikely. The true memory of the feeling, of being inside it, of truly knowing what it was like, had already diminished to a dry historical fact« (*CB* 98). Her consciousness, therefore, is active in order to find a way out of her uncomfortable situation. She even finds a similarity between what she is experiencing in the present situation and what she experienced in her past situation when his father, like Edward at present, was undressing. The resemblance triggers in reader's mind Florence's perception of Edward's would-be action as rape, most probably in the same manner her father did in the past[97]. Nevertheless, such an

---

96 Palmer defines the term as the »process whereby readers create the illusion of a continuing consciousness for a character out of the scattered, isolated mentions of that person. The character continues to exist in the storyworld even when not present at a particular point in the text« (»The Mind« 81).

97 Many critics believe that Florence's rape by his father is understandable from the textual hints. Ingersoll, for example, states that »The novel does, however, drop maddeningly vague but irresistible hints that the source of Florence's repugnance

analogy does not help Florence because her present situation does not seem to be a memory but a »fact,« hurting her. Despite that, she tries to »pretend convincingly« in order to »whittle her anxieties away« (*CB* 101). The narrative, however, shows the way she is stuck in this difficult situation. She grabs at whatever she perceives to be helpful as she does not know what to do. In other words, she creates the convention itself when she finds herself not knowing one. In doing that, she takes Edward's behaviour as a model: »But beyond the obvious three words [I love you.], what could she herself say that did not sound contrived or foolish? And since he was silent, she thought this must be the convention« (*CB* 102).

In such scenes, when Florence is assessing their situation at that particular moment, the character's and narrator's voices get so closer to each other that their differentiation becomes very difficult. The reader, nevertheless, knows that the recounted subjectivity belongs to Florence. At the same time, the extradiegetic narrator's illustrative and explanatory comments on the characters' situation do all resemble Edward's and Florence's internal discourses. Moreover, they show the impact of their personality traits, time, family, culture, class etc. on their mental functioning. The affinities between the two discourses (the characters' and the narrator's), moreover, signify the conformity of the two concerning the represented problems in the storyworld. In the following passage, for example, it seems that the narrator's voice does conform to Florence's perception of the necessity to rely on Edward in order to feel »assurance«:

> She needed to feel close to him in order to hold down the demon of panic she knew was ready to overwhelm her. She had to know he was with her, on her side, and was not going to use her, that he was her friend and was kindly and tender. Otherwise it

---

toward sexuality may be her father« (»The Moment« 136). Nevertheless, referring to such observations, particularly to Dominic Head's position »who ascribes the girl's insecurity and subsequent repulsion for sex to child abuse by her father«, Puschmann-Nalenz claims that »Several hints point to a different psychological constellation: she replaces a son in her father's eyes [...]. Being sensitive, she sees both her parents as unattractive and distant, her younger sister as a nuisance, [...]. It is difficult for her to regard herself as part of a group or community outside her professional occupation with music« (203–204).

> could all go wrong, in a very lonely way. She was dependent on him for this assurance, beyond love. (*CB* 102)

To find out such »assurance,« she gives several interpretations to every action of Edward. For example, when he gazes at her while his »lips quivering a little,« Florence's inferences are as following, »nerves perhaps, or a nascent smile, or a thought evolving into words« (*CB* 102). Florence's internal struggles, accordingly, grow mild, the more she reminds herself of the necessity of keeping up »appearances« in order to »please him.« Florence is aware of her problem, his expectations and the things she can do in order to both keep up appearances, and manage or control Edward:

> But her immediate preoccupation—an improvement on revulsion or fear—was to keep up appearances, not to let him down or humiliate herself, or seem a poor choice among all the women he had known. She was going to get through this. She would never let him know what a struggle it was, what it cost her, to appear calm. She was without any other desire but to please him and make this night a success, [. . .] Her panic and disgust, she thought, were under control, she loved Edward, and all her thoughts were on helping him have what he so dearly wanted and to make him love her all the more. It was in this spirit that she slid her right hand down between his groin and hers. (*CB* 103–104)

In spite of all her care and calculations, she cannot read Edward's mind or misreads it although she makes her efforts to be truly aware of his tense situation. They mutually continue keeping up appearances without cooperation as they intramentally try to overcome the tough situation or their sexual anxieties. Despite that, their precautions do not seem to have a consciously built shared point. It is, in other words, the separate nature of their unspoken cautions that make the problem more tense. She, for example, taunts herself after Edward »emptie[s] himself« (*CB* 105). Provided by the narrator with the knowledge that Edward's problem is »arriving too soon,« the reader, nevertheless, knows beforehand that he is prone to immature orgasm. She immediately condemns herself for her »terrible mistake«—pulling Edward's testicles:

> It was a calamity, and she knew immediately that it was all her fault, that she was inept, ignorant and stupid. [. . .] She should not have interfered, she should never have believed the manual. [. . .] she should have known well enough that her attitude

> in rehearsals for the string quartet had no relevance here. [. . .] She knew how loathsome, how unmannerly her behaviour was, how it must add to his misery to see her so desperate to remove this part of himself from her skin. (*CB* 105–106)

McEwan in this scene, according to Ingersol, »offers in excruciating detail what it might feel like to be sprayed with a copious shower of hot, stinging, and then cold, caking semen« (»The Moment« 140). Such a detailed report anchors firmly to the reader's world experiences or frames. Moreover, if she knew that he had the problem of arriving too soon and if she were aware of his anxieties and even fears concerning their copulation, she would never condemn herself for being »inept, ignorant, and stupid.« Furthermore, what she considered as her »cooperation« with him turns out to be merely misinterpretations because the outcome of cooperation should be the consolidation of intermental minds through bringing about a consciously shared activity. Nevertheless, her embedded narratives change into presentation of the conflicts between her two selves. While one hates herself, the other hates Edward:

> [1] She was two selves—the one who flung the pillow down in exasperation, the other who looked on and hated herself for it. [2] It was unbearable that he should watch her, the punishing, hysterical woman he had foolishly married. [3] She could hate him for what he was witnessing now and would never forget. She had to get away from him. (*CB* 106)

Florence is represented as coming out of herself and looking at herself from both her own perspective and that of Edward's [1 and 2] or as Courtney points out:

> she becomes aware of two simultaneous parts of herself: the reactive part and the analytical part. The analytical part of her watches with disgust as the reactive part cannot help itself from indulging in primary psychological and physical reactions in the moment. As a character, Florence demonstrates a developed mind—she is not simply reacting instinctively, she is also simultaneously assessing her actions and feeling disgust because they contradict how she thinks she should feel. Even in her moment of frenzied crisis, Florence has enough time to perform complex thought processes concerning her situation. (*CB* 193)

Based on her own assumption, as shown in [2], she draws the conclusion that she should »get away« immediately. The aftereffects of this decision will never leave the newlyweds. Her tolerating capacity terminates when she finds herself responsible for the problem that »her other watching self appeared to be telling her calmly, but not quite in words, But this is just what it's like to be mad. She could not look at him. It was torture to remain in the room with someone who knew her like this« (*CB* 106). She runs to the beach in order to clear her mind or, according to Wondrich, »Florence flees their botched lovemaking to reach the beach for shelter.« Nevertheless, after lying on the bed for a while and ascribing all the faults to Florence, Edward rushes to the beach where their bitter argument arises. That is the final stroke to their fragile relationship.

The opening of the first section at the final part presents the narrative events, after Edward's leaving, from Florence's perspective. Unlike Edward, she is worried about what might happen or about the consequences of her action. When she unexpectedly sees Edward coming along the shore towards her, we are told:

> [1] She watched him, willing him to go slower, for she was guiltily afraid of him, and was desperate for more time to herself. [2] Whatever conversation they were about to have, she dreaded it. As she understood it, there were no words to name what had happened, there existed no shared language in which two sane adults could describe such events to each other. And to argue about it was even further beyond her imagining. There could be no discussion. She did not want to think about it, [3] and she hoped he felt the same. [4] But what else were they to talk about? Why else were they out here? The matter lay between them, as solid as a geographical feature, a mountain, a headland. Unnameable, unavoidable. [5] And she was ashamed. The aftershock of her own behaviour reverberated through her, and even seemed to sound in her ears. (*CB* 139–140)

Florence's anticipation about the nature of their would-be meeting is telling considerably. She still feels that she is »guilty« about what happened in the bedroom. As a result, she counterfactually wishes to be alone because she »fears« Edward [1]. Her prospect of their next conversation is tantalizing because she is aware of the lack of a »shared language« about the problem [2]. At the same time, she expects Edward to have the same feeling too [3]. She knows that they should talk about the problem because it is the only observable, »solid,« thing that they share [4]. Accordingly, she feels

»shamed« for the second time which »reverberates' in her ears [5]. Her situation is similar to a catch-22 or hopeless situation. She goes through a circle which begins from hopelessness, passes through hopefulness and finally leads in absolute hopelessness again. To put it in narratological terms, she is represented as being firstly in a disequilibrium state, then in an equilibrium state and finally in a different kind of disequilibrium which brings about some fundamental changes to her thoughts and actions too. Florence, moreover, seems to be considering the problem from a broader perspective. She is aware of her problem, she is willing to find a beneficial way out of that tense situation and, at the same time, she is aware of the difficulty of speaking about their problem. Her peace-seeking self ascribes all »disgrace« and »shame« to herself. By the same token, she is repressing the desires of her other disrupting self she escaped from in the bedroom. For example, she tries to examine whether Edward had a role in the »disgrace« or not. She patiently finds out the reasons of his silence on their problem. In other words, she imagines the way Edward thinks about the situation. The narrative represents her cognitive activities in this moment:

> [1] Did she dare admit that she was a tiny bit relieved that it was not only her, that he too had something wrong with him? How terrible, but how comforting it would be if he suffered from some form of congenital illness, a family curse, the sort of sickness to which only shame and silence attach, the way it did to enuresis, or to cancer, a word she superstitiously never spoke aloud for fear it would infect her mouth—silliness, for sure, which she would never confess to. [2] Then they could feel sorry for each other, bound in love by their separate afflictions. And she did feel sorry for him, [3] but she also felt a little cheated. If he had an unusual condition, why had he not told her, in confidence? [4] But she understood perfectly why he could not. She too had not spoken up. [5] How could he have begun to broach the matter of his own particular deformity, what could have been his opening words? They did not exist. Such a language had yet to be invented. (*CB* 140–141)

Florence is primarily imagining that Edward should have a role, for example »something wrong with him,« in this situation [1]. She feels relaxed in this revelation imagining Edward and herself »bound in love by their separate afflictions« [2]. Nevertheless, she expands the possibility condemning and censuring Edward for hiding the truth from her. As a result, she feels »cheated« [3]. Still, she is able to put herself in Edward's place finding that they both suffer from the same problem. Having remembered that she could not speak up too, she forgives Edward for a moment [4]. The last part [5] is focalized from the narrator's perspective. It highlights Edward's difficulty in talking about his »particular deformity« because of language deficiency. The narrator's comment, moreover, elucidates what Florence cannot understand. Florence cannot persuade herself that Edward is also responsible for the situation. Her beliefs or presuppositions in this case seem to be unchangeable. She feels sure that Edward has no fault in her »disgrace,« as revealed in this FIT statement: »Even as she elaborately thought this through, she knew very well there was nothing wrong with him. Nothing at all. It was her, only her« (*CB* 141).

Therefore, during all their tense moments in the bedroom and after that in the beach, Florence is haunted with the thought of not being cruel to Edward and not giving him any chance of taking her as a »fraud.« For example, even though she fears him, »she thought it would be too cruel to run away« (*CB* 142). At the midst of her broodings and before Edward's arriving, Florence is reminded of her earlier thought or her »daring proposal.« She still thinks the only way by which they can continue on their shared life is to »love and set each other free.« She believes that her proposal is beneficial to both sides. She is aware of her own problem, she hates penetration, and understands that Edward expects her to be his wife like any other woman. She is not, however, aware of Edward's personal problem—arriving too soon. Her proposal, therefore, is totally aspectual. Holding different values, they have »conflicting approaches to life« (Wells, *Ian McEwan* 92). Considering Florence, for example, the narrator observes that: »She never could quite get the full measure of her own ignorance, because in some matters she thought she was rather wise« (*CB* 142). The following passage reveals Florence's internal conflicts portraying her indecisive mental state when Edward is approaching. She tries to find an appealing way in order to communicate with him:

> It was another of her failings that she had no idea what attitude to take with him, no feelings beyond her dread of what he might say, and of what she would be expected

> to say in return. She did not know if she should be asking for forgiveness, or expecting an apology. She was not in love, or out of love—she felt nothing. She just wanted to be here alone in the dusk against the bulk of her giant tree. (*CB* 142–143)

The degree Florence's mind is perplexed at the moment is portrayed in this passage. This situation, according to Spitz, is the sign of the fact that:

> ensuing dispute is not pre-planned. [. . .] Rather it appears that once Edward and Florence begin producing sequential oppositional moves and thereby establish a conflict frame, the exchange takes on a life of its own, dragging the speakers along—whatever their original intentions might have been. (202)

Florence is caught between two states. No longer does she make hypotheses about Edward since she does not know »what attitude to take with him.« The above passage, like Florence's many embedded narratives, gives the reader the impression of not knowing what to do. Despite that and quite astonishingly, Florence's mood changes abruptly when she, while exchanging some words with Edward, finds out that in that warm weather »he had brought his jacket with him there.« This moment her »good opinion« disappears and cannot be restores later: »how irritable she suddenly felt, when minutes ago she was so ashamed of herself. She was usually so keen to have his good opinion, and now she did not care« (*CB* 143).

Florence's embedded narratives, accordingly, represent her mental activities in order to solve a terrible problem or dilemma in her relationship with Edward. Moreover, the impact of the complicated moments in the bedroom and at the beach on Florence's mental functioning and their subsequent contributions to her decisions and actions all reveal the centrality of the presentation of fictional minds' operation and what it's like for them to experience some moments in the storyworld. Likewise, these are the central concepts to both Palmer's and Herman's discussion of the respectively fictional minds and narrativity.

5.4 The Question of Aspectuality in the Embedded Narratives: Edward Mayhew

Edward's patriarchal mind is represented as pursuing its own goals and desires. His second or hidden self is so strong that it presupposes its centrality in every situation. Throughout their strenuous moments in the hotel room, Edward's intramental self proceeds only with its strongly aspectual perceptions without taking into account Florence' perspective. He is unable to reconstruct his strongly held perspectives or aspectuality. While he tries to overcome his conventionalised intramental dispositions since he loves Florence, he ironically finds himself desperate to do so. His internal conflicts, therefore, act as the main drive for his actions. Accordingly, his embedded narratives show his mental functioning moment by moment representing the impact of narrative situations on his decisions and actions. From the very beginning, his mind is presented as being troubled with his unspeakable problem without finding a way out until their wedding night. This anxiety leaves no room for Edward to think about Florence's states:

> [1] For over a year, Edward had been mesmerised by the prospect that on the evening of a given date in July the most sensitive portion of himself would reside, however briefly, within a naturally formed cavity inside this cheerful, pretty, formidably intelligent woman. [2] How this was to be achieved without absurdity, or disappointment, troubled him. His specific worry, based on one unfortunate experience, was of over-excitement, of what he had heard someone describe as ›arriving too soon‹. The matter was rarely out of his thoughts, but though his fear of failure was great, his eagerness—for rapture, for resolution—was far greater. (*CB* 6–7)

Thinking very highly of her, Edward desires Florence [1]. She is more than a sexual tool for him since he thinks of her as »cheerful,« »pretty« and »formidably intelligent.« Such a physical as well as intellectual combination of beauty, however, remains the biggest cause of Florence's charm to Edward. He is aware of his own problem. His one »unfortunate experience« provokes his anxiety over consummating his marriage [2]. In the early passages, Edward ascribes the main cause of his problem not to Florence but to himself. It shows his ability and capacity to evaluate the issues from different perspectives. As a result, for a while his ensuing evaluations and judgments are based on shared interests. It moreover indicates the rational side of his thought that is able to control and orient his actions in the early parts of the narrative. Nevertheless, he suffers from being in a kind of dilemma between two states—»his fear of failure,« and his »eagerness«.

Unlike Florence, Edward is presented as being primarily concerned about the appearances or signs. Since he is mostly driven by his sexual desires, he is unable to take into account Florence's mental states. For example, to satiate his desires, as we are told, »he longed for them [the waiters] to leave« (*CB* 12). He does not even make theories about her mind; instead, he is presented as being enchanted with her beauty, »But the hand that held the wine glass trembled as he struggled to contain his sudden happiness, his exaltation. She appeared to glow before him, and she was lovely -beautiful, sensuous, gifted, good-natured beyond belief« (*CB* 12). Edward, moreover, exaggerates about his own character. He compares himself with some historical figures he has prepared in a list. His wayward intramental perceptions and judgments are notable in his broodings recounted in such passages:

> As he dressed for the wedding that morning [. . .] he had decided that none of the figures on his list could have known his kind of satisfaction. His elation was a form of greatness in itself. Here he was, a gloriously fulfilled, or almost fulfilled, man. At the age of twenty-two, he had already outshone them all. (*CB* 13–14)

Such emotional fulfilment is, nevertheless, transient because Edward is unaware of the intensity of his problem as he is totally ignorant about Florence's painful feeling at this moment. However, the moment he encounters with his ineluctable anxiety, the sense of fulfilment gives way to painful sensations and finally to disappointment.

Furthermore, Edward is unaware of the duality in Florence's behaviour since he fundamentally pays attention to her outward beauty and music performance. Counterfactually, he thinks that all Florence's »thought and emotion appeared naked to him.« Such a simplistic interpretation takes him to misread her real thoughts and feelings since he misinterprets her actions. Therefore, as far as he is controlled by his intramental anxieties, he is also restricted by the outward aspects of Florence's behaviour:

> How could he fail to love someone so strangely and warmly particular, so painfully honest and self-aware, whose every thought and emotion appeared naked to view, streaming like charged particles through her changing expressions and gestures? Even without her strongboned beauty he would have had to love her. And she loved

> him with such intensity, such excruciating physical reticence. Not only his passions, heightened by the lack of a proper outlet, but also his protective instincts were aroused. But was she really so vulnerable? (*CB* 16)

Moreover, in his experiences with Florence before the wedding night, Edward finds her »determined to lead« in music, influential on her »frightening« father and possessing some »womanly osmosis« (*CB* 17). Her »osmosis,« however, does not influence him as he thinks it does. Following such perceptions, Edward thinks that Florence is exactly the woman he wants although he reconstructs such perceptions during their restless wedding night. Besides that, he reconstructs his own ideas and perceptions about Florence many years after that night when it is too late to help their lost intermental bond return.

Referring to Florence's earlier proposal to see the beach for themselves, Edward thinks, »Trudging along the beach would have been better than sitting here« (*CB* 19). Such ironic thought shows his helplessness in the room. As a result of his passionate waiting to embrace Florence, Edward feels a »terrible pressure narrowing his thoughts, onstraining his speech, and he was in acute physical discomfort-his trousers or underwear seemed to have shrunk.« In addition, we are told that »all he wanted, all he could think of, was himself and Florence lying naked together on or in the bed next door, confronting at last that awesome experience that seemed as remote from daily life as a vision of religious ecstasy« (*CB* 19–20). His »thought-confining desire« (*CB* 20) finally persuades him to submit to Florence's requests and needs. Edward's engagement with sexual desires is reported to be with him from the moment he was twelve years old after which he »indulged constantly in what one enlightened authority was now calling ›self-pleasuring‹,« in order to »release« himself from the »urgent, thought confining desire« (*CB* 20). The narrator, ironically, recounts that Edward's only contribution to the wedding arrangements »was to refrain« from self-pleasing for over a week. This memory reincarnates in Edward's contemplations in the bedroom. It is moreover a »euphemistic way of thinking about sexual activity, whereas Florence has no language in which to represent what she thinks of as a frightening social obligation« (Wells, *Ian McEwan* 94). Accordingly, it is an unavoidable possibility that Edward's marriage was more for the sake of having sex than finding a shared mind. He wrongly perceives that it is Florence's main reason too. Such a reasoning leads him to misreads her »shyness« as a common trait:

> [1] Why did he not rise from his roast, cover her in kisses and lead her towards the four-poster next door? [2] It was not so simple. [3] He had a fairly long history of engaging with Florence's shyness. He had come to respect it, even revere it, [4] mistaking it for a form of coyness, a conventional veil for a richly sexual nature. In all, part of the intricate depth of her personality, and proof of her quality. [5] He persuaded himself that he preferred her this way. He did not spell it out for himself, but her reticence suited his own ignorance and lack of confidence; a more sensual and demanding woman, a wild woman, might have terrified him. (*CB* 21)

The narrator's voice in this passage overlaps with the character's thoughts delivered in FIT mode. The narrator examines the reasons for Edward's inability to take Florence towards the next door [1]. The second sentence, however, indicates the difficulty of the action from both the character's and the narrator's perspectives [2]. From the narrator's perspective, Edward finds taking Florence into the bedroom »not so simple« since he fear that, doing so, he might commit a mistake or misinterpret her real intentions. He has been ascribing it to her »shyness« [3]. This shows his continual misreading of her mind. He always takes her internal dilemmas as signs of her »coyness.« Moreover, he associates it with the conventional belief that shyness is a »veil for richly sexual nature« which proved, from Edward's perspective, her »quality« [4]. He even allows himself to enlarge the fantasy by binding her problem to his own. Based on such a wrong proposition, he attenuates his own »ignorance and lack of confidence.« Therefore, when he imagines himself marrying a »sensual and more demanding, a wild woman.« Edward finds it »terrifying.« Therefore, Edward's reading of Florence's intentions and his inferences concerning her behaviour in the hotel room fundamentally derive from his strongly aspectual attributions to Florence. The extradiegetic narrator's analysis of Edward's conscious and unconscious mental functioning, moreover, shows the impact of that night, their wedding night, on his consciousness. The narrator, nevertheless, ascribes their reticent or controlled behaviour to each other to some factors beyond their personal realms, to the realm of time, language, science etc.:

> Their courtship had been a pavane, a stately unfolding, bound by protocols never agreed or voiced, but generally observed. Nothing was ever discussed—nor did they feel the lack of intimate talk. These were matters beyond words, beyond definition. The language and practice of therapy, the currency of feelings diligently shared, mutually analysed, were not yet in general circulation. While one heard of wealthier people going in for psychoanalysis, it was not yet customary to regard oneself in everyday terms as an enigma, as an exercise in narrative history, or as a problem waiting to be solved. (*CB* 21)

Having indicated the difficulty of any progression in their relationships from Edward's perspective, the narrator draws some inferences about Florence's behaviour towards Edward too. The more Edward proceeds, the more she retreats although carefully. Her primary purpose is pleasing him or at least keeping a balance between her internal dilemmas and his expectations. She endeavours to manage both of them and she is represented successful at doing so until their confrontation in the beach when she feels forced to follow her own intramental perceptions. Their opposing orientations are represented in the following scene:

> he took her hand and plunged it between his legs set the process back weeks. She became, not frosty, or even cool—that was never her way—but imperceptibly remote, perhaps disappointed, or even faintly betrayed. She retreated from him somehow without letting him ever feel in doubt about her love. (*CB* 22)

The »imperceptibility« is their shared characteristic. It mainly derives from some social, historical and linguistic factors as much as from their personality traits. Nevertheless, Edward's insistence on intramental desires, regardless of the other side's feelings and sensations, lead to their final intramental dissent. Even in his proposal to her, his emotions, more than his intellect, control his thought and actions. As we are told, »she let her hand rest briefly on, or near, his penis. For less than fifteen seconds, in rising hope and ecstasy, he felt her through two layers of fabric. As soon as she pulled away he knew he could bear it no more. He asked her to marry him« (*CB* 22).

Nevertheless, Edward tries to overcome his own internal conflicts and anxieties by separating himself from the socio-political issues echoed off the walls downstairs. He dares to conclude that »It could not go on. It was time to act.« The intention to »act« instead of thinking about acting provokes Edward into doing something in order to break the ice between them. His ironic expression, »We could go downstairs and listen properly,« entices in Florence's mind a series of strongly aspectual, and at the same time intramental, inferences. For example, we are told, »She thought he was criticising her for preferring the wireless to him« (*CB* 26). She is in fact right in inferring that Edward is criticising her. She is also aware of the fact that Edward's primary concern in the bedroom is to make her be aware of their primary job at the room. As a result, she gets excited simply because she thinks that Edward does not understand her internal dilemma. Therefore, she finds herself obliged to return a mutual ironic possibility to Edward, »Or we could go and lie on the bed« (*CB* 26). She knows that what Edward wants more than anything else is going to bed and she is aware of impact of her words on his consciousness. Therefore, she relentlessly chooses her words in order to take her revenge on him. The ironic tone of her statement, however, does not change his intramental intentions.

When the narrative perspective changes to Edward, or it is his viewpoints that are presented through internal focalization, we encounter a dramatically different thought. Following his own interpretation of Florence's (re)actions, Edward continues his misreading of her thoughts. Besides that, he persists on what he considers to be his appropriate reaction to her thoughts:

> [1] Ever in his exalted, jittery condition he thought he understood her customary reticence. [2] All the more cause for joy then, that they faced this momentous occasion, this dividing line of experience, together. [3] And the thrilling fact remained that it was Florence who had suggested lying on the bed. Her changed status had set her free. (*CB* 28)

In this FIT passage, Edward wrongly thinks that he understands the chief reason of Florence's »reticence« state, which has become »customary« too. His interpretation of her silence or reticence, however, is in opposition to her actual feelings and perceptions. Edward takes her thoughts for granted in many situations. Since he presupposes that he understands her behaviour correctly, he grounds his expectations and proposals on such flawed perceptions. Following that, he adjusts his later reasoning to such counterfactual inferences while facing their »dividing line of experience« [2]. Furthermore, Edward finds it a »thrilling fact« that Florence was the initiator of the ceremony. He also thinks that her marriage, »her changed status,« has liberated her [3]. Unlike him, the reader is aware of the fact that Edward's discourse gets more aspectual and intramental, the more time it takes to go to bed.

Edward, therefore, is the person who is mostly pushing himself and Florence towards their break since he exacerbates the existing imbalance in their intramental minds through his continuous misinterpretations. For example, when he gets closer to her whispering, »You're very beautiful,« that triggers in Florence's mind intentional reminding of her feelings towards him, »She made herself remember how much she loved this man. He was kind, sensitive, he loved her and could do her no harm. She shrugged herself deeper into his embrace, close against his chest, and inhaled his familiar scent, which had a woody quality and was reassuring« (*CB* 28). While Florence wants to make herself at ease with him reminding herself about his significance, Edward continues his assertiveness, which is imbued with his wrong inferences and associations. (Un)knowingly, he continues his misinterpretations and intramental behaviours. For example, as it is told, »He knew well enough she did not like this kind of kissing,« or he did know that he should not put his tongue into her mouth as she does not like it, still he could not resist doing so: »and he had never before been so assertive« (*CB* 29).

Without having a plan and being »weary of books and birdsong and country peace« (*CB* 46), Edward leaves his family home in Turville Heath one day. Similarly, in the Henley railway station he quite accidentally chose to go to Oxford where he, out of chance, »saw a handwritten sign advertising a lunchtime meeting of the local CNL, and hesitated. [. . .] Still, he was a paid-up member, he had nothing else to do and he felt a vague pull of obligation. It was his duty to help save the world« (*CB* 47). Even in the meeting hall, the first person Edward sees is Florence. His assumptions, inferences and mindreading about her character display Edward's personal desires and intentions before even opening his conversation with Florence. Moreover, he tries to make a theory of mind about Florence although he does not seem to be able to enter into her mind:

> [1] As his eyes adjusted, the first person he saw was Florence, [. . .] He thought for a moment she was a nurse—in an abstract, conventional way he found nurses erotic, because—so he liked to fantasize—they already knew everything about his body and its needs. [2] Unlike most girls he stared at in the street or in shops, she did not look away. [3] Her look was quizzical or humorous, and possibly bored and wanting entertainment. It was a strange face, certainly beautiful, but in a sculpted, strongboned way. In the gloom of the hall the singular quality of light from a high window to her right made her face resemble a carved mask, soulful and tranquil and hard to read. [...] [4] He was walking toward her with no idea of what he would say. In the matter of opening lines, he was reliably inept. (*CB* 47–48)

Through making an analogy between the nurses and Florence, Edward concludes that she should be fairly »erotic.« With such a presupposition, he continues his subsequent examinations of her appearances and nature. Edward, moreover, extends the comparison to the girls he had already seen in the streets [2]. Again, he finds Florence in better condition. Following that, he tries to infer her thoughts from her facial expressions [3], but he finds her face »quizzical or humorous,« »bored,« »wanting entertainment,« »strange,« »soulful« and finally »tranquil.« Such uncertain inferences bring Edward to finds it »hard to read« her feelings and thoughts based on her facial expressions. Nevertheless, he is driven towards her even though he does not know how to open his conversation or what to say to her [4]. Furthermore, he allows more flawed inferences about Florence when he takes the movement of her finger at the moment of giving him the CNL pamphlet as an intentional act from her side: »As he took it from her, her finger trailed, surely not by accident, across the inside of his wrist« (*CB* 48). The sense of possessing her appears in Edward when he interprets the man beside Florence as »looking venomous«: »The fellow with her was looking venomous as he waited for him to move away, but Edward stayed right where he was« (*CB* 48). As this TR shows, Edward stays in the hall simply in order to show the man who he is or to make him recognise his existence. This stubborn or obstinate characteristic plays a significant role in Edward's life before meeting Florence, at the moment of meeting her for the first time and on their wedding night. Therefore, it gradually leads Edward towards intramentality forcing him to focus on his own perceptions and desires or his thoughts.

Edward is represented as being aware of his own ignorance or lack of experience of making love. As we are told, »he did not quite know what to do.« The ignorance makes him unable to decode the »perturbation beneath his hand« (*CB* 89). At the same time, he is excited and curious about the prospect. For a moment, he is concerned about his own readings of Florence's signs although we know that he mostly misreads them. In other words, in a similar manner to Florence, he lives in an uncertain situation but in different terms. Thus, his self-knowledge about his tendency to »misread the signs« (*CB* 99) reveals his own in-between situation. However, unlike Florence, he takes it for granted that she is »eager« and after such a perception, he endeavours to make up for her tacit requests: »[1] his caution was surely absurd. This hesitancy was a madness of his own. [2] They were married, for goodness' sake, and she was encouraging him, urging him on, desperate for him to take the lead. [3] But still, he could not escape the memories of those times when he had misread the signs« (*CB* 90). In FIT mode, Edward is represented as ascribing »madness« to himself since he considers his »caution« as foolish [1]. Therefore, he grounds his own perception on some personal reasons—they are married, she encourages him etc.—in order to justify his action [2]. Nevertheless, as indicated by the conjunctive word »but,« Edward, drawing on his earlier experiences, is haunted by his inclination towards misreading signs [3]. Thus, to highlight his misreading experiences, the narrator in this part recounts the occasions of Edward's misreadings in order to show to what extent he is capable of doing so. Therefore, Edward feels growing unease throughout the two significant moments—at the bedroom and at the beach:

> [1] He regarded his state of excitement, ignorance and indecision as dangerous because he did not trust himself. [2] He was capable of behaving stupidly, even explosively. He was known to his university friends as one of those quiet types, prone to the occasional violent eruption. According to his father, his very early childhood had been marked by spectacular tantrums. (*CB* 91)

The first part, in FIT mode, reveals Edward's self-knowledge. Drawing on his experiential repertoire, he finds himself distrustful [1]. In the second part, the narrator provides some background information in order to support Edward's assumption. According to the narrator's report, there had been an intermental thought among his friends concerning Edward's »occasional violent eruption.« Likewise, his father ascribed »spectacular tantrums« to his childhood [2]. Moreover, in all his violent moods »there is an implied personal inadequacy. [. . .] Edward's volatility, as well as his moral and emotional lack, [. . .] is made to hang over the wedding night« (Head, »*On Chesil Beach*« 120). In addition, Puschmann-Nalenz makes a connection between Edward's violent mood and his social class stating that »To Edward Mayhew with his isolated, disorderly upbringing and his keen interest in fanatical medieval religious cults violence seemed to be a part of life, until he became familiar with the standards of the educated classes. Violence there is judged unethical« (206). The inclusion of such passages in Edward's embedded narratives holds a teleological importance because, as we are told, through the »occasional violent eruption[s]'« or »spectacular tantrums.« Edward found a »thrilling unpredictability, and discovered a spontaneous, decisive self that eluded him in the rest of his tranquil existence« (*CB* 91). Edward felt finding such a »decisive self« when he unexpectedly and out of blue hit a man who had hit his friend, Harold Mather. He did so because, as the narrator recounts, »his anger had lifted itself and spiralled into a kind of ecstasy« (*CB* 94). Nevertheless, Edward reconstructs his perception that his fighting was a necessity when he figure out the indirect rejection of his street fighting by his friend:

> Edward realised that what he had done was simply not cool, and his shame was all the greater. Street fighting did not go with poetry and irony, bebop or history. He was guilty of a lapse of taste. He was not the person he had thought. What he believed was an interesting quirk, a rough virtue, turned out to be a vulgarity. He was a country boy, a provincial idiot who thought a bareknuckle swipe could impress a friend. It was a mortifying reappraisal. He was making one of the advances typical of early adulthood: the discovery that there were new values by which he preferred to be judged. Since then, Edward had stayed out of fights. (*CB* 95)

Therefore, Edward does possess the propensity to get nervous or angry, to behave irrationally and then regret after a while when it is too late. His sequences of actions against Florence in the bedroom are similar to this situation. He tries to control his anger, but when he loses his control, it violates the balance in their relationship. Moreover, he reconstructs his behaviour when it is too late. Therefore, this »madness« story prepares the scene for Edward's nervous and disruptive reaction after his abrupt ejaculation. In spite of his attempts to control his »anger« in the past, Edward still »did not trust himself« when he was in the bedroom. Accordingly, frightened by his own »savage impatience« (2007b: 95), he is unable to make out of Florence's fear. Instead, he keeps thinking that if they just take one more step, they can enter into freedom. At the same time, he does not know why they are unable to do so: »It was so simple! Why weren't they up there now, instead of sitting here, bottled up with all the things they did not know how to say or dared not do?« The narrated FIT passage, therefore, reveals Edward as being aware of his tacit anger, his ignorance about sexual matters and his own weaknesses in that case. In spite of all these, he does not know anything about Florence's mental states. Unlike Florence, who tries not to offend him through her actions, Edward does not even make inferences about her internal feelings. He only feels confused about the reason Florence does not let him in easily. For a moment, the narrative perspective changes to the omniscient narrator who reveals in TR mode the actual obstacle to the newlyweds' intermentality: »And what stood in their way? Their personalities and pasts, their ignorance and fear, timidity, squeamishness, lack of entitlement or experience or easy manners, then the tail end of a religious prohibition, their Englishness and class, and history itself. Nothing much at all« (*CB* 96). It is not, however, accidental that the narrator points to »personality« as the first obstacle on their way to intermentality. Edward and Florence are, in fact, personally different people regardless of the other obstacles since, according to Childs, in this passage »McEwan suggests that temporal orientation is achieved by the behaviour of people situated at points along a stretch of time« (»Contemporary« 31). They both depend on their intramental thoughts mostly because of their peculiar »pasts.« The last phrase, »nothing much at all,« seems to be ironic because the enumerated obstacles making totally »a high wall« (*CB* 88) between them, are the fundamental problems. Moreover, according to Wells, the narrator in this passage »wryly sums up their problem as one endemic to British culture at the time« (*Ian McEwan* 93).

Edward, nevertheless, attempts to control his thoughts. For example, when he thinks that »back through time« all the couples were »surely more adept« in the bedroom where they are now, he controls himself not to laugh at his own imagination of the people standing in a row back. In doing that, Edward takes into account their situation and Florence's possible reaction to his behaviour: »It was important not to think about them; comedy was an erotic poison. He also had to hold off the thought that she might be terrified of him. If he believed that, he could do nothing.« Nevertheless, he is uncertain because, as in the previous moments, »her face [was] slack and difficult to read.« Therefore, Edward continues his misreading signs, as he himself was »nervous with desire and indecision« (*CB* 97). While »desire« is something personal, the state of »indecision« comes mostly from the lack of his knowledge about Florence—he not only does not know anything about sex, but he is also ignorant about Florence's feelings and thoughts in the same way he is ignorant about his own feelings and actions. It seems that Edward, more than Florence, looks at the signs without being able to decode them or go beyond them as well as beyond his own mind or thoughts. They both know that they are in a tense situation; despite that, they, particularly Edward, tenaciously insist on their desires in order to go on—Florence does so mostly in order not to hurt Edward, while Edward does so simply because he wants to insatiate his desires. Therefore, it is possible to argue that while Edward is heading towards its disruption seemingly, Florence consciously tries to preserve the already established cognitive unit between them. Further, concerning her attempts to maintain the intermental unit, Florence's ability and capacity do not appear to be unbound. When she finds the proper chance at the beach, she contributes to the total breakdown of their intermentality with her insistence on her dissenting intramental perspectives. Her aggressive behaviour derives from both her obstinacy and her sense of seeking revenge.

After Florence leaves the room (*CB* 106), the narrative does not immediately focus on Edward's reaction. Instead, in order to go to the roots of his reaction to the raised situation, it provides some part of their life stories after encountering: Edward's stormy relationship with Florence's father, George Ponting, his discussions and disagreements with Florence's mother, Emily, besides the other issues (*CB* 112–130). Edward is reminded of these memories in the bedroom and, in a similar manner to his experience in different situations, he is filled up with »contrary emotions« after Florence leaves the room. As we are told: »He was feeling the pull of contrary emotions, and needed to hold on to all his best, his kindest thoughts of her, or else he thought he would fold, he would simply give up« (*CB* 130). After seeing the »liquid heaviness in his legs,« Edward lingers for a while with his trousers in his hands. The internal focalization reveals his intentions in taking Florence responsible for his »shame.« These perceptions, nevertheless, will lead to the total breakdown of their intermental unit because the more Edward ponders on the situation, the more he taunts Florence:

> [1] This over-obvious fact was too harsh. How could he get by, alone and unsupported? And how could he go down and face her on the beach, where he guessed she must be? [2] His trousers felt heavy and ridiculous in his hand, these parallel tubes of cloth joined at one end, an arbitrary fashion of recent centuries. Putting them on, it seemed to him, would return him to the social world, to his obligations and to the true measure of his shame. Once dressed, he would have to go and find her. And so he delayed. (*CB* 131)

The first part of this passage seems to be a TR focalized primarily by the narrator revealing Edward's »alone and unsupported« state. In its second part, the boundary between private and social domains is emphasised. Edward is aware of the impact of the »social world« on his behaviour. Furthermore, he knows that the »true measure of his shame« beside his »obligations« vary considerably in social and private realms. Accordingly, he prefers not to put on his clothes in order to control his reaction or at least alleviate it. He tries to postpone his reaction to Florence through the »snatches of memories.« For example, he draws the conclusion that »Oh yes, he should not doubt it, she was a good person« (*CB* 132). Nevertheless, through his recollection of the last experiences, Edward at last could not

> hold back the advance of an element that initially he did not care to admit, the beginnings of a darkening of mood, a darker reckoning, a trace of poison that even now was branching through his being. Anger. The demon he had kept down earlier when he thought his patience was about to break. How tempting to give in to it, now that he was alone and could let it burn. After such humiliation, his self-respect demanded it. (*CB* 133)

Edward yields to these thoughts, the more he broods on the situation. The impact of his »arriving soon« on his mental functioning increases, the more he finds himself in a »humiliating« situation. He ascribes this problem to Florence finally. Further, the feeling of being insulted grows in Edward when he reviews Florence's reaction to the situation. Having considered Florence's action as an »insult,« a sign of »contempt,« and »a twist of scalpel,« Edward draws the conclusion that she has left him alone with »all the burden of failure.« Therefore, as recounted in FIT mode in part [2], he finally perceives that she »wanted to punish him.« Nevertheless, when he is reminded of her »touch« once more, he gets a bit milder and is tempted to forgive her [3]. Despite that, his intramental reasoning, which is against Florence's, is so strong that he cannot resist his intentional propensity to do so:

> [1] What an insult it was, what contempt she showed for him with her cry of revulsion and the fuss with the pillow, what a twist of the scalpel, to run from the room without a word, leaving him with the disgusting taint of shame, and all the burden of failure. [2] She had done what she could to make the situation worse, and irretrievable. He was contemptible to her, she wanted to punish him, to leave him alone to contemplate his inadequacies without any thought for her own part. Surely it was the movement of her hand, her fingers, that had brought him on. [3] At the memory of that touch, that sweet sensation, fresh sharp-edged arousal began to distract him, enticing him from these hardening thoughts, tempting him to start forgiving her. [4] But he resisted. He had found his theme, and he pushed on. He sensed there was a weightier matter just ahead, and here it was, he had it at last, he burst into it, like a miner breaking through the sides of a wider tunnel, a gloomy thoroughfare broad enough for his gathering fury. (*CB* 133–134)

As indicated by the narrator's analogy in the last part [4], in his reaction to the situation, Edward not only relies on his perceptions at that moment but also, »like a miner breaking through the sides of a wider tunnel,« he breaks through his already forgotten experiences in different situations. He intentionally does so in order to encounter with her with appropriate »gathering fury.« This new discovery puts Edward in a new situation in which he reconstructs his perceptions concerning Florence too, giving all the rights to himself. Therefore, his aspectuality changes into a new phase in which they are totally strangers to each other since their cooperation is intentionally replaced with dissents. They no longer belong to the intermental unit that they both have struggled in order to maintain. All Edward's perceptions about his expectations of her come true when, based on them, he condemns Florence. His internal focalization reveals the transformation of his thought:

> [1] It stood clear before him, and he was an idiot not to have seen it. For a whole year he had suffered in passive torment, wanting her till he ached, and wanting small things too, pathetic innocent things like a real full kiss, and her touching him and letting him touch her. The promise of marriage was his only relief. And then what pleasures she had denied them both. Even if they could not make love until after they were married, there was no need for such contortions, such agonies of restraint. He had been patient, uncomplaining—a polite fool. [. . .] [2] the fault was hers. [. . .] She was unsensual, utterly without desire. She could never feel what he felt. [. . .] she had deceived him. She wanted a husband for the sake of respectability, or to please her parents, or because it was what everyone did. Or she thought it was a marvellous game. She did not love him, she could not love in the way that men and women loved, and she knew this and kept it from him. She was dishonest. (*CB* 135)

In the first part of the above passage [1], Edward re-evaluates their shared experiences which, towards the end of their experiences in the storytime, act as a defining platform for their present actions. His account reveals his innocence and submissiveness as »a polite fool.« He needs such a presentation in order to feel strong to ascribe all faults to Florence. Thus, he finds her »unsensual,« »without desire« and »dishonest.« This misreading, or what Puschmann-Nalenz calls, »Edwards' misapprehension« (203), motivates Edward to go after Florence, towards the beach where their mutual poisonous ascriptions and intramental dissents bring their cognitive unit to end. After such a self-centred evaluation of the situation, Edward, now determined, thinks that it »would be meaningless if it [his surging anger] remained unspoken« (*CB* 135). It is in fact Edward whose readjustment and re-evaluations lead to an imbalance in their relationship. Thus, the presentation of ejaculation scene from Edward's and Florence's aspectual perceptions reveals both the wide divergence between the two and its »taunting« impact on their mental workings at that moment. At the same time, while Florence is represented as willing to maintain the intermental unit already established between them, Edward apparently yields to disrupting their established bond.

After Florence's leaving, the narrative speeds up and in less than ten pages, (*CB* 57–166), it covers Edward's life until his sixties. The temporal and perspectival changes indicate the far-reaching importance of the two short moments, the bedroom and beach scenes, on Edward's mental states. A large part of narration is allocated to the presentation of those moments. In a TR mode and using prolepsis or flash-forwards, Edward's reaction to Florence's last words before parting is recounted from Edward's perspective after many years. As it is highlighted, the more time passes, the more Edward ponders about Florence's proposal. Finally, understanding its true nature, he is able to reconstruct his perceptions towards Florence's proposal:

> Her words, their particular archaic construction, would haunt him for a long time to come. He would wake in the night and hear them, or something like their echo, and their yearning, regretful tone, and he would groan at the memory of that moment, of his silence and of the way he angrily turned from her, of how he then stayed out on the beach another hour, savouring the full deliciousness of the injury and wrong and insult she had inflicted on him, elevated by a mawkish sense of himself as being wholesomely and tragically in the right. (*CB* 157)

When Edward returns to hotel after Florence leaves, he still thinks that he is not guilty. In order to defend himself, he even confides, in his imagination, their case to a »stern impartial judge who understood his case completely.« When he finds out that the judge supports his views too, he feels »noble« and this temporarily saves him from his internal conflicts. Moreover, lying on the bed in the hotel after their confrontation in the beach, Edward ascribes the reasons of his action or behaviour to what he calls her »humiliations«:

> His thoughts chased themselves around in a dance, in a delirium of constant return. To marry him, then deny him, it was monstrous, wanted him to go with other women, perhaps she wanted to watch, it was a humiliation, it was unbelievable, no

> one would believe it, said she loved him, he hardly ever saw her breasts, tricked him into marriage, didn't even know how to kiss, fooled him, conned him, no one must know, had to remain his shameful secret, that she married him then denied him, it was monstrous. (*CB* 158–159)

Edward's mental states in this FIT passage are presented as experiencing a flux. His calculations and ascriptions are all counterfactual because, presented Florence's perspective with an emphasis on her perceptions about their stern situation, the reader already knows that she did not intend to humiliate, trick, cone, deny or fool Edward. Through her proposal, she just wanted to solve her personal fear of sex while it was in fact Edward's anger or rage that destroyed their relationship. Unlike Edward, Florence was aware of her own weakness and she tried to overcome it although she just could attenuate it. Edward, nevertheless, is presented as giving himself fully to his anger as well as to some unchangeable opinions. However, the more time passes, the more his anger subsides. The time he gains more experience, he becomes more competent to reconstruct his interpretations of Florence's proposal. In other words, during the passage of time and retrospectively, his intramental dissent decreases. Although Florence no longer exists in the stroyworld, but she is present in his mental life:

> Towards the end of that celebrated decade, when his life came under pressure from all the new excitements and freedoms and fashions, as well as from the chaos of numerous love affairs—he became at last reasonably competent—he often thought of her strange proposal, and it no longer seemed quite so ridiculous, and certainly not disgusting or insulting. In the new circumstances of the day, it appeared liberated, and far ahead of its time, innocently generous, an act of self-sacrifice that he had quite failed to understand. (*CB* 160)

Florence's desired intermental unit is achieved at last when she is absent both from the storyworld and from Edward's actual life. He not only regrets misreading her proposal but also, in retrospection and »under pressure from all the new excitements and freedoms and fashions,« he finds her proposal as »an act of self-sacrifice that he had quite failed to understand.« Despite that, nothing is recounted about Florence's life and destiny after her leaving except something about her performance with »the Ennismore

Quartet's triumphant debut at the Wigmore Hall in July 1968« (*CB* 162). Edward, however, did not know about it. He had not read the Time magazine reviewer's comment on Miss Ponting's »lilting tenderness of her tone and the lyrical delicacy of her phrasing, played, if I may put it this way, like a woman in love, not only with Mozart, or with music, but with life itself« (*CB* 162). Moreover, as the narrator's account shows, Florence's love to Edward continues after their separation:

> if Edward had read that review, he could not have known—no one knew but Florence—that as the house lights came up, and as the dazed young players stood to acknowledge the rapturous applause, the first violinist could not help her gaze travelling to the middle of the third row, to seat 9C. (*CB* 162–163)[98]

Nevertheless, Edward reconstructs meaningfully his interpretation of her proposal and their relationship towards the end of narrative. Doing that, he comes to know how much she loved him while he gradually become aware of his love for her. He also finds out for the first time how totally different his life would have been if they remained together: »In later years [. . .] it seemed to him that an explanation of his existence would take up less than a minute, less than half a page. What had he done with himself? He had drifted through, half asleep, inattentive, unambitious, unserious, childless, comfortable. His modest achievements were mostly material« (*CB* 163). Accordingly, Edward, now in his sixties, is finally able to overcome his egoistic intramental perceptions about Florence:

> At last he could admit to himself that he had never met anyone he loved as much, that he had never found anyone, man or woman, who matched her seriousness. Perhaps if he had stayed with her, he would have been more focused and ambitious about his own life, he might have written those history books. [. . .] He preferred to preserve her as she was in his memories. (*CB* 165)

---

98 9C refers to Edward's promise to Florence once he accompanied her to the rehearsal room in the Wigmore hall. There he witnesses her leading performance in the Quartet. When Florence tells him that one day her group, the Ennismore Quartet, will play in the Wigmore hall, Edward mutually promises her to be there on that special day: he »vowed that whatever happened, he would be here on that day, in this very seat, 9C, and he would lead the applause and the bravos at the end« (McEwan, *CB* 125).

Edward is able to share Florence's thoughts only when he is in his sixties and is free from the dominance of his anger. This revelation makes him connected to the cognitive unit Florence was looking for. Nevertheless, such an intermentality is an imaginary one since he did »nothing« on Chesil Beach. The last part of narrative is, therefore, given to Edward's perspective after some forty years. The narrator's comments also reveal a deep melancholy in Edward's consciousness:

> [1] When he thought of her, it rather amazed him, that he had let that girl with her violin go. [2] Now, of course, he saw that her self-effacing proposal was quite irrelevant. All she had needed was the certainty of his love, and his reassurance that there was no hurry when a lifetime lay ahead of them. Love and patience [. . .] [3] This is how the entire course of a life can be changed—by doing nothing. On Chesil Beach he could have called out to Florence, he could have gone after her. [4] He did not know, or would not have cared to know, that as she ran away from him, certain in her distress that she was about to lose him, she had never loved him more, or more hopelessly, and that the sound of his voice would have been a deliverance, and she would have turned back. Instead, he stood in cold and righteous silence in the summer's dusk, watching her hurry along the shore, the sound of her difficult progress lost to the breaking of small waves, until she was a blurred, receding point against the immense straight road of shingle gleaming in the pallid light. (*CB* 166)

This is one of the few scenes where Edward is able to come out of his own perspective and imagine looking at Florence's proposal and behaviour from her own perspective. In doing so, he regrets that let Florence go then. Referring to such a closure, Puschmann-Nalenz states that »Using this structural imbalance as closure the author explores only the regret and futility in the young man's later life, whose achievements do not attain the public acknowledgement of Florence's« (205). Likewise, he is »amazed« when he recollects Florence's going away [1]. Moreover, he finds her proposal as »self-effacing« through which Florence just wanted to be certain about his »reassurance.« If he would be patient, Edward thinks, they would settle down their problems through time. He blames himself since he did not do so [2]. Furthermore, reconstruction of his perspective is in fact the result of intellectual growth as we are told that for him »Decision–making appeared as a process and a sign of maturity on the threshold of young adulthood

[. . .] Individual responsibility proves again determined by society, historical situation and accidental circumstances« (Puschmann-Nalenz 207). Florence in part [3] is seen, according to Wondrich, as »walking away for ever, into the distance along the shore, into the resonant, emotional closure which conflates images of singleness and uniformity.« Moreover, for the first time Edward ascribes all the faults to himself acknowledging that if, instead of doing nothing, he did something, their destiny would have been different. Further, in this passage Edward »reflects melancholy and resignation« (Puschmann-Nalenz 207). The last part is focalized through the narrator's perspective revealing Florence's internal feelings while leaving Edward on the beach. The narrator emphasises that if he had been aware of her perception at that moment, he would have done something in order to prevent her from going away. In this way, the narrator, like Edward himself, ascribes the main cause of their break up to Edward, to his »righteous silence.« Moreover, according to Childs, the final two sentences of the passage suggest that the »characters are fixed in time before a heavily analogised moment in social history« (»Contemporary« 32). Furthermore, Wondrich points out the historical importance of beach in the presentation of the newlyweds' final shared moments:

> The whole course of a life, of two lives, in fact, is thus retrospectively figured as displaced on the indifferent, effacing space of that famous shore which echoes and replicates Arnold's «darkling plain.« Individual histories, History and the progress of Nature coalesce, once again, within the culturally inscribed space of the beach, where shingle forms an endless road, though with no ends and without an aim.

Despite all aimless implications along the beach, when he recollects those moments after some forty years, he feels its impact afresh. As a result, he acknowledges his guilt. Although in vain, he longs for his lost intermentality with now-absent but famous Florence. In other words, we infer that throughout the long years of their separation, Edward has been mentally concerned with the thought of reconstructing his past. Therefore, through such revaluation, the narrative reader also rearranges his/her perception of Edward back through the time of their open confrontation. Through following Edward's embedded narratives as well as the omniscient narrator's reports, s/he can imagine Edward's difficult process in rearranging his thoughts and interpretation about Florence's proposal. This perspectival change, however, has mostly been possible through the effect of time. Accordingly, the operation of his mind as his experience of what it's like for such a person to experience a perspectival transformation throughout some forty years are the focal concerns of Edward's embedded narratives.

Examination of Edward's and Florence's embedded and doubly embedded narratives shows the reasons their incipient small intermental minds change into two separate minds that dissent intramentally. This brings about the total disintegration of their intermental thoughts and relationship. Therefore, Palmer's argument over the presentation of the functioning fictional minds as the primary function of narrative and Herman's emphasis on the representation of experience in narrative as well as the cognitive activities of the experiencing fictional minds, or the way they undergo particular experiences throughout the narrative, in many ways help us to understand narrative meaning. They help us effectively to analyse the construction of Edward's and Florence's minds in *CB* narrative, their narration or presentation and the way we, as readers, can psychoanalyse the function of their minds based on our own real world knowledge and experiences. Besides that, they help us to engage closely in the presentation process of the sequences of events that lead to the newlyweds' separation through representing the impact of particular moments on their thoughts and actions. Edward's embedded narratives represent a dogmatic mind that solely pursues its own intentions without attempting to go beyond its perspective in order to include Florence's, or the other self's, perspective as well. While Florence is aware of the way his mind works, she is not able to overcome her own internal conflicts at the last moment in the beach. On the one hand, conforming to Edward's possible expectations, she endeavours not to offend him in order to help their delicate intermental activity go on. On the other hand, she is experiencing an internal conflict between love and sex. Accordingly, she wrongly thinks that her proposal, to love and set each other free, encompasses both sides of her problem. Nevertheless, her proposal does not seem to take into account Edward's personality both from his perspective and from the reader's perspective as well. In putting forward such a proposal, Florence does not use her own experiential repertoire of Edward. At the same time, she feels desperate to find any other alternative to her condition. If Edward, through presupposition, is unable to take into account her condition, Florence cannot overcome her appalling dilemma, which finally leads her towards uttering her intramental proposal although she is aware of Edward's possible adverse reaction. The narrative, moreover, displays how two minds experience the uncomfortable situations on their wedding nights. Supporting their pasts through flashbacks and anticipating their future through flash-forwards, the narrative explores the contribution of some particular moments to the fictional mind's present moment decisions. The application of FIT along with the narrator's TRs for the representation of the characters' mental functioning engages the reader deeply in the process of the couple's passage from intermentality into their vigorous intramental dissents. Thus, it is possible to argue that the narrativity level of *CB* is considerably high since it mainly presents the cognitive activities of the fictional minds.

6. Conclusion

> Imagining yourself into the minds of other people is, I think, a fundamental human act of empathy, which lies at the base of all our moral understanding. (»Ian«)

> Just as in real life the individual constructs the minds of others from their behavior, so the reader infers the workings of fictional minds and sees these minds in action from observation of characters' behavior and actions. Novels contain a wide variety of material or evidence on which readers base their conjectures, hypotheses, and predictions about fictional minds. (Palmer, *Fictional* 246)

> Narrative affords not just a means of expressing what it's like to experience events but moreover a basis or context for the having of (an) experience in the first place. (Herman, *Basic* 212)

Fictional worlds are constructed by using literary imagination. To reconstruct, re-imagine or experience them, readers naturally use their cognitive or subjective abilities. As a result, narrative fiction both represents mental states and is rich in terms of cognitive cues. Such cues enable readers to reconstruct the represented world in their minds more easily. Narrative meaning, understanding or communication is the result of such interaction. In this case, both Palmer's and Herman's theories of fictional minds and narrativity show how some interdisciplinary concepts, mostly coming from the field of cognitive studies, can help readers to have a more effective interpretation of narrative. They also try to explain some universal processes through which narrative experience takes place. CN, accordingly, highlights the interrelationships between the subjective abilities of the reader and the reading experiences. Besides reinforcing the reader's cognitive abilities, the result of such interaction is comprehending the storyworld in general and mental functioning of the fictional characters in particular.

This study has shown how Palmer's theories related to the construction and operation of fictional minds—embedded and double embedded narratives, intermental/intramental minds and the modes for consciousness representation—are highly beneficial to narrative interpretation. In addition, it has discussed the ways Herman's theories relate to the basic elements of narrative and narrativity in general, and his fourth basic element—what it's like or qualia aspect of narrative—in particular, are useful devices for understanding the workings of fictional minds. Such theories enable narrative interpreter to analyse the manner of fictional minds' functioning and, at the same time, explore the role of experience or the impact of the narrative events and situations on fictional minds behaviour. In this way, they enrich the reader's role in the interpretation act of the narratives such *AM, AT* and *CB*. Accordingly, following the principles of CN, this study showed the way narrative meaning is realised simultaneously by the role of reader, his/her own world knowledge and experiences, and the textual cues. It follows that, in CN reader constructs the fictional minds through his/her actual world experiences, scripts and frames since at the heart of any narrative lies representation of some experiencing minds.

As shown by the analyses of McEwan's narratives, a great deal of information about a character comes from the representation of its mental workings. Narrative reader experiences the fictional world through observing their (inner) speeches, decisions, actions, as well as the content of the narrator's reports. This means that readers principally rely on their real world experiences in order to understand the mental aspects of any storytelling practices. This study explains the processes through which the three intermental units in *AM, AT* and *CB* break down. The distinguished characteristic of McEwan's narratives turns out to be the supremacy or dominance of intramental (private) thought over intermental (joint) one. The ongoing conflict between the two aspects of the characters' mental orientations finally end in their pure intramentality. Re-experiencing of the past events and situations contributes considerably to their passage from shared to private thoughts. As CN argues, reader's narrative experience passes through both textual markers and personal experiences. This means that narrative meaning is not in the text to be actualized by the reader. Likewise, it does not belong to the reader's horizon totally. Instead, narrative interpretation, meaning or experience is the outcome of the convergence between the textual horizon and that of the reader's.

The fundamental problem in *AM*, *AT* and *CB* seems to be the impossibility of maintaining, let alone constructing, the intermental thoughts between the characters. The narratives are not only presentation of the already established intermental thoughts' disintegration process but also they are portrayals of the impossibility of maintaining such units. Furthermore, the mental functioning of the four focal characters is presented not only through their own private thoughts and perceptions but also by the thoughts and perceptions of the other character(s) about them as well. In other words, throughout the narratives, they both think, about themselves as well as about the other(s), and are thought by the other(s). Because of that, their whole minds are represented mostly through a combination of FIT and TR modes. Such a combinatory narrative technique enables the author, McEwan, to construct and represent his fictional minds from different perspectives. Likewise, through providing two perspectives, it allows reader to perceive and evaluate the manner of fictional characters' mental functioning. Clive and Vernon in *AM* have been close friends for a long time but with the death of their shared friend, Molly, at the narrative's beginning, the gradual breaking process of their intermental unit takes place. That finally makes the two old friends change into two enemies destroying mutually each other's life in the end. Likewise, in the newlyweds' narrative in *CB*, the impossibility of fulfilling an intermental activity lies at the heart of the storytelling practice. Edward and Florence are unable to build a joint activity or make a decision to solve their seemingly insurmountable problem. In *AT*, the emerging intermental unit between Cecilia and Robbie is aborted by an external factor. Briony's misperceptions, caused by a sequence of events, about their romantic relationship finally ends in her big crime. As a result, the couple are separated forever.

AM, *AT* and *CB* cultivate intramental behaviour. Instead of breeding intermental activities, they represent fictional minds operating primarily according to their intramental or private perception or orientations. They are unable to read or know for certain what the other character is thinking and hence their false inferences exceedingly deteriorate their condition. Edward, for example, is unable to think what Florence might be thinking or feeling at their tense moment in the bedroom and he continues this intramental behaviour at the beach scene too. When Florence asks him to forgive her, Edward disregards her suggestive request only repining for his egoistic passiveness forty years after that moment. Belatedly, he gets to understand that what they needed was not the momentary rushing for an action driven by a totally intramental thought, but at least realizing the necessity of agreeing in their intramentality. Their problem is not primarily their inability to construct intermental bond or thought between themselves in order to have an intermental activity but it is mostly their intramental dissents. Not only do they fail in constructing intermental thoughts, but also they do not agree about their intramental perceptions. Edward insists on fulfilling the wedding night sex while Florence, being anxious about it, intends to postpone it. As a result, the imbalance in their thoughts finally bring about their separation. Similarly, Clive and Vernon as two close friends in *AM*, intentionally insist on their own counterfactual perceptions of their both private and public issues. While Clive accuses Vernon of being immoral in publishing Garmony's transvestite photographs, Vernon mutually accuses Clive in preferring his artistic creation over his moral duty when he intentionally dispensed with saving a woman in the rocks. The basic implied problem in Clive-Vernon and Edward-Florence relationship seems to be not the lack of an intermental unit but the unattainability of an assent in intramental states. In other words, the chief problem is that the characters intramentally dissent. Not only do they disagree but also, in their disagreement, they are unable to imagine the perception of narrative events and situations from the minds or perspectives of the others. In the like manner, the plot structure in the first part of *AT* represents the gradual development of Briony's intramentality and its negative impact on the only intermental potential in the narrative.

Palmer's emphasis that the social context of the fictional minds, in a similar manner to real minds, cultivates their intermentality does not apply to the *AM* , *AT* and *CB*. The two pairs in the narratives under consideration are presented as possessing both subjectivity and intersubjectivity at the same time; nevertheless, their intersubjectivity do not lead to intermental minds because they tend to put their subjectivity higher than their intersubjectivity. In other words, being subjective-first characters, there is no balance between their two sides. Moreover, the examined fictional minds are disseminated in each other's minds in a way that if we subtract the version of another character(s) in one character's mind, the remaining part cannot be called a character at all. That is so because it lacks fundamentally any mental operations or cognitive/subjective activities representation of which, according to cognitive narratologists, should be taken as the primary condition of narrativity. The existence of these characters greatly depends on their attribution of mental states to the other character(s). They continuously attempt to infer what is going on in the other characters' minds so that they can prepare their (re)actions according to the other characters' thoughts and plans.

The main problem in McEwan's examined characters is the lack of a balance between their private and social or intramental and intermental parts. The narratives are in fact presentation of the gradual process of the expansion in the growing rift between them. What the characters appear to be unable to do is the restoration of a mutually acceptable balance between their private perceptions and those of the others. Since every one of them—Clive, Vernon, Edward, Florence and Briony—fail at taking or imagining the other character's perspectives and since they cannot accept in right terms the existence or legitimacy of such perspectives, they are unable to restore the lost balance to their relationship. In other words, they are incapable of reaching out beyond the confines of their own perspectives in order to take part in a joint action although they are intersubjective fictional minds without possessing its intermental aspect. In each of these narratives, when the narrative begins, the dividing or breakdown process has already begun. Furthermore, the characters are represented as being unable to build up intermental minds throughout the narrative progression. In addition, the narrative structure or plot does not seem to control the fictional minds' mental functioning too. Instead, it is the operation of fictional minds that add up gradually to the construction of narrative plot. It follows that, *AM, AT* and *CB* are primarily about cognitive activities of the intramental fictional minds.

Through some narrative techniques, the author in these narratives attempts to present the impact of narrative events and situations on the construction, operation and presentation of fictional minds or consciousness. The present study was in search of the analysis of this aspect in the chosen narratives in the light of Herman's theory of narrative and narrativity.

Application of Herman's theory to *AM*¸ *AT* and *CB* does reveal the reasons why they are appealing narratives. According to Herman, representation of what it's like or qualia in narrative is the most important aspect among the four basic narrative elements—situatedness, event sequencing, worldmaking/world disruption, and what it's like (or qualia). It refers to the representation of the impact of the events in the storyworld on the experiencing minds or what it's like for them to undergo some experiences within the stopryworlds or perceive, read and imagine, or not to be able to do so, the other minds. Thus, the fictional minds' experience becomes central part of narrative and, according to Herman, the degree a narrative represents the impact of narrative events and situations on the characters' consciousness, its narrativity level grows too.

In *AM*, *AT* and *CB* the primary concern of the narratives seems to be the representation of the impact of narrative events and situations on fictional minds in particular moment of their life. *AM* represents how Clive and Vernon receive the shared and private events totally differently. It explores the way Molly's death, Garmony's transvestite photographs, the rape scene in the Lake District and Clive's artistic creation as well as Vernon's professional dilemmas (re)construct the close friends' minds in a way that their asymmetric orientations bring about their mutual murder towards the end of narrative. This aspect is so strong in *CB* that one can reduce it to the representation of the qualia or what it's like aspect of narrative. In this way, the narrative examines closely the internal operation of the two minds in a parallel manner delineating their intramental orientations. Although Clive knows that Vernon knows that he is stuck in his career as well as he failed his humane responsibilities in the rocks, he persists on his own pretensions. Likewise, Vernon is aware of Clive's disagreement with his decision to publish the photographs. He knows that his action is against Molly's wish or Clive's assent. Despite that, he insists on his own position pretending it to be for the advantages of the public. Likewise, Clive pretends his indifference to the rape scene to be for the sake of his duty towards art, which is going to serve the public, not towards individuals. They are, therefore, mutually aware of their pretensions or they are intersubjective persons who are able to read each other's minds. Nonetheless, they are represented as being incapable of intermental thoughts because they do not have any shared or joint actions. There is no cooperation between them other than their mutual contribution to their fatal end. As a result, the *AM* narrative changes into presentation of two obstinate characters whose intramental perceptions are delineated through representation of the impact of narrative events and situations on their minds and their unlike reactions to those events as well. The lack of a cooperative activity and exploration of its reasons lie at the core of McEwan's attempt in *AM*. The narrative presents the process of diverging experiencing minds.

Likewise, in *CB* the disparity between internal-external, thought-action, self-other, subjective-intersubjective and intramental-intermental aspects seem to be the primary focus of narrative. Edward desires Florence's body disregarding her own feeling an behaviour. He finds himself unable to surmount his intramental perceptions while Florence is able to go beyond her own dimension and look at their condition form both of their perspectives. Therefore, Edward is not primarily intersubjective with Florence as he lacks any intermental bond with her, while Florence is intersubjective and intermental with Edward, represented by her total cooperation with him, until the conflict scene in the beach. Therefore, *CB* examines the impact of the same situation on the two experiencing minds closely. Edward's frenzied enchantment with the thought of penetrating into Florence and Florence's internal conflicts lie at the focus of narrative. The characters, particularly Florence, are ascribing mental states to each other grounding their inferences on each other's actions. The outcome of Edward's sheer persistence to fulfil his desires, regardless of Florence's state, is Florence's reliance on her intramental orientations at last. From the opening scenes, she is represented as struggling to maintain the balance between her subjective-intersubjective and mental-intermental orientations. Florence cooperates with Edward until her intramental dispositions dominate her mental functioning. Moreover, the impossibility of copulation or the impracticality of marriage consummation can be read as the lack of their intersubjectivity and hence their intermentality. The reasons for inaccessibility of the intermental minds, shared/joint action(s) or co-participation in *CB* are both personal and social and the narrative is presentation of the (im)possibility of the dialogue between the too. Moreover, it registers the impact of both dimensions on the continuously reported consciousness of the couple. It is only through the passage of time that Edward is able to overcome the social aspect in order to construct an intermental mind with Florence. That was, nevertheless, the defining obstacle to his way to reach intermentality with Florence. The narrative, therefore, attempts to represent the difficult process of an intermental mind's construction.

In the same way, the limited borders of one's perspective are shown in *AT* through following Briony's desire to transcend the limits of her mind as well as experience. McEwan presents us with two opposing modes of Briony's mental functioning. In the first part, it is her intramental, egoist, subjective-first or self-contained mental functioning that manipulates her behaviour and finally brings about her big crime against Robbie and, indirectly, Cecilia. In other words, her evaluative thoughts destroy the promising intermental unit between them. In the last part, it is her intermental, intersubjective first or sympathetic mental functioning that moulds her authorial thought. (Re)Evaluating her own younger perspective continuously, it is only through time and experience that she has been able to imagine the other perspectives. In this way, the analysis of *AT* shows the fact that although intermental units between and among character are constructed, they are continuously threatened by the dominant presence of intramental minds. In other words, intramentality is a prevalent mode of mental functioning. The novelist, however, can act against this course as, through imagination, s/he can let the intermental unit last forever.

This study, accordingly, has shown how CN, as defined by Herman and Palmer, can help us to experience the represented fictional minds' functioning in *AM*, *AT* and *CB*. Herman's terminologies help us to explore the relationship, or nexus, between narrative and mind or consciousness and its relationship with narrativity. He primarily considers narrative as the representation of cognitive activity and measures its narrativity in a gradient manner arguing that the more a narrative represents mental activity the more it can be considered as narrative. Likewise, Palmer considers presentation of fictional minds' operation as the fundamental aspect of narrative. His terminologies, therefore, help us to analyse the construction, operation and presentation of fictional minds within the stroyworlds. Moreover, according to Palmer, intermental thought or unit is not the average of the two or more thoughts but different thought over which there is agreement. Such different cognitive unit is not obtained between Clive and Vernon as well as between Edward and Florence because they are unable to merge their intramental thoughts in order to gain access to a sustainable intermental unit.

The analyses of *AM, AT* and *CB* imply two reasons for the central characters' final situation: one refers to the extra textual or contextual factors such as the socio-historical ones that encourage the intramental aspects of people's thoughts. The other refers to the individual characteristics internalised in the central characters' mentality as they find themselves unable to overcome them. Throughout this study, we have seen how the four central characters desperately struggle to maintain the fragile intermental unit among themselves. Moreover, it has shown how narrative reader, as cognitive approach to narrative emphasises, is central to narrative interpretation since s/he, drawing on her/his real world knowledge, frames and experiences, attempts to unfold the manner fictional minds within storyworlds are functioning either self-containedly in themselves or with the other minds.

Human relationships are continuously built and broken in any reader's real world. Similar to this experience, *AM, AT* and *CB* narrate the breaking-down process of two close relationships. By the help of CN's terminology, this study explored the reasons apparently safe relationships can break-down by some unexpected, but latent, events. The overlapping or interconnection between reader's real world experience and the reading act experience functions as a fundamental frame based on which reader's narrative experience is actualised. Such interdependence not only adds to the reader's engagement in the reading act but also it activates his/her subjective or conscious and unconscious abilities too. In this way, reading act enhances the reader's ability in coping with the similar storyworld situations in his/her real world context. From this perspective, which is also emphasised by both Palmer and Herman, McEwan's selected narratives prove to be rich in terms of providing universal mental models, which engage the readers widely. Besides highlighting the cognitive activities of the central characters, representation of the impact of some historical moments on the operation of the central fictional minds is seemingly their primary goal. Accordingly, McEwan in *AM, AT* and *CB* uses intramental characterisation as a narrative technique to reveal the degree egocentrism and inability to take into account the opposite perspective(s) can end in catastrophic results.

7. BIBLIOGRAPHY

Abbott, H. Porter. »Narrativity.« *The Living Handbook of Narratology*. Ed. Peter Hühn et al. Hamburg: Hamburg University Press, 2009. 309–328. Print.

Albers, Stefanie and Caeners, Torsten. »The Poetics and Aesthetics of Ian McEwan's *Atonement*.« *English Studies* 90.6 (2009): 707–720. Print.

Bal, Mieke. *Narratology: Introduction to the Theory of Narrative.* 3rd ed. Toronto: University of Toronto Press, 2009. Print.

---. »Notes on Narrative Embedding.« *Poetics Today* 2.2 (1981): 41–59. Web. 16 July. 2012.

Bentley, Nick. *Contemporary British Fiction.* Edinburgh: Edinburgh University Press, 2008. Print.

Bernaerts, Lars et al. »Introduction: Cognitive Narrative Studies: Themes and Variations.« *Stories and Minds: Approaches to Literary Narrative.* Eds. Lars Bernaerts et al. Lincoln: University of Nebraska Press, 2013. 1–22. Print.

Bortolussi, Marisa. »Response to Alan Palmer's ›Social Minds‹.« *Style* 45.2 (Summer 2011): 283–287. Web. 06 Apr. 2012.

Brooker, Joseph. *Literature of the 1980s: After the Watershed.* Edinburgh University Press: Edinburgh, 2010. Print.

Brewer, William Florence. »Schemata.« *The MIT Encyclopedia of the Cognitive Sciences.* Ed. Robert A. Wilson and Frank Clive. Cambridge: MIT Press, 1999. 729–730. Print.

Caracciolo, Marco. »Experientiality.« *The Living Handbook of Narratology.* Eds. Peter Hühn et al. Web. 10 Oct. 2013.

----. »Fictional Consciousness: A Reader's Manual.« *Style* 46.1 (2012): 42–65. Web. 28 Dec. 2012.

---. »Notes for a(nother) Theory of Experientiality.« *Journal of Literary Theory (JLT)* 6.1 (2012): 177–194. Web. 12 May. 2012.

---. »Phenomenological metaphors in readers' engagement with characters: The case of Ian McEwan's Saturday.« *Language and Literature* 22.1 (2013): 60–76. Web. 12 Feb. 2013.

Catrinescu, Dana. »Rethinking Spatiality: The Degraded Body in Ian McEwan's *Amsterdam.*« *B. A. S.: British and American Studies/Revista de Studii Britanice si Americane,* 7 (2001): 157–165. Web. 22 Dec. 2013.

Childs, Peter. »Contemporary McEwan and Anosognosia.« *Ian McEwan: Art and Politics*. Ed. Pascal Nicklas. Heidelberg: Winter, 2009. 23–38. Print.

---. *The Fiction of Ian McEwan*. Ed. Peter Childs. New York: Palgrave, 2006. Print.

Cochran, Angus R. B. »Ian McEwan.« *British Writers: Supplement iv*. Eds. George Stade and Carol Howard. New York: Charles Scribner's Sons, 1997. 389–408. Print.

Courtney, Hannah. »Narrative Temporality and Slowed Scene: The Interaction of Event and Thought Representation in Ian McEwan's Fiction.« *Narrative* 21.2 (2013): 180–197. Web. 10 June. 2013.

Duncan, Susan. »Language and Communication.« *The MIT Encyclopedia of the Cognitive Sciences*. Ed. Frank C. Keil and Robert A. Wilson. Cambridge: MIT Press, 1999. 438–441. Print.

Emmott, Catherine and Alexander, Mark. »Schemata.« *Narratologia / Contributions to Narrative Theory: Handbook of Narratology*. Eds. Peter Hühn et al. Berlin: Walter de Gruyter, 2009. 411–419. Print.

Fludernik, Monika. »Narratology in the Twenty-First Century: The Cognitive Approach to Narrative.« *PMLA-Publications of the Modern Language Association of America* 125.4 (2010): 924–930. Print.

---. *The Fictions and the Languages of Fiction*. London: Routledge, 1993. Print.

---. *Towards A Natural Narratology*. London: Routledge, 2005. Print.

Fludernik, Monika and Olson, Greta. »Introduction.« *Current Trends in Narratology*. Ed. Greta Olson. Berlin: Walter de Gruyter, 2011. 1–33. Print.

Gaedtke, Andrew. »Cognitive Investigations: The Problems of Qualia and Style in the Contemporary Neuronovel.« *Novel: A Forum on Fiction* 45.20 (2012): 184–201. Web. 09 Oct. 2013.

Gaydosik, Victoria. *The Facts on File Companion to the British Novel, Volume II: 20th Century*. New York: Facts on File, Inc. 2006. Print.

Genette, Gerard. *Narrative Discourse: An Essay in Method*. Trans. E. Jane Lewin. Ithaca: Cornell University Press, 1980. Print.

Green, Susan. »Consciousness and Ian McEwan's Saturday: »What Henry Knows?« *English Studies* 91.1 (2010): 58–73. Print.

Groes, Sebastian. »*A Cartography of the Contemporary: Mapping Newness in the Work of Ian McEwan.*« *Ian McEwan: Contemporary Critical Perspectives*. Ed. Sebastian Groes. London: Continuum, 2009. 1–12. Print.

Head, Dominic. »*On Chesil Beach*: Another ›Overrated Novella?« *Ian McEwan: Contemporary Critical Perspectives*. Ed. Sebastian Groes. London: Continuum, 2009. 115–122. Print.

---. *The Cambridge Introduction to Modern British Fiction, 1950–2000.* Cambridge, Cambridge University Press, 2002. Print.

Henry, Patrick. »Amsterdam by Ian McEwan; Atonement by Ian McEwan; Saturday by Ian McEwan; On Chesil Beach by Ian McEwan.« Rev. *Modern Language Studies* 38.1 (2008): 75–84. Web. 05 Oct. 2012.

Herman, David. *Basic Elements of Narrative*. Oxford: Wiley-Blackwell, 2009. Print.

---. »Cognition, emotion, and consciousness.« *The Cambridge Companion to Narrative*. Ed. David Herman. New York: Cambridge University Press, 2007. 245–259. Print.

---. »Cognitive Narratology.« *Handbook of Narratology*. Eds. Peter Hühn et al. Berlin: Walter de Gruyter, 2009. 30–43. Print.

---. »Narrative: Cognitive Approaches.« *Encyclopedia of language & linguistics*. Eds. Edward K. Brown et al. Volume 1. Elsevier, 2006. 452–459. Print.

---. »Narrative Theory after the Second Cognition Revolution.« *Introduction to Cognitive Cultural Studies*. Ed. Lisa Zunshine. Maryland: The John Hopkins University Press, 2010. 155–175. Print.

---. »Narrative Ways of Worldmaking.« *Narratology in the Age of Cross-Disciplinary Narrative Research*. Eds. Sandra Heinen and Roy Sommer. Berlin: Walter de Gruyter, 2009. 80–96. Print.

---. »Narratology as a Cognitive Science.« *Image [&] Narrative* 1 (2000). Web. 12 Nov. 2012.

---. »Post-Cartesian Approaches to Narrative and Mind: A response to Alan Palmer's Target Essay on ›Social Minds.‹« *Style* 45.2 (Summer 2011). 265–271. Print.

---. »Scripts, Sequences, and Stories: Elements of a Postclassical Narratology.« *PMLA* 112.5 (1997): 1046–1059. Print.

---. *Story Logic: Problems and Possibilities of Narrative*. Lincoln: University of Nebraska Press, 2002. Print.

---. *Storytelling and the Sciences of Mind*. Massachusetts: The MIT Press, 2013. Print.

---. »Storytelling and the Sciences of Mind: Cognitive Narratology, Discursive Psychology and Narrative in Face-to-Face Interaction.« *Narrative* 15 (2007): 306–334. Web. 18 May. 2012.

Herman, Luc and Bart Vervaeck. *Handbook of Narrative Analysis*. Lincoln: University of Nebraska Press, 2005. Print.

Hoff, Molly. *Virginia Woolf's Mrs. Dalloway: Invisible Presences*. South Carolina: Clemson University, 2009. Print.

Hogan, Patrick Colm. »Palmer's Anti-Cognitivist Challenge.« *Style* 45.2 (2011): 244–248. Web. 04 Oct. 2012.

Ingersoll, Earl G. »City of Endings: Ian McEwan's *Amsterdam*.« *Midwest Quarterly* 46.2 (2005): 123–138. Web. 12 March. 2012

---. »The Moment of History and The History of the Moment: Ian McEwan's *On Chesil Beach*.« *Midwest Quarterly* 52.2 (2011): 131–147. Web. 12 March. 2012.

Jahn, Manfred. »Cognitive Narratology.« *Routledge Encyclopedia of Narrative Theory*. Eds. David Herman et al. London: Routledge, 2005. 67–71. Print.

---. »Frames, Preferences, and the Reading of Third-Person Narratives: Towards a Cognitive Narratology.« *Poetics Today* 18.4 (Winter 1997): 441–468. Web. 12 August. 2012.

---. »Windows of Focalization: Deconstructing and Reconstructing a Narratological Concept.« *Style* 30.2 (Summer1996): 241–268. Web. 14 May. 2007.

James, David. »A boy stepped out': Migrancy, visuality, and the mapping of masculinities in later fiction of Ian McEwan.« *Textual Practice* 17.1 (2003): 81–100. Web. 16 May. 2012.

Kohn, Robert Edward. »The Fivesquare Amsterdam of Ian McEwan.« *Critical Survey* 16.1 (2004): 89–106. Web. 22 Feb. 2012.

Malcolm, David. *UNDERSTANDING Ian McEwan*. South Carolina: University of South Carolina, 2002. Print.

Margolin, Uri. »CHARACTER.« *Routledge Encyclopedia of Narrative Theory*. Ed. David Herman et al. London: Routledge, 2005. 52–57. Print.

---. »Focalization: Where Do We Go from Here?« *Point of View, Perspective, and Focalization: Modeling Mediation in Narrative*. Ed. Peter Hühn et al. Berlin: De Gruyter, 2009. 41–57. Print.

---. »From Predicates to People like Us: Kinds of Readerly Engagement with Literary Characters.« *Characters in Fictional Worlds: Understanding Imaginary Beings in Literature, Film, and Other Media*. Eds. Jens Eder et al. Berlin: De Gruyter, 2010. 400–415. Print.

Mathews, Peter. »After the Victorians: The Historical Turning Point in McEwan's *On Chesil Beach*.« *Critique* 53 (2012): 82–91. Web. 28 August. 2012.

---. »The Impression of a Deeper Darkness: Ian McEwan's *Atonement*.« *ESC* 32.1 (March 2006): 147–160. Print.

McEwan, Ian. *Amsterdam*. London: Vintage, 2005. Print.

---. *Atonement*. London: Anchor, 2003. Print.

---. »Journeys without Maps: An Interview with Ian McEwan.« Interview. By Jon Cook et al. Ed. Sebastian Groes. *Ian McEwan: Contemporary Critical Perspectives*. London: Continuum, 2009. 123–134. Print.

---. »Ian McEwan.« Interview. *PBS*. Web. 12 July. 2013. <*pbs.org/wgbh/pages/frontline/shows/faith/interviews*>.

---. »Missing You.« Interview. By Bryan Appleyard. *The Advertiser.* 13 April. 2007. Web. 18 March. 2012.

---. *On Chesil Beach.* London: Jonathan Cape, 2007. Print.

---. »Only love and then oblivion. Love was all they had to set against their murderers.« *The Guardian.* 15 (Sept. 2001). Web. 12 Feb. 2012.

---. »On making love work in fiction.« Video. *LUISIANAchannel.* Web. 25 Sep. 2013.

---. »The Art of Fiction N. 173« Interview. By Adam Begley. *The Paris Review.* Web. 05 Sep. 2013.

McHale. Brian. »Transparent Minds Revisited.« *NARRATIVE* 20.1 (January 2012): 115–124. Web. O4 Feb. 2012.

Nicklas, Pascal. »The Ethical Question: Art and Politics in the Work of Ian McEwan.« *Ian McEwan: Art and Politics.* Ed. Pascal Nicklas. Heidelberg: Winter, 2009. 9–22. Print.

O'Hara, David K. »Briony's Being-For: Metafictional Narrative Ethics in Ian McEwan's *Atonement.*« *Critique* 52.1 (2011): 74–100. 2011.

Palmer, Alan. »Attribution of Madness in Ian McEwan's Enduring Love.« *Style* 43.3 (2009): 291–308. Web. 12 Dec. 2012.

---. »Construction of Fictional Minds.« *Narrative* 10.1 (Jan. 2002): 28–46. Web.13 Jul. 2012.

---. *Fictional Minds.* Lincoln: University of Nebraska Press, 2004. Print.

---. »Small Intermental Units in Little Dorrit.« *Yearbook of Research in English and American Literature.* Berlin: Walter de Gruyter, 2008. 163–180.

---. »Social Minds in Fiction and Criticism.« *Style* 45.2 (Summer 2011). Web. 08 Jan. 2012.

---. »Social Minds in *Little Dorrit.*« *Theory of Mind and Literature.* Eds. Paula Leverage et al. Indiana: Purdue University Press, 2011. 27–40. Print.

---. *Social Minds in the Novel.* Columbus: the Ohio State University Press, 2010. Print.

---. »Storyworlds and Groups.« *Introduction to Cognitive Cultural Studies.* Ed. Lisa Zunshine. Maryland: The John Hopkins University Press, 2010. 176–192. Print.

---. »The Lydgate Storyworld.« *Narratology beyond Literary Criticism*. Ed. Jan Christoph Meister. Berlin: Walter de Gruyter, 2005. 151–172. Print.

---. »The Mind Beyond the Skin in Little Dorrit.« *Current Trends in Narratology*. Ed. Greta Olson. Berlin: Walter de Gruyter, 2011. 79–100. Print.

---. »Thought and Consciousness Representation (Literature).« *Routledge Encyclopedia of Narrative Theory*. Ed. David Herman et al. London: Routledge, 2005. 602–607. Print.

Pamuk, Orhan. *The Naive and the Sentimental Novelist: Charles Eliot Norton Lectures, 2009.* Trans. Nazim Dikbaş. London: Faber and Faber, 2010. Print.

Prince, Gerald. *A Dictionary of Narratology (Revised Edition).* Lincoln: University of Nebraska Press, 2003. Print.

---. *Narratology: The Form and Functioning of Narrative.* Berlin and New York: Mouton Publishers, 1982. Print.

Puschmann-Nalenz, Barbara. ›Ethics in Ian McEwan's Twenty-First Century Novels. Individual and Society and the Problem of Freewill.« *Ian McEwan: Art and Politics.* Ed. Pascal Nicklas. Heidelberg: Winter, 2009. 187–211. Print.

Ridley, Matt, »Forward: Ian McEwan and the Rational Mind.« *Ian McEwan: Contemporary Critical Perspectives.* Ed. Sebastian Groes. London: Continuum, 2009. vii-x. Print.

Rimmon-Kenan, Shlomith. *Narrative Fiction: Contemporary Poetics.* Second Edition. London: Routledge, 2002. Print.

Segalla, Rosemary. »The Therapeutic Work of the Group: Finding the Self through Finding the Other.« *Self Experiences in Group, Revisited: Affective Attachments, Intersubjective Regulations, and Human Understanding.* Ed. Irene Harwood et al. New York: Routledge, 2012. Print.

Schaeffer, Jean-Marie and Iona Vultur. »MIMESIS.« *Routledge Encyclopedia of Narrative Theory*. Ed. David Herman et al. London: Routledge, 2005. 309–310. Print.

Schneider, Ralf. »Toward a Cognitive Theory of Literary Character: The Dynamics of Mental-Model Construction.« *Style* 35.4 (Winter 2001): 607–639. Web. 22 June. 2012,

Schwalm, Helga. »Figures of Authorship, Empathy, & The Ethics of Narrative (Mis-)Recognition in Ian McEwan's Later Fiction.« *Ian McEwan: Art and Politics*. Ed. Pascal Nicklas. Heidelberg: Winter, 2009. 173–185. Print.

Semino, Elena. »Blending and characters' mental functioning in Virginia Woolf's ›Lappin and Lapinova‹.« *Language and Literature* 15.1 (2006): 55–72. Web. 20 Dec. 2012.

Shakespeare, William. »Julius Caesar.« *Shakespeare-online*. Web. 26 Sep. 2012.

Shen, Dan. »DIEGESIS.« *Routledge Encyclopedia of Narrative Theory*. Eds. David Herman et al. London: Routledge, 2005. 107–107. Print.

Spitz, Alice. »The Music of Argument: the Portrayal of Argument in Ian McEwan's *On Chesil Beach*.« *Language and Literature* 19.2 (2010): 197–220. Web. 15 July. 2013.

Stanzel, Franz K. »Teller-Characters and Reflector-Characters in Narrative Theory.« *Poetic Today* 2.2 (1981): 5–15. Web. 14 Nov. 2012.

Stockwell, Peter. »Changing Minds in Narrative.« *Style* 45.2 (2011): 288–291. Web. 15 Sep. 2013.

Susan, Green. »Consciousness and Ian McEwan's Saturday: »What Henry Knows.« *English Studies* 91.1 (2010): 58–73. Web. 13 Jan. 2010.

Tsai, Jen-chieh. »Question of Reception Ethics: Amity and Animosity in Ian McEwan's *AM*.« *Integrams* 12.1 (2011). Web. 02 July. 2013.

Vygotsky, Lev. *Language and Thought*. Trans. Alex Kozulin. London: The MIT Press, 1986. Print.

Walters, Natasha. »Young Love, Old Angst.« Review Section. *The Guardian*. Web. 25 Feb. 2013.

Watt, Ian. *The Rise of the Novel: Studies in Defoe, Richardson and Fielding.* California: University of California Press, 1957. Print.

Wells, Lynn. »Ian McEwan.« *The Encyclopedia of Twentieth Century Fiction: Twentieth Century British and Irish Fiction.* Volume 1. Ed. Brian W. Shaffer. Oxford: Wiley-Blackwell, 2011. 250–253. Print.

---. *Ian McEwan.* New York: Palgrave, 2010. Print.

Wertsch, James Vernon. »Vygotsky, Lev Semenovich.« *The MIT Encyclopedia of Cognitive Sciences.* Eds. Robert A Wislon and Frank Clive Keil. Massachusetts: The MIT Press, 1999. 878–879. Print.

Woolf, Virginia. »Modern Fiction.« *The Essays of Virginia Woolf: Volume 4: 1925 to 1928.* Ed. Andrew McNeille, London: The Hogarth Press. 157–165. 1984. Print.

Wondrich, Roberta Gefter. »«these heavy sands are language»: the beach as a cultural signifier from *Dover Beach* to *On Chesil Beach.*« *Academia.* Web. 15 March. 2013.

Zlatev, Jordan et al. »Intersubjectivity: What makes us human?« *The Shared Mind: Perspectives on intersubjectivity.* Eds. Jordan Zlatev et al. Amsterdam: John Benjamins Publishing Company, 2008. 1–16. Print.

Zunshine, Lisa. »Introduction: What is Cognitive Cultural Studies?« *Introduction to Cognitive Cultural Studies.* Ed. Lisa Zunshine. Maryland: The John Hopkins University Press, 2010. 1–34. Print.

---. *Why We Read Fiction: Theory of Mind and the Novel.* Columbus: The Ohio State University Press, 2006. Print.

ibidem-Verlag / *ibidem* Press
Melchiorstr. 15
70439 Stuttgart
Germany

ibidem@ibidem.eu
ibidem.eu